R. J. Dodds

Chronicles of Wasted Time

2: The Infernal Grove

MALCOLM MUGGERIDGE

Chronicles of Wasted Time

Chronicle 2:
The Infernal Grove

Till I turn from Female Love,
And root up the Infernal Grove,
I shall never worthy be
To step into Eternity.
— Blake

William Morrow & Company, Inc.
New York 1974

Published in the United States in 1974.

Copyright © 1973 by Malcolm Muggeridge.

Published in Great Britain in 1973.

All rights reserved. No part of this book may be reproduced or utilized in any form or by any means, electronic or mechanical, including photocopying, recording or by any information storage and retrieval system, without permission in writing from the Publisher. Inquiries should be addressed to William Morrow and Company, Inc., 105 Madison Ave., New York, N.Y. 10016.

Printed in the United States of America.

1 2 3 4 5 78 77 76 75 74

Library of Congress Cataloging in Publication Data

Muggeridge, Malcolm (date)
  The infernal grove.

  (His Chronicles of wasted time, 2)
   1. Muggeridge, Malcolm (date)   I. Title.
II. Series.
PR6025.U5Z5152 vol. 2 070′.92′4 [B] 74-1258
ISBN 0-688-00300-1

FOR MY EVER-DEAR CHILDREN:
LEONARD, JOHN AND VALENTINE,
AND THE OTHER THREE THAT HAVE
COME TO US THROUGH THEM:
SYLVIA, ANNE AND GERRIT-JAN

Contents

Chronicles of Wasted Time

2: The Infernal Grove

1 *The Iron Gates*

Let us roll all our strength and all
Our Sweetness up into one ball,
And tear our pleasures with rough strife
Through the iron gates of life
                    – Andrew Marvell

O! dreadful is the check – intense the agony –
When the ear begins to hear, and the eye begins to see;
When the pulse begins to throb, the brain to think again;
The soul to feel the flesh, and the flesh to feel the chain.
                    – Emily Brontë

A passionate tumultuous age will overthrow everything, pull everything down; but a revolutionary age that is at the same time reflective
and passionless leaves everything standing but cunningly empties it
of significance.
                    – Kierkegaard

IN THE AUTUMN of 1933 I came to Geneva from Rosinière, where I
had been staying after my Moscow adventure, to take a temporary job
at the International Labour Office, then part of the now defunct League
of Nations. Kitty and the two children and I had a small apartment in
the Rue de Lausanne overlooking the Lake and the Jardin des Anglais.
    The stern, forbidding Kremlin seemed far away, with its Red Flag
endlessly flying; by night arc-lit to make a pool of blood in the surrounding darkness. As were also the brown-shirted bully-boys and braided
embonpoint maidens roaming the streets of Berlin in search of cowering
Jewish shopkeepers. It was a snug little retreat, tucked away among
mountains; more like a stage-set or a willow-pattern than an actual
place, with steamers puffing to and fro across the Lake, and pretty
Renaissance-style houses, their gardens reaching down to the Lake

shore, recalling Mme de Staël, with her tall, red-headed Benjamin
Constant in attendance, and their interminable rhythm of meals and
talk and talk and meals. Then, as now, a great storm raged beyond the
snow-capped mountains, standing guard like majestic sentries; their
heads rosy at dawn, shining white by day, and in the evening scarlet.
I comforted myself by recalling the many honourable precedents for
thus taking refuge in this particular sanctuary. For instance, Rousseau
wearing Armenian dress and seated at his crochet work; or Voltaire, an
earlier version of Bernard Shaw, growing rich and famous by shocking
and thrilling those for whom the tumbrils were already waiting. As today
there are the millionaire colonists of Gstad, and the lords of show business scattered about the cantons where the Inland Revenue men cease
from troubling and the wealthy are at rest.

It was through David Blelloch that I came to hear of the ILO job, and
thanks to his kind offices that I got it; he being the son-in-law of Robert
Dell, *Guardian* Paris correspondent during my time in Manchester,
who had now been transferred to Geneva to report the doings of the
League of Nations. I used to run into Dell there from time to time;
still gloved, cane in hand, shoes of patent leather, soft hat rakishly
tilted, reminiscing about Anatole France and the villainies of the Quai
d'Orsay. Employment of some kind I urgently needed, as once again I
had practically no money. So I was greatly beholden to Blelloch and his
wife Sylvia, who were uniformly kind and generous to Kitty and me
while we were in Geneva.

The ILO, brain-child of Albert Thomas its first Director-General,
was set up at the same time as the League of Nations in the mood of
ebullience which followed the 1914–18 war, the intention being to reinforce the League's machinery for safeguarding international peace by
equivalent machinery for promoting social justice, on a basis of fair
wages and humane working conditions. Alas, despite Albert Thomas's
valiant efforts and ardent oratory, as little progress seemed to have been
made towards the realisation of social justice as of peace. By the time I
arrived on the scene, Thomas was dead, and his place had been taken
by an English don and sometime civil servant named Harold Butler,
who accorded me a brief interview when I took up my temporary post.
He had to a marked degree the curious, disconcerting way dons had in
those days, when one was supposed to be conversing with them, of
seeming to have dozed off and to be muttering in their sleep.

The section of the ILO to which I was posted had overflowed from
the newly constructed main building into a temporary structure in the

grounds, and was engaged in preparing a survey of co-operative movements throughout the world. It was to assist in this work that I had been appointed. The head of the section was a tiny, pedantic Frenchman, M. Prosper, with a large moustache that seemed quite out of proportion with the rest of him; like the luxuriant bushes you sometimes find sprouting out of a minute crack in a rock face. I never discovered that he had any particular interest in co-operative movements; any more, for that matter, than I had myself. This, despite lingering memories of going shopping for my mother at the Croydon Co-op, and of the confidence of my father and his friends that a retail trader whose profits were distributed as divi to the customers must ultimately put out of business competitors who kept them for themselves.

When asked to pronounce upon some point of policy or principle in connection with the work of his section, M. Prosper invariably retreated behind his moustache, and exclaimed in a voice that was quite remarkably deep and resonant for so tiny a frame: '*J'ai mes règles, j'ai mes règles!*' What these rules were, who had drafted them, and to what end, no one was ever able to find out. Contrasting with his laodicean attitude to co-operative movements, even in his native France, let alone in China or Peru, was the relentless concern with which he followed anything to do with the ILO's internal organisation; more particularly, promotions, salary scales and superannuation arrangements. When these were under consideration, he would become enormously vehement and excited, waving his arms about, and injecting into his voice a note of passionate concern, which, as things turned out, met with its just reward. I like to think of M. Prosper living out his days comfortably in some agreeable spot in Provence, noting with quiet satisfaction that his monthly cheque, drawn on the Banque de Genève, maintains its value in a shifting world. I only once encountered him outside the office, and that was in the Rue de Lausanne, just when I was turning into the apartment block where we lived. 'Ah!' he said to me, with, as I thought, a note of accusation in that deep voice of his, '*vous avez planté votre tente*'. It made me feel quite uneasy, as though he had caught me out in some nefarious enterprise, and I tried to reassure him by muttering confusedly: '*Mais non, Monsieur, nous sommes seulement des locataires*'. He gave me a distant, condescending nod, and passed on, presumably to some tent of his own, where Madame Prosper awaited him, maybe some children, shouting, as he hove in sight, '*Voilà Papa!*'; a dog barking, a *grandmère* serenely smiling, a servant laying the table – just like the Bontemps family from whose doings I learnt my first French words and grammar.

There were some six or seven of us in his department engaged in preparing the survey of co-operative movements. The only one of my colleagues who made much impression on me was H, a Lithuanian Jewess, with whom I spent a lot of my time talking. She had contracted polio as a child, and now needed to wear metal braces; because of her condition, walking painfully and slowly with two sticks. Everything she did required an enormous effort, which somehow resulted in the upper part of her becoming magnified. Her head and bust were a caricaturist's drawing, the face being particularly huge and swollen, yet in its own way, beautiful – like one of those lurid flowers that grow in stony wildernesses. After Kitty and I returned to London, she came and stayed with us there, and I took her round sight-seeing – something I hate anyway. She was avid to go everywhere and see everything. Her audacious refusal to accept the limitations of her crippled state drove her to undertake the most difficult operations. She went traipsing through Hampton Court and the Tower of London, climbed up into the dome of St Paul's, and, shaking and straining over her two sticks, and dragging along her two helpless legs, got on and off moving-stairways and made her way onto the tops of buses. I admired, and in a way loved her, and yet was also horrified by her, and glad when her visit came to an end.

Inevitably, however we might begin, much of our talk had a way of veering towards the Soviet regime, with which, as a Lithuanian, she was all too familiar. Although we heaped obloquy in unison on the GPU, the forced labour camps, and all the other horrors, I sensed in her a certain reservation, as though deep down in her heart, despite everything, she nourished an unquenchable expectation that somehow the socialist hopes she had invested in the Russian Revolution would be, if not realised in the USSR, made more realisable by what was happening there. In the unacknowledged world-wide civil war that was going on then – still is, for that matter – cutting across all existing loyalties, all accepted values and codes of behaviour, H was on one side and I on the other, and, ultimately, as I well knew, nothing could change either of our allegiances. Not even, in her case, such incidents as when, during the operation of the Nazi–Soviet Pact, at the Brest-Litovsk Bridge – Margaret Buber-Neumann has described the scene – the GPU handed over to the Gestapo, German-Jewish Communists who had taken refuge in the USSR, with Soviet and Nazi officers jointly checking the lists. Nor, in my case, the realisation that, as grows ever more obvious to me, what is still called our free way of life turns out to be neither free nor a way of life; safeguarding nothing that makes it worth defending, and with no future prospects that make it worth protracting.

After H's visit to us in London, I never saw or heard of her again until I happened to read the Royal Commission Report on the Canadian Spy Case resulting from the defection of Gouzenko, a cipher-clerk in the Soviet Embassy in Ottawa. One of the names Gouzenko handed over of Soviet agents operating in Canada was H's. It seemed that she had been sent to Montreal by the ILO, and there, no doubt partly through pressure on her family in Lithuania, by this time incorporated into the USSR, induced to perform minor espionage services in a Soviet spy ring. So, in the end, her true allegiance did come out. I wonder if mine ever will. Or if I really have one.

In our temporary building where we toiled on M. Prosper's behalf it used to get very hot owing to an uncontrollable heating system, and this made me sleepy. From time to time a trolley brought in tea or coffee and biscuits. I used to long for its coming, as I had for the tea-tray when I was wrestling in my room in the *Guardian* office with a leader; maybe one on this very ILO – an institution held in high esteem in Cross Street. The biscuits, when they came, were all stamped with the initials BIT (Bureau International de Travail), which some-how made them like sacerdotal wafers; if so, presumably munched in remembrance of the lantern-jawed Princetonian, Woodrow Wilson.

I cannot pretend that I threw myself with much zest into collecting and collating data about co-operative movements. For one thing, the information came exclusively from government sources, and was therefore highly suspect. Some of it, indeed, was manifestly absurd, suggesting, as it did, that co-operative enterprises were more numerous and advanced in countries like Cuba and Afghanistan than in France and Switzerland. When I raised this point with M. Prosper, he rather crossly remarked that it was not our business to question the genuine-ness of the data provided for us by member States; our business was to present it, as clearly and cogently as possible. So, with these dubious bricks, we constructed our great statistical edifice. When I left, it was still far from completion. Perhaps even to this day it exists somewhere or other as a work of reference, to be quoted from, or used in arguing a thesis or making a case. Cholerton's famous comment on the Moscow Trials – that everything about them was true except the facts – might well be applied to it; as, indeed, to much of the output of the League and its affiliates. I well remember a senior official coming one evening into the canteen, and telling me with the utmost satisfaction that eight years

of earnest endeavour had just been brought to a successful conclusion.
So, it was a gala-day for him. It seemed that he had been engaged in
drafting a Convention banning the employment of women in mines,
and at last, with only two member States – Poland and India – entering
a reservation, his draft had been unanimously approved. It came
out afterwards that Poland and India were the only two countries
among those adhering to the Convention in which women did work in
mines.

As the winter came on, chill winds began to blow, mists to gather, so
that we were often quite shut in, with even the Lake lost to view. Nonetheless, I doggedly took my walks along the Quai Woodrow Wilson,
noting League delegates and their hangers-on similarly bent. Men in
overcoats with astrakhan collars, sometimes cigar-smoking, or talking
vehemently; maybe arm-in-arm with a single companion, or in groups,
gesticulating, pausing to spread out their arms as though making some
dramatic point. The solitaries often trying to open their newspapers in
the wind – _Journal de Genève, Gazette de Lausanne_ – a quick, anxious
peek preliminary to subsequent more particular study. More important
ones with a plain-clothes man or two trotting behind to ensure that no
harm should befall them, or maybe a secretary or PA respectfully in
attendance in case some need should arise for their services.

Occasionally, a face was vaguely recognisable. As Briand, somnolent-
eyed, heavily moustached, nicotine-stained, or his opposite number,
Laval, sallow complexion and white tie contrasting; the two of them like
figures in a weather-gauge, one going in as the other comes out. Or
Politis, Titulescu, Benès – names to conjure with in their day, but who
remembers them now? Or fat little Litvinov waddling along to propose
once more the total disarmament of one and all, unconditionally and for
ever; in his train, three or four GPU men, with wide trousers, and
bulges under their arms, and little, dry, expressionless eyes. Or Arthur
Henderson in his bowler, still presiding over the Disarmament Conference to which Litvinov's proposal would be put, and still wearing
that lost look I had noticed when I ran into him on a channel steamer
just after the Labour holocaust of 1932. Or the then British Foreign
Secretary, Sir John Simon, reptilian, a snake in snake's clothing if ever
there was one, with Strang – whom I had known in Moscow – at his
elbow, so that a distant greeting could be exchanged, and, for adjoint,
a newcomer to the international scene, none other than young Anthony
Eden, a spring in his step, a song in his heart, moustache likewise
vibrant, homburg-hatted (headgear, as his fame increased, to be named

after him), *ce jeune homme extraordinaire qui aime tant la paix*, as the French newspapers referred to him. Who could then have foreseen the stormy course that lay ahead for him? From glory to glory; the Foreign Office, the War Office, and finally Downing Street, and then that weird withdrawal to the Jamaican Bondhouse, Goldeneye, and, reappearance as a ghostly earl or belted ghost. And, finally – was it really he? Looking out across the Lake from a hotel balcony in the early morning? That grey straggling moustache, those floating locks and flashing eyes, that air of woebegone self-satisfaction – was it, could it be . . . ? Yes, it was. None other than our Prime Minister, the Rt Hon. Ramsay MacDonald. 'Good-morning, sir,' I said as cheerfully as possible. In return he gave me one of his slow, lugubrious looks, and then delivered himself of a characteristic line: 'The day is for the wurruld, but the morrrning is for myself!' I left him to enjoy his own morning in preparation for the world's day.

The League of Nations in those days focused the hopes of the enlightened everywhere; all eyes were upon it in the confident expectation that it would succeed in making war as obsolete as duelling, and armed forces as unnecessary to nations as wearing a sword had become to individual citizens. In some mysterious way, just willing this would bring it to pass; by renouncing armaments, nationalistic policies and other works of the evil one, good would triumph, and peace reign for evermore. Sooner or later, everyone who was anyone came to Geneva to celebrate this new era of universal peace that was being inaugurated there. As well as the delegates themselves and their suites, there were innumerable campaigners of one sort and another, male and female, clerical and lay, young and old; all with some notion to publicise, some pet solution to offer, some organisation to promote. They gathered in droves, fanning out through the city, and settling in hotels and pensions, from the Lakeside ones down to tiny obscure back-street establishments. Ferocious ladies with moustaches, clergymen with black leather patches on the elbows of their jackets or cassocks and smelling of tobacco smoke, mad admirals who knew where to find the lost tribes of Israel, and scarcely saner generals who deduced prophetic warnings from the measurements of the pyramids; but one and all believers in the League's historic role to deliver mankind painlessly and inexpensively from the curse of war to the great advantage of all concerned.

What a time that was for Geneva! Not since Calvin has the spotlight of history so shone on it; and, of course, with the spotlight, came the world's newspapermen, their favourite haunt being the Café Bavaria, whose walls were lined with appropriate cartoons in deference to this special clientele. Thither they came, hot-foot from Berlin or Paris or London or New York, their stringers respectfully in attendance, with stories to write, expense accounts to draw on – *Garçon, encore des scotchs!* I occasionally dropped into the Bavaria myself to join an acquaintance for a drink, breaking off my researches into co-operative movements and my talks with H to get the feel again of news-gathering and the news-gatherers. More often than not, there would be present one or other of the famous American special correspondents – John Gunther, Vincent Sheean, Negley Farson, H. R. Knickerbocker – who in those days roamed the world, and would touch down at Geneva from time to time to cover a meeting of the League Council or Assembly, or in the vague expectation that even the Disarmament Conference as it meandered on, like Charles II taking an unconscionable time in dying, might yet yield a story. There was always the possibility, too, of something actually happening; as when Herr Greiser, President of the Danzig Senate, cocked a snook at the League delegates, or when the German delegates scornfully withdrew from the Disarmament Conference, leading the President, Arthur Henderson, to remark, on being asked what his reaction was, that it was 'a bit awkward'.

They were the knight-errants of our time; rescuers of nations in distress, champions of the downtrodden and oppressed, who smote the offending dragons hip and thigh with breathless words rattled off on their typewriters, and, later, caparisoned, cap-a-pie, cantered more sedately, but no less lucratively, round the lecture circuits. Above the tobacco smoke and the clatter of glasses, words and phrases resounded. Civilian bombing. . . . Would they be able to re-phrase the resolution to make it acceptable to the Great Powers? . . . Drafters hard at work . . . Eden optimistic and sees light at the end of the tunnel. . . . Even Briand awake and optimistic. . . . Even Sir John Simon wearing a frosty smile. . . . Begins: HOPE RISING GENEVA LEAGUE CIRCLES RESOL-UTION NOW DRAFTING BANNING CIVILIAN BOMBING UNCON-DITIONALLY RECEIVING QUASI-UNANIMOUS SUPPORT MORE. In the warmth of the Bavaria, three or four *fines* under my belt, I joined in the talk with a sense of being at the hub of events. Here, one knew what was happening; felt the world's pulse, and listened to its heartbeat. Here, as the *Guardian* would have put it, 'a new way of conducting international relations was being forged; quiet reasonable discussion round a table instead of bluster and gun-boats. Nor should the clownish gesture of a Herr Greiser be taken too seriously, and certainly not allowed to jeopardise the promising prospects for a wide-ranging peaceful settlement. . . .'

Outside, breathing in the cold damp air, the glow I had felt in the Café Bavaria soon wore off. News, like sensuality, is a passing excitement; perhaps the ultimate fantasy of all. A shadow's shadow, the scenario of the film of the play of the book. TRIUMPH FOR MR EDEN . . . DISCOURS MAGNIFIQUE DE M. BRIAND VAUT À LA FRANCE UNE JOURNÉE INOUBLIABLE . . . STRONG SUPPORT FOR POLITIS–TITULESCU COMPROMISE RESOLUTION. . . . Such items flashed round the world, shouted down telephones, set up by compositors, tapped out on teleprinters, subbed and digested and commented upon. Seemingly so momentous, and so soon cold. Who is Briand? What next Politis? Whither Titulescu? And the League itself? What was it but another Tower of Babel, climbing inanely into the sky? Through the mist I could just see the outline of the great new Palais de Nations, then under construction. Cedars from Lebanon, marble from Italy, precious metals from the Andes; contributions of one sort and another from every corner of the globe. A Palace of the Nations as stupendous as Kubla Khan's in Xanadu.

Alas, as it turned out, barely was the Palais des Nations completed and ready to be occupied than the second world war was ready to begin. While Hitler's panzers were actually roaring into Poland from the west, and Stalin's divisions lumbering in to meet them from the east, the League was in session in its new premises, discussing – the codification of level-crossing signs. At the time I remember feeling a sort of relief. At least there would be no more compromise resolutions, whether devised by MM. Politis and Titulescu or anyone else; no more triumphs for Mr Eden, or magnificent discourses by M. Briand. How wrong I was! Another Tower of Babel, taller, more tower-like and more babulous, would spring up in Manhattan, to outdo the League many times over in the irrelevance of its proceedings, the ambiguity of its resolutions and the confusion of its purposes. What will they be discussing there, I ask myself, when the guided missiles begin to fly?

By this time, Kitty and the children had gone back to London to set up house in preparation for my return, and I had told M. Prosper that the tent I had planted I now proposed to roll up and be gone. He kindly provided me with a testimonial to the effect that I had performed my duties with diligence and conscientiousness. It was, I fear, even less deserved than such statements usually are; my contribution to the massive report on co-operative movements throughout the world having been minute, and shaky at that. My last days in Geneva were solitary and morose, and largely spent pounding along beside the Lake, which seemed particularly leaden and ill-omened on those dark winter days. It, too, had I but known it, had a future destiny as the last hiding place of the world's hoarded gold, deposited there in fear as, in my time, its hoarded peace had been deposited there in hope.

As a place of pilgrimage, Geneva lacked the melodrama of Moscow; its cult more fatuous than sinister. Yet, just as, pounding round the Red Square, I endlessly asked myself how it came about that the choicest spirits of the age – all the gurus and dancing dervishes of enlightenment – prostrated themselves before a brutish tyrant like Stalin, so, pounding along the Quai Woodrow Wilson, I kept wondering what Pied Piper had been able to lead them to the shores of this sullen Lake, confidently expecting to find there Tennyson's Parliament of Man and Federation of the World. In both cases, as it seemed to me, the significant thing was the ready acceptance of fantasy as reality; even a predilection in favour of fantasy, and a corresponding abhorrence of reality. Why?

It was the question of questions; confronting it, I could only wail and lament by the Lake shore, cursing its dark waters, its chill mists, its icy winds, as I remembered my own readiness to take to the plastic wings of fantasy; to listen with Caliban to the sounds and sweet airs which give delight and hurt not, so that when we wake – but we never do – we cry to sleep again. All I could claim – so miniscule a claim – was that I knew, had always known, would always know, that the alternative reality existed, and that, all too desultorily and faithlessly, I had looked for it, aware that the quest was the only true and serious purpose life held. Trying to tear it out of the sky, or out of other flesh; searching for it in grains of sand, and on the stony tops of mountains. Pursuing and pursued, stumbling on as it breathed down my neck, and chasing after it as it disappeared from view; crying for mercy as I waited for it to pounce, shouting myself hoarse as I tried to call it back – like a shipwrecked man shouting hopelessly after a distant ship. Glimpsing for an instant the fearful symmetry, the mystery and the meaning of things; then, the vision lost, as it seemed, for ever, and I left stranded. Borne down by the mountains, sightless in the darkness, chilled as though the Lake water flowed in my veins.

Coming back to London, it seemed as though I had been away for years; actually only for eighteen months. Everything looked differently to me;

especially the assumption on which I had lived from my earliest years, that such and such changes, brought about peacefully through the ballot-box, or drastically through some sort of revolutionary process, would transform human life; making it brotherly, prosperous and just, instead of, as it had always been, and still was for most people, full of poverty, exploitation and conflict. I no longer believed this, nor ever would again. The essential quality of our lives, as I now understood, was a factor, not so much of how we lived, but of why we lived. It was our values, not our production processes, or our laws, or our social relationships, that governed our existence.

This conclusion was by no means as clear-cut then as it subsequently became. I still felt rather dazed, like a clergyman from under whom the mat of orthodoxy has been pulled. Also – quite unreasonably, I admit, in view of the way I had written and spoken about them – I was upset at having become a kind of moral leper in the eyes of old friends and acquaintances like Kingsley Martin and other former *Guardian* colleagues. I was still in the happy position of not receiving press-cuttings, but when *Winter in Moscow* was published, soon after my return from Geneva, I found myself called a liar and a renegade in most publications of the Left. In the case of the *New Statesman* I was foolish enough to send in a letter of self-vindication and protest, but, needless to say, it was not published. It was only when Khrushchev, in his famous speech at the twentieth Party Congress, disclosed the full magnitude of the calamity the forced collectivisation of agriculture had brought about in the USSR, that what I had reported received official confirmation. No one, however, apologised for having called me a slanderer and running dog of Capitalism, or thought any the less of Shaw, the Webbs and all the others who had so ardently and indignantly denied there had been a calamity at all.

Kitty, with her usual skill, had set up in a modest flat in Parliament Hill Fields, but it involved sharing a staircase and various other domestic arrangements, which, with two small children, presented difficulties. Shortly after my arrival on the scene, the landlord asked us to go. Kitty, in any case, was six months pregnant, and in no condition for house-hunting with practically no money. Asking the *Guardian* for a testimonial would have involved approaching Crozier – something that was infinitely repugnant to me. I had, it is true, the good M. Prosper's one but, not surprisingly, it failed to register in Fleet Street. From Geneva I had written to *The Times* to know if there was any chance of being taken on, but received an answer from Barrington Ward which held out little hope. A similar feeler put out to the BBC likewise met with no response. Altogether we were in a mess.

This was a low point in my fortunes; not just materially, but in every sense. I saw no prospect of making a living as a free-lance writer; the articles I wrote and submitted to various publications all came back to me. *Winter in Moscow*, it is true, was reprinted in England, and published in America; but the financial results of this were relatively meagre, and the professional consequences disastrous. Most of the minor patronage in the world of journalism and communications, even in the early thirties, was in the hands of lib-leftists to whom I was now anathema, while in Conservative eyes I was, rightly, suspect. In a rather self-pitying note I jotted down at this time, I described how isolated I felt myself to be, and how I knew that henceforth I should always be so; whereas, to get along in the world, it was necessary to support a ticket, whether Left, Right or Centre. One could love the Soviet Union and detest the British Raj, or vice versa; but to hate both, and for the same reasons – which was my case – was not permissible. So, when I called on the editor of the *Morning Post*, H. A. Gwynne, who had published my articles on my time in the USSR, I found him most friendly and charming but, on the subject of a job, evasive. Similarly, Gerald Barry, then still editor of the *Week-End Review*, and later of the *News Chronicle*. This was to be increasingly an age of polarised loyalties. A review I wrote for the *Spectator*, which predicted the eclipse of liberalism as a moral and political irrelevance, was returned as being inadmissible in its columns; likewise an article submitted to *The Times* about the impossibility of functioning as a conscientious and honest journalist in the conditions imposed by the Soviet authorities.

I had finished my novel, *Picture Palace*, about the *Guardian*, and the publishers of *Winter in Moscow*, Eyre & Spottiswoode, had accepted it for publication. At the same time, out of the blue, Jonathan Cape asked me to write a book about Samuel Butler, the author of *Erewhon* and *The Way of All Flesh*, to appear on the centenary of his birth. The proposal was made over a meal at the Etoile in Charlotte Street; an excellent restaurant that I never enter nowadays, if I can possibly avoid it, because, for me, it is haunted by the ghosts of the books I haven't written and the contracts I haven't fulfilled. Between the hors d'œuvres and the cheese, I hear them incessantly groaning and rattling their (or maybe my) chains. Cape, a tall, solid man with a muddy complexion and ill-fitting false teeth, had originally been a travelling book salesman, but, branching out as a publisher himself, had been remarkably successful.

He enjoyed the great advantage of rarely reading his books, having, in Richard Garnett, a chief reader who read them on his behalf with great acumen. This left him free to estimate their possibilities in other, more subtle ways; holding and weighing them in his hand, turning over their pages, perhaps even smelling them or nibbling at the end-papers. I imagine that a successful picture-dealer operates similarly; Cape was a sort of Duveen, with Garnett as his Berenson. His first bold venture was to publish *Arabia Deserta*, which was an immediate success, and put him in the way of taking over T. E. Lawrence as a literary property. Another great coup was a collected edition of Mary Webb, which he launched to coincide with a speech in praise of her works by the then Prime Minister, Stanley Baldwin, about which Cape had prior knowledge from Tom Jones, the trusted counsellor of a whole series of Prime Ministers. A real relish would come into Cape's voice as he described how he went round from publisher to publisher buying up the rights in Mary Webb's hitherto unsuccessful novels for quite small sums in preparation for his own collected edition, which in the end sold something like a million copies. When he came to this part of the narrative, he would observe: 'Money talks!' Cape, certainly, made it talk, if not sing.

In his innocence – often a quality of worldly success, as sophistication is of worldly failure – he took it for granted that I should admire Butler's works, and find his character and personality congenial. I encouraged him in this view, though actually I knew next to nothing about Butler, and was only very scantily conversant with his works. It was agreed between us that I should take on the book, and appropriate financial arrangements were made. From Cape's point of view, the project ended badly; the more I explored Butler's life and outlook, the less I liked him. By the time I had finished, the result could not but be unacceptable to Cape, as the publisher of Butler's collected works, as well as of Festing Jones's adulatory biography, and much other Butleriana. In the end, another publisher took over my book. I consider it a great compliment that nonetheless Cape several times approached me subsequently with a view to getting me on his list. Perhaps, after all, he shared my feelings about Butler more than he cared to say.

The last time I saw him, we lunched together alone in his flat in Bedford Square, shortly before the outbreak of the 1939–45 war. He was extremely indignant about the state of the world, which he attributed largely to H. G. Wells, one of whose books he had lately published with a substantial advance which had not, as of then, been earned. He told me how he had approached Wells and demanded an explanation, not so much of the book's poor sales, as of all the fraudulent hopes Wells had held out for the future as a result of the discoveries of science and the alleged enlargement of human understanding. The thought of this encounter appealed to me greatly, even though, not surprisingly, it failed to provide Cape with any satisfaction. He also complained bitterly about women novelists, who, he said, were either hideously unattractive but considered their publisher owed them a pass, or so alluring that if he offered one he was liable to be repulsed. My impression is that he was more often in the latter than the former case.

With the Butler book to do, and *Picture Palace* coming out, this was another point in my life when I might have plausibly given up journalism and settled down to be a writer. It was lucky I didn't, because, shortly after my novel had been sent out for review, I received an intimation from the publisher that the *Guardian* had applied for an injunction and threatened an action for libel, which, he explained, could only be fought if I was prepared to put up at once several thousand pounds to cover costs. Otherwise, a settlement would have to be made, necessarily involving the withdrawal of the book. As I had no money at all, only an overdraft, and no possibility of laying hands on any, the publisher's proposal was purely a formality, as he, I am sure, knew; and a settlement was duly reached, whereby the book was withdrawn and all existing copies destroyed. I kept one myself, which I still have; and I believe one or two others are extant. Otherwise, the novel, along with all the work I had put into it and the hopes I had invested in it, was sunk without trace. This was the heaviest blow I ever received as a writer, and it came just when I was least equipped, financially or in any other way, to withstand it. At the time I raged inwardly at the *Guardian*'s – as it seemed to me – contemptible hypocrisy in thus bringing about the suppression of a book, which, though critical of itself, could not, by any stretch of the imagination, be said seriously to damage it commercially – the ground of its complaint. Even now, I have to admit, if my eye happens to fall on some ardent protest in its columns against a move to ban an obscene publication or entertainment, on the ground that any infringement of the right of self-expression is indefensible, I remember – more, I hope, with a grin than a groan – how little such considerations weighed when it was a question of preventing the publication of *Picture Palace*.

The situation was saved for me, financially speaking, by noticing, in the Situations Vacant column in *The Times*, that applications were invited for the post of assistant-editor of the *Calcutta Statesman*. I applied at once, though in a somewhat desultory way, and, to my great surprise, was appointed, at what seemed to me a princely salary. My feelings about this sudden prosperity were mixed. In matters like money and sex, in which the ego is heavily engaged, no satisfaction is attainable; what one wants is to be both rich *and* poor, to be Don Juan *and* St Francis at one and the same time – which cannot be managed. Kitty and I found a pleasant little Regency house in Grove Terrace, overlooking Hampstead Heath, and there I was to leave her once more; now with three children, my daughter Valentine having got herself born with reasonable ease and celerity. Next to Kitty herself, she is the person I have most loved and watched over in this world.

Before leaving for Calcutta, I was required to wait upon Lord Reading, a former Viceroy and Lord Chief Justice, who acted as general adviser to the financial trust which owned the *Statesman*. His office was in a large building at Blackfriars, on the Embankment. I found him seated at a desk with nothing on it, looking immensely old and Jewish and worldly. The very texture of his face was like a parchment deed made out in his favour; with his beak of a nose, a flourishing signature, and his tight red mouth, the seal. Actually, as I soon discovered, he was in a mood of jubilation, and for a strange reason. Gandhi had been going through one of his occasional phases of unpopularity because of a clash with Hindu orthodoxy – the same thing that led ultimately to his assassination – and that very day it had been reported in the papers that he had been stoned by fellow-Indians. Nothing could have pleased Reading more. When he had been Viceroy, the stones were all thrown at him on Gandhi's behalf; now they were being thrown at Gandhi. His parchment face was positively beaming, and, if not actually rubbing his hands together, he seemed to be on the point of doing so. So overpowering was his delight at the turn of events that I wondered if he really remembered the purpose of my being there in his office, apart from a vague awareness that it had something to do with my going to India. Anyway, we talked briefly about my own, scarcely Viceregal, time in Travancore, and I mentioned that Gandhi had visited Alwaye when I was there. This set him off, and again he was far away, watching the grotesque little figure in the loincloth, the hostile crowd pushing towards him, the stones falling round him; instead of the everlasting '*Mahatma Gandhi ki jai*' which had so often assailed his ears (though only distantly, as he sat secure in his Viceregal carriage), this time, angry, derisory shouts. It was, in his eyes, a delectable reversal of fortune. When he got up to

shake hands and indicate that my audience was over, I was quite surprised to find that he was wearing an ordinary lounge suit. I had all
along been seeing him in buckskin breeches and a gilded coat shining
with orders and decorations. A secretary took me to lunch in a canteen
in the basement; he told me that Reading had recently been married
for the second time, to a lady a good deal younger than himself. She
had particularly instructed him, the secretary said, to see that her celebrated husband did not eat oysters – a difficult assignment because he
was greatly addicted to them.

Another call I was required to make before leaving for Calcutta was
on the then Secretary of State for India, Sir Samuel Hoare. He received
me at the India office, very suave and genial. Reading looked back on
Viceregal days; Hoare perhaps saw himself as one day becoming Viceroy. Meanwhile, the Reforms! He was for them heart and soul; and,
indeed, piloted them through the House of Commons with skill and
subtlety, warmly cheered on from Printing House Square and Cross
Street, for once in unison. He asked me to write to him from time to
time about how things were going at the Indian end, which I gladly
undertook to do. Face still Quakerish, but with worldly accretions,
Hoare's Bank intervening between the Society of Friends and Rt Hon.
Hon., Gallant and Learned ones in the House of Commons; neatly
attired, sleek, with white kid tops to his boots, he felt himself to be in
charge of India's destiny. In that same office of his, seated at that self-
same desk, had not successive Secretaries of State settled the affairs of
India and its hundreds of millions of inhabitants, far, far away though
they might be. As I tried to point out in our correspondence, duly engaged in when I got to India, things were different now. He might push
the tiller this way or that, but the ship would not respond. Surely, it
couldn't be quite as bad as that, he wrote back. But couldn't it? All
that grinding of Parliamentary mills; all those divisions, sometimes
through the night; the flushed faces and dishevelled hair, Churchill on
his feet, papers waved – Here! Here! Shame! Resign! At last, *le roy le
veult*. A triumph for the Secretary of State, *The Times* and the *Guardian*
intoned, and a tribute to his patience and persistence. Even so, when
the hour struck, the Raj fell, like others before it, and what had happened, or was to happen, in Westminster and Whitehall had little or no
bearing on the manner of its falling, or on the sequel.

How different was my journey to India and arrival in Calcutta this
time, from the previous occasion ten years before! On the boat, *Viceroy
of India*, and the train from Bombay to Calcutta, I travelled, of course,

first-class. Now I had become a Burra Sahib indeed, however much I might try, conversationally and in my attitude of mind, to pretend otherwise. This was gratifying to my conceit, but otherwise a source of wretchedness, which was crystallised in an incident, trivial in itself, which nonetheless made a deep impression on me. A missionary who was travelling second-class on the same boat, and who had known me when I was at Alwaye, sought me out for a chat. We greeted one another affectionately, and then, after we had exchanged a few words, he looked at me strangely and said: 'You've changed, you're quite different.' I knew exactly what he meant, but I tried to pass his remark off facetiously; saying something about being older, though not wiser. Shortly afterwards, he got up abruptly and left me. I never saw him again, but what he said stayed with me.

The year I spent in Calcutta was easily the most melancholy of my life. For once I kept a diary regularly, which I find now so full of misery and self-pity as to be barely readable. I lived in a flat above the *Statesman* office with a man named Wordsworth – he claimed to be some sort of descendant of the poet – who was acting-editor of the paper when I arrived. He had been in the Indian Educational Service; then had moved over to journalism. A short, plump, pasty man, who had all the correct liberal views and attitudes of mind; believing, for instance, that it would be possible, through constitutional changes, to transform the British Raj peaceably into a Westminster-style self-governing democracy. Also that the League of Nations, given the proper support, might be relied on to keep the peace while remedying Germany's legitimate grievances. And so on. I must have been a disagreeable member of the household. His soft persistence in upholding such views led me to go out of my way to pour scorn and ridicule on them, as well as on all his heroes, like Anthony Eden, Noel Baker, Robert Cecil and Gilbert Murray.

Among some old papers I kept from this time in Calcutta, I came across a leader I had written when Wordsworth was in the chair, heavily scored by his editorial pencil. It was headed 'Towards A Repetition of 1914', and began: 'It is interesting to look back and see how, little by little, Germany has shuffled out of the Treaty of Versailles,' and goes on to point out that this process did not begin with Hitler and the Nazis, nor was it a consequence of the harsh treatment Germany suffered at the hands of the Allies; it started before the Treaty was even concluded. 'No sooner, that is to say, was the war over than Germany began to prepare for another.' This sentence was deleted, and Hitler given a 'Herr'. Thereafter, when his name occurred, it was usually replaced by 'the Nazis', as though to indicate that there was a distinction between him and his followers. I was not allowed to say that there were plenty of people, including the Foreign Secretary, 'who appear to think that, although Germany has just publicly repudiated one treaty, peace may be safeguarded by persuading her to sign another'. Nor that trying to coax Germany back into the League of Nations in the hope that thereby European security might be safeguarded, was like sending a criminal who has broken all the laws in one country, into another where the laws were different, in the expectation that there he would be law-abiding. Even in my concluding sentence: 'While Sir John Simon tries to soothe Hitler back to Geneva, and Mr Anthony Eden carries his load of well-worn platitudes from one capital to another, everything is being prepared for the final stage – a repetition of 1914, only worse', 'platitudes' is altered to 'arguments'. This old, dog-eared leader with its rash of heavy pencilled deletions, is, in its tiny way, an historical document, providing, as it does, a true image of the spirit of appeasement which had already captivated so many of the righteous and the enlightened, like Wordsworth. I cannot now remember whether or not, as editorially amended, it ever appeared in the paper; if it did, it would have made no conceivable difference to anyone or anything, even though the concluding prediction was to come true, and more than true, before five years had passed.

Over my desk there was a large fan, which, turning, scattered the papers on my desk, and blew the sheet in my typewriter back on itself, with disastrous consequences to my typing. On the other hand, to turn the fan off left me sitting with a stagnant mind in stagnant air. So, I was always turning it on and off; as I did, likewise, such thoughts as I could muster – two parallel processes. It was the period when some White Paper, or Blue Book, or Royal Commission Report relating to India was always coming out. Since they were all accorded editorial treatment, they needed to be studied, analysed, criticised, even though they had little, if any, relevance to the actual existing situation – a tottering Imperial Power confronted with a rising tide of nationalism, still attached to the bizarre figure of Gandhi, but with other Indian leaders – mostly western-educated, like Nehru, and Moslem zealots like Jinnah – increasingly taking a hand. It seemed obvious to me that there could only be one outcome; the British would have to go. Yet they themselves, in their clubs and offices, at their mah-jong and bridge tables, on their polo-grounds and tennis-courts, were serenely convinced that, with some adjustments here and there, the Raj, in one form or another, would go on for centuries yet. A favourite saying among them was that, if the British left, within six months the Indians would be down on their knees begging them to come back. It seems almost inconceivable now, but this was seriously believed. Certainly, I cannot recall meeting a single British business man or government official, soldier or even missionary, who would have considered it possible that the Raj was to end before the twentieth century had half run its course.

This made it difficult to talk seriously with them about the Raj and its outcome; still more to write seriously about it in the *Statesman*, which was the organ of British business interests, particularly in Bengal, and largely dependent on them for its very substantial advertising revenue. So I just did what I had to do, without bothering too much about it. Bored in a way, and yet not bored; for instance, finding something vivid and captivating in the scene each night when the paper was going to press. The humid heat hanging over everything, muffling sounds and smudging galleys; the strange chant of the proof-readers, in which stock prices, cricket scores, and even at times maybe words of my own, were all mixed up, and addressed, as it seemed, to some deity. But who? Their Excellencies? Sun Life? BP? Perhaps returning after dinner, rather tipsy, cigar-smoking, white dinner-jacketed, to drop into the subs' room to see if there was any news. There, inscrutable faces, and such a variety of heads; some of them shaved, wholly or partially, maybe with a shaved strip down the middle like an airport runway; others tousled, turbaned, with or without buns, bent over copy or Linotype machines. Despite the noise and the chatter, like the night itself, all so still. Anglo-Indian girls, rather beautiful and hopeless, beautiful in their hopelessness – Ivy, Gladys, Renee; barely contained in their dresses. Down below, the rotaries, recently installed, pounding away; they, too, leaving intact that brooding stillness, heavy and fathomless. Holding a galley in my hand to look at it – 'Before any forward step can be taken, terrorism must stop; that is the first condition . . .'; damp patches marking where I had held it, the ink running. When we were filming *Twilight of Empire*, I turned over the pages of bound volumes of the *Statesman* covering the time that I worked on it, and read out sentences as empty and as turgid. Did I write them? Honesty compelled me to admit that I might have.

The greatest alleviation of my dismal life in Calcutta was a friendship I had with four Indians. It started with Shahid Suhrawardy, who had heard of my coming to Calcutta from Hugh Kingsmill's brother, Brian Lunn, and so he sought me out. I liked him at once. He had the virtues

of his faults; heavily pock-marked, a great fantasist, reputedly a dedicated womaniser, and belonging to one of the leading Moslem families
in Bengal. The adventure of his life had been to go to Russia, where he
fell in with a theatrical company and became the lover of the leading
lady. Though he was separated from her, he continued to send her a
substantial part of his salary as Professor of Fine Arts at Calcutta University; a post that made little demands on his time and energies, there
being few students, and they not particularly diligent, and no arts, fine
or otherwise. Through Shahid I met the others – Sudhindranath Datta,
a Bengali poet who had been Rabindranath Tagore's secretary, Apurbo
Chanda, a large, jovial man, a civil servant, at that time Calcutta's acting
Director of Education, and Tulsi Goswami, a rich landowner and Congress politician. Sudhin was the most elegant and cultivated of them, and
the one I came in the end to know and love best; Tulsi the most dazzling,
whose wearing of *kadi*, or homespun cloth, as a good follower of Gandhi,
did not prevent him from looking like a dandy and living a life of great
extravagance and self-indulgence; Chanda large, cheerful and amicable.

We met often, and at least once a week dined together, either at one
of their houses, or in a restaurant – often a Chinese one because Shahid
had romantic notions about China; sometimes in the Bengal Club, of
which I was now a member. This necessitated having a private room,
Indians not being allowed in the club dining-room. I must say, as I
often told them, they missed nothing by being excluded; but even so it
was vaguely embarrassing. It seems extraordinary now that such absurd
arrangements were maintained almost up to the end of the Raj.

The motive of the Calcutta Sahibs and their Memsahibs for thus
guarding their exclusivity so jealously was social rather than racial or
political. Service in India, whether in Government, commerce or even
as a missionary, provided, in its day, a ready means of instant social
climbing. It was perfectly possible to acquire an upper-class way of life,
with servants, playing polo, changing for dinner and other intimations of
gentility in a single generation. Furthermore, a socially aspiring Sahib,
by sending his progeny to public schools, could ensure that they took
this changed status for granted, and so were firmly integrated into the
upper classes from the beginning. This was one of the attractions of
Empire for its lowlier devotees, and maybe, too, why its loss has tended
to produce revolutionary impulses among those who would have been its
beneficiaries – the Brushwood Boys with nowhere to go, the Sanderses
without a River, the Bulldog Drummonds hopelessly studying the
classified advertisements in the *Daily Telegraph*.

On my first visit to India none of this arose, but in Calcutta it did. I used to go riding in the early morning on the Maidan, or out at the Jodhpur Club. Being up on a horse is a great assertion of social distinction – being a knight rather than a pawn; the riding schools flourish with the gossip-columns. Fortunately for me, by some special mercy, whenever I have been caught up in knightly fancies, something has always happened to make me look ridiculous. Don Quixote rather than Sir Galahad has been my prototype. Thus, riding in the Maidan one morning, my horse ran away with me; pounding along, I noticed a little compact group of horsemen, one of whom detached himself, and came racing after me. As my horse lost its momentum – due to fatigue rather than to anything I did – he caught up with me, and angrily asked me whether I realised that I had galloped past His Excellency, the Governor. I said I hadn't realised it, but even if I had I shouldn't have been able to do anything because my horse had run away with me. Whereupon, he muttered something about how riders as incompetent as I obviously was, ought not to be allowed to use the Maidan; and anyway not to let it happen again. The governor in question was none other than Sir John Anderson, a portentous civil servant who subsequently became Churchill's Home Secretary in the war, and gave his name to an air-raid shelter, ending up as Viscount Waverley.

Some fifteen years later, when I was a newspaper correspondent in Washington, Walter Bell, the then British Ambassador, Lord Inverchapel's PA, telephoned to say that they had Lord Waverley staying at the Embassy, and could I possibly arrange some sort of journalistic party for him. This was duly done. In the course of the evening I mentioned the incident on the Maidan in Calcutta, but it did not please him; however it was told, it presupposed a certain pomposity on his part. I did not add that it cured me for ever of feeling important on a horse. In appearance, he was more like a bronze statue of a man than a man and might, in the ordinary way, have expected to figure on one in the streets of Calcutta. The cities of the Empire used to be full of such statues of British soldiers and administrators. Now they have mostly been removed, the few left standing, forgotten and neglected, for the birds to use; one or two of the very famous – a General Gordon, a Kitchener – sent home at great expense. The process of change has been speeding up so fast that already some of their indigenous successors have fallen out of favour and likewise been removed – for instance, Nkrumah in Accra. History is written in statues as well as in blood.

My four Indian friends were, of course, all nationalists, or *Swarajists*, though Tulsi was the only practising militant. At the same time, in education and tastes, and even habits, they were completely Anglicised. Indeed, it was I who often found myself arguing most strongly against the cultural and spiritual consequences of the Raj, and insisting that it would only truly come to an end if it were pulled up by the roots, not just sliced off. Otherwise the white Sahibs would be dismissed, only to be replaced by brown ones. Sudhin alone really agreed with me about this; he felt differently, perhaps, because Bengali was his true language and medium of expression, whereas, in the case of the others, it was English. Shahid regarded himself, anyway, as a cosmopolitan; in Europe he spoke nostalgically about the sensual delights offered by Oriental women, and in India he was in raptures over the pleasures he had experienced in the arms of European ones. *Kharma Sutra* abroad, *Fanny Hill* at home. Tulsi, who had made a runaway marriage with the daughter of the only Indian peer, Lord Sinha, was by upbringing and temperament an aristocrat, and seemingly perfectly at ease in all circumstances; Chanda likewise, by virtue of the sheer ebullience of his nature.

Yet in all of them I sensed an undercurrent of melancholy, corresponding to my own. This was especially true of Sudhin; but Shahid, too, despite his outward show of being a contented sensualist, looked tired and lost when his face fell into repose. In Tulsi's case, he drank excessively, and, in the end, self-destructively, to evade thoughts that might sadden him; and even Chanda was liable to fall unaccountably into long silences. Deep inside them they knew that this western culture they had so brilliantly acquired, this very English language they spoke so fluently and idiomatically, and, in Sudhin's case with great artistry, these ancient seats of learning (they had all been at Oxford or Cambridge) where they had been so proud to be alumni that it had all seen its best days, and was now in a decline, and they with it. Though in a sense I was in the same case, it was at least a home-produced gold brick that I was landed with; whereas, what they had acquired at such great trouble and expense was an imported product. Sudhin called the elegant fragment of autobiography he left behind him '*The Twilight World*'. No one has described this no-man's-land between a dying Indian culture and a debased western one more subtly and delicately than he. It was the habitat of all my four friends, and, in somewhat different terms, my own. A twilight growing ever darker.

We went on a visit together to Santiniketan, the *ashram* founded by Rabindranath Tagore; it, too, a confluence of cultural streams. William Morris knights-at-arms, on elephants instead of white horses; there's shade under the banion tree, brother; arrows of non-desire building a garden city in India's dry and dusty land. In the morning we were awakened by acolytes singing under our windows, and in the evening we sat at the Poet's feet, listening, along with the other *ashram* residents, to an address by him. He was a majestic figure with a long silky beard, robed rather than dressed, hair parted in the middle – a sort of ethereal Rasputin; a steeple to Gandhi's gargoyle. The two of them represented the poles of Indian nationalism; Poet and Mahatma, with Miss Slade, an admiral's daughter, shuttling between them. A German lady, spectacled, head shaved, and wearing a saffron robe, continued to spin as the Poet exhorted us to turn away from western materialism. I preferred her in saffron to dirndl.

My four friends looked forward to Indian Independence, but also, in their different ways, consciously or unconsciously, dreaded it. Even Tulsi, who for a time was actually a Congress Minister in the Bengal Government, and who would certainly have given everything he had – including his life – for the Swarajist cause, as I well knew, kept hidden deep down in his heart some reservations. Our parts in history are allotted, not chosen; and theirs belonged to the Raj, which they hated, rather than to the Swaraj, whose coming to pass they sought. Curiously enough, the one who in worldly terms throve most when Independence came was Shahid, who cared least about it. As a Moslem, western-educated and with some academic distinction, he had a rarity value in the newly constituted Pakistan, and was made chairman of the Civil Service Commission responsible for appointments to government posts. I met him briefly when he occupied this position, and he complained wryly that, though he could appoint others, himself he could not appoint. In time, he must somehow have overcome this difficulty, because he was posted as Ambassador to Madrid; a congenial appointment, Spain being a country he liked, and, as he was happy to find, harbouring few Pakistani nationals, which made his duties correspondingly unexacting. I saw him several times during this period; he had grown very deaf, but his face had come to wear an expression of great serenity and benevolence. Soon after he retired and returned to Karachi, I heard that he had died.

The other three were less fortunate. Tulsi ran through his fortune, and his health collapsed. Once when I happened to be passing through Calcutta, Sudhin took me to see him. We found that he had recently suffered a stroke, which had partially paralysed him, and made it difficult for him to speak. As we sat with him, he was struggling to say something, which turned out to be that he was distressed I should see him in so poor a state. I tried to tell him – I hope so much that I succeeded – that it was a joy to me to see him always. This was true. Even then, a dying man, something of the charm, the gaiety and profligacy, which had so captivated me when we first met, still remained. I knew I should never see him again, and was glad of an opportunity to say good-bye. He died a few weeks later. Sudhin himself, as a Bengali poet and writer of the highest reputation, might have been expected to thrive in post-Raj India. Instead, he chose to make himself partially an exile, and went with his wife, Rajeshwiri, an accomplished singer and musician, on a protracted foreign tour. I saw him several times in the course of it, but had the feeling even then that he was taking a last look at the places and people and things he cared most about. I thought I detected something muted in him; a smiling disregard for the projects – in his case, among others, a definitive biography of Tagore – the world always heaps in the laps of those with no zest to undertake them. Back in Calcutta, one night he just died. As for Chanda – in the last conversation I had with him, in one of the Calcutta clubs some years after India had become independent, he complained bitterly about the dreadful people who, under the Nehru Raj, managed to get themselves elected as members; for all the world like some ferocious Indian Colonel Blimp. Now he, too, has died and I alone remain.

Though I was nominally living in Calcutta, I was not really living there at all. It was extraordinary how, as a Sahib in India, this could be done. For instance, I had a car with a driver, and he drove me wherever I wanted to go, from door to door; the shops and restaurants and cinemas and clubs frequented by Sahibs were clean and orderly, insulated from the teeming town. In the crowded streets, my driver would sound his hooter persistently, and a way would be opened before us; shadowy figures melting away, gibbering and grimacing. If, as I sometimes did, I walked through the bazaar, I might actually rub shoulders with fellow-pedestrians, but if they saw it was a Sahib, as likely as not they would draw aside. Again, if I showed interest in a particular shop, the shop-keeper would drop whatever he was doing, leave any customer he happened to be serving, to attend to my requirements. Though such treatment in some ways appealed to my vanity and egotism, it was a hateful feeling to be thus cut off from the life and people of the city. Sometimes I would stand on the balcony of the flat above the *Statesman* office, and look down at the street below – Chowringee – envious of passers-by pushing and elbowing their way along the pavement, the road likewise packed with jostling vehicles, trams and cars and rickshaws and bicycles all mixed up. Below me, the noise of an Indian street, with its jabber and bells and shouts; and I up above there, cut off from it all, isolated in the absurdity of the additional caste the English had created in India, over-topping all the others.

On one occasion I did get involved, and then too nearly for my taste. Driving me to a dinner party for which I was rather late, my driver ran a man over. I felt the jerk as it happened. The driver naturally stopped the car, and at once a crowd began to gather; faces peering in at me angrily through the windows, shaking their fists, shouting, suddenly wild and furious. There were no policemen about, and no one, as far as I could see, had sent for an ambulance. Was there even one available for such lowly casualties? I began to wonder what was going to happen, when my driver, with great presence of mind, got out of the car, picked up the injured – or, for all I knew, dead – man, deposited him beside the driving-seat, and drove off as fast as he could go to the nearest hospital. It all happened so quickly that there was no time for the crowd to react. A few stones came hurtling after us, that was all. At the hospital, the man was taken to the emergency ward to be examined, and I trailed along, thinking that perhaps, as a Sahib, I might be able to get him attended to more quickly. I felt particularly absurd in my dinner jacket; the more so because, in order not to get any blood on it, I kept well away from the injured man. Everywhere bodies were stretched out, overflowing from the wards into the corridors. It was difficult to avoid treading on them. To my great relief, it appeared that my man had suffered no serious injury, and was only shaken. While I was arranging matters for him – inevitably producing some money, the only thing I had to give; rupees, pieces of paper, too easily earned, with the King-Emperor's head on them – another emergency case was brought in. This time, it was a man who had cut his throat.

I shuddered at the gaping hole in his neck; at the blood, and his grey, inert face. Who was he? No one seemed to know, or to care much either. All I wanted to do was to get away. Back to my dinner party, a drink, talk, spoons dipping into soup, servants in red cummerbunds passing round plates of food and bottles of wine – a scene calculated to put out of sight and mind this other one of sprawling bodies, and the man with the gashed throat who was too inconsequential even to have a name, or arouse curiosity as to why he should have cut a gaping hole in his windpipe; his single gesture of defiance against a world which seemed indifferent whether he lived or died.

At our dinner-table conversation I mentioned the incident, giving rise to a number of sage observations. Calcutta medical services very inadequate, traffic control deplorable; anyway life held cheap in the East – look at the way they treat animals! – in contradistinction to the West, where the individual was valued. Yes, admittedly in the recent war there'd been retrogression, but that wasn't going to happen again. We were learning; hence the League of Nations. What about transmigration? Maybe my man hoped to have a better break in another incarnation; to be born in Croydon, say, instead of Calcutta, and pass matriculation, and take books out of the public library. In Calcutta we'd reduced infant mortality, certainly, which, of course, was a good thing – no one was going to deny that – but led to the other difficulty; too many people, my man being one of the surplus. So it went on through the evening, until it was time to call for our cars and go; but I still hadn't managed to exorcise that other scene in the hospital. Even years afterwards, when I was back in Calcutta with Mother Teresa, it came back more vividly than ever. I could not but contrast my attitude with hers; not just in the sense that we moved in opposite directions – she to where the poor and afflicted were, and I away from them. It was in her response to them that the true contrast lay; she seeing in each sorrowing, suffering human being, neither a body surplus to a population norm, nor a waste product, but the image of a sorrowing, suffering Saviour, so that in solacing them she had the inestimable honour and joy of solacing him. A *Via Dolorosa* that was also a *Via Gloriosa*.

In my office, I worked more often at Samuel Butler than on contributions to the *Statesman*'s editorial columns. I daresay the conditions under which I wrote about him – with the fan churning up the stagnant, humid air, and my stagnant mind needing to be churned up likewise if it was to function at all – affected my view of him and his books. Sentences came laboriously, and the very physical effort of typing left me limp and exhausted. Visitors occasionally dropped in, breaking the thread of my thoughts; mostly Indians, who had a disconcerting way of sitting on and on in total silence. There was, for instance, B, a barrister-at-law who had been at Harrow and Oxford. His ostensible purpose was to collect a book for review (books, even new ones, soon had a damp, musty smell in Bengal's humid climate), but, as he put it, he'd just pushed his head through the door to say Salaam. His appearance still bore some traces of Inns of Court formality – alpaca jacket, winged collar, watch-chain, but with the lost eyes, weak mouth and sometimes tremulous hands of a drunkard. He had legal tales to tell – repartee of a Birkenhead, eloquence of a Patrick Hastings, skill of a Birkett. 'My *guru*,' he said to me once, 'is Hilaire Belloc.' It was almost unbearably poignant; after all, B was our creation.

In such circumstances, I saw Butler more luridly than I might otherwise have done, as symbolising everything I most abhorred. In my estimation, the poor fellow might have drafted the League of Nations Covenant, been a founder-member of the Fabian Society and a Friend of the Soviet Union, instead of holding strongly conservative views about everything except homosexuality and patricide; he being homosexual himself, and hating his father for persistently refusing to die and leave him his money. Like Columbus stumbling upon America when he thought he was finding a route to India, Butler, all unconsciously blazed a trail which many have subsequently followed. Thus, through *The Way of All Flesh*, published posthumously, he helped to make it as fashionable to detest parents as formerly it had been to revere them. His sentimental, timid homosexuality likewise went down well among the enlightened; as also did his profound respect for money as the source of all happiness, and the condition of personal freedom. 'No gold, no Holy Ghost' he jotted down in one of his grotesquely over-praised Notebooks.

Excoriating Butler through leaden Bengal afternoons and evenings, seated under a fan; breaking off to cope with the Report of the Joint Select Parliamentary Committee on Indian Constitutional Reform ('A state paper of the highest importance whose language is adequate to the gravity of the scene . . .'); then back to Butler, and his weekly visits to a French lady in Handel Street, whom he shared with his friend and future biographer, Festing Jones, though on different days – in the circumstances, I consider it quite a feat that the book was somehow finished and dispatched to the publisher. A good part of the credit was due to Kitty, who patiently went through the Butler papers, lodged with Geoffrey Keynes, the brother of Maynard; copying out for me what she thought would be of interest or significance, and doing it so skilfully that pretty well every scrap of material she sent me was usable. I had been to see Keynes and his fellow literary executor before leaving for India, and found him a fussy, finicky man, with whom I should have found it difficult to deal. Needless to say, when he read my book he hated it, and I half-feared that there would be a repetition of what happened with *Picture Palace*. It was within his power to prevent publication because of my use of copyright material. However, though less liberal in principle than the *Guardian*, to my great relief he behaved more liberally, and contented himself with just expressing his own personal distaste and disapproval.

It was from Mr Cathie, Butler's servant, whom I met shortly before leaving for India, that I got the details of the visits Butler and Festing Jones paid to Handel Street each week. Cathie was a respectable-looking man in a dark suit, stiff collar and shirt-front, who had set up in a grocery business after Butler's death, and who proved to be a true disciple of his late master by at once raising the question of remuneration. We agreed on a fiver in advance, to be followed by another at the end of our confabulations. 'The Governor,' he told me, 'would go every Wednesday afternoon. "Oh, bother, Alfred," he'd say. "It's Wednesday today, and I've got to go to Handel Street." He'd leave about two-thirty and be back by five, walking both ways.' Jones, it appeared, went on Thursdays, but how long he stayed, and whether he, too, walked both ways, Mr Cathie did not know, or particularly care. 'He was always crying,' he said of Jones, whom he obviously disliked. Of the French lady herself, he said that she was dark and large, a fine-looking woman, whom the Governor had picked up one evening at Islington. He and Jones paid her a pound a week each, including their holidays. While they were away, Mr Cathie handed over the money in person, and, as he put it, took her out once or twice himself. Rightly or wrongly, the impression I formed was that on these occasions he considered himself to have been more than the equal of the other two together.

Their hearts, anyway, whatever may have been the case with their bodies, were not in Handel Street, but with a Swiss youth named Hans Faesch, a lock of whose hair they wore, turn and turn about, in a locket suspended from their watch-chains. Together, they saw Hans off from Holborn Viaduct Station when he went to Singapore. Butler celebrated the occasion with some verses beginning:

> Out, out, into the night,
> With the wind bitter north-east and the sea rough.
> You have a racking cough and your lungs are weak,
> But out, out into the night you go.
> So guide you and guard you, Heaven, and fare you well.

which he considered to be 'the best thing I ever wrote'. He sent the verses to the *Spectator* for publication, but later withdrew them because, as he wrote to Hans, 'things have happened in England which make Jones and me decide not to publish them even anonymously'. On Butler's copy of this letter there is a note to the effect that the event in question was the trial of Oscar Wilde. Just before we separated, and after he had received his second fiver, Mr Cathie paused to remark: 'There's one man I didn't care for. Now what's his name? I've got it –

Bern*ard* Shaw [accentuating the second syllable of 'Bernard']. I didn't care for the way he spoke at the Erewhon Dinner. Not at all. And the Governor didn't care for him either. "He's a beast," he said when he came back from seeing him. "He's a beast!"' Mr Cathie departed chuckling. After being thus briefed by Mr Cathie, I visited Handel Street with Hugh Kingsmill and Hesketh Pearson to identify the house. While we were there, Kingsmill drew so hilarious a picture of these weird transactions, including the French lady's imagined comparison between M. Mercredi and M. Jeudi, and a recitation of 'Out, out, out into the night', that by the time he had finished, Hesketh and I were holding onto lamp-posts, helpless with laughter.

My book on Butler, when it appeared, offended all the critics, E. M. Forster called it a cross-patch of a book, and Desmond McCarthy, the reigning pundit at the time, devoted two whole articles in the *Sunday Times* to demolishing it. Needless to say, the Butler cult has continued unabated, and even to this day Mr Cathie's Governor is held up as a Voltarian exploder of Victorian humbug and complacency; whereas, in point of fact, he was himself – if there is such a thing – the quintessential Victorian. It is curious how often the cult figure turns out, on investigation, to be the antithesis of the cult he is supposed to have initiated. Who, for instance, would have disliked *O! Calcutta* more than D. H. Lawrence? Or Stalinism more than Karl Marx?

By this time, the editor of the *Statesman*, Arthur Moore, had returned from leave. He had only lately been appointed to the editorship, after his predecessor, Alfred Watson, had been shot at by a Bengal terrorist for some articles that Moore had written. It was a rather embarrassing basis for inheriting the position, especially as Watson would have been well content to stay on. However, the proprietors considered this would be imprudent, and so Watson returned to London, where he frequented the National Liberal Club and was knighted. Moore had worked for *The Times* as correspondent in Persia, and very much belonged to that tradition. In happier circumstances he might well have been offered the throne of Albania, or have sent long delayed messages from Mecca or Tibet, or trudged through Outer Mongolia. As it was, he had turned up in Calcutta, where his mercurial temperament took him from the out-and-out imperialist position which might have cost Watson his life, and did cost him his job, to one of close affinity with the Swarajists. He was a gifted, unstable, Northern Irishman, fated to make a mess of his career, not through being too rigid – which is one way of doing it – but through being too flexible – which is another. I noticed that Europeans living in India either grow duskier or whiter; Moore was in the latter category. Belieing his political views, he grew whiter and whiter, the impression being intensified when, after he left the *Statesman*, he stayed on in Delhi and grew a black beard. Towards the end of his life he fell on evil days, and came to see me once about some project or other. I received him sympathetically, but, I regret to say, offered no effective help.

Kitty came to Calcutta for a short visit at Christmas. It was an unhappy time for both of us, and the nearest our marriage came to breaking up. Just before she left, we found ourselves briefly at one again, and, after she had gone, I sent her a long telegram saying that nothing could ever part us – as, indeed, has proved to be the case. Of all the memories I have to confront, the most hateful are occasions such as this, when I racked my mind to think of words which would hurt and allusions which would stir up bitterness. If there were any possibility of unsaying anything – which, of course, there isn't – this is what I should most wish unsaid. The immediate cause of strife was, inevitably, infidelities. I think of them with a kind of wonder. Can I really have been so obsessed by a relationship which made so little lasting impression that now I have difficulty in recalling the person concerned? Did I really wait like that, with my heart furiously beating, for a telephone call? Ring a door bell, and listen with such a concentration of excitement to approaching footsteps? Scribble notes so ardently? Tear open others received so eagerly? In the consequent pin-pointing of emotion and desire, feel the warmth of the sun on my back, breathe in the fragrance of jasmine in a garden, with sharpened senses? Aware, as never before, of the bright colours and silken texture of a sari, and the touch of fingers so soft and supple that they might have been boneless. Overwhelmed likewise by the sudden onslaught of night, velvety black, dancing with fire-flies; the stars themselves so near and bright that one of them might be a tiny jewel fixed in a nostril, and, at the same time, so distant that they seemed to be beyond the furthest limits of space, in the eternity that sensuality cannot reach? Was it really so?

Don Juan, more even than Raskolnikov, is the hero of our time; his impersonation, our most gruelling servitude, the quest for his Unholy Grail our most tortuous journey. He is everywhere – on the motorways in his GB-ed car, at cocktail parties recce-ing the company; a huntsman in a game-reserve. Once, in a Stockholm roof café, the people I was with happened to mention that one of the waiters – a Canadian named Harry – was in the habit each evening of picking on one of the customers to come home with him. They pointed him out to me; like the other waiters, wearing a sort of smartly cut red hunting jacket, and weaving his way among the tables while holding aloft his tray loaded with bottles and glasses. Examining him curiously, I noticed that his face had a rapt, almost mystical expression, as though his thoughts were far removed from the mundane business of serving drinks and collecting tips; at the same time, full of the ineffable sadness that comes of seeking the attainable. A People's Byron; the egotist persisting in his egotism to the point of becoming disinterested; the carnal so ardently pursued that it becomes a kind of spirituality. Looking more closely, I saw that he was older than I had thought. There were wrinkles, a certain thinning, and even perhaps greying, of the hair; a dry parchment look about the flesh. Did he always, I asked, manage to pull off his evening conquest? Nearly always, I was told, but there might be occasional evenings when something went awry – when he made the wrong choice, or when he or the chosen one happened to be out of sorts. The pale Scandinavian light – it was summer and the days scarcely ended – hung over the scene, adding a macabre unearthly touch.

Who can be expected to look for a God when there isn't one? Or for perfection when there is nothing beyond the ticking of the clocks. What is to be done but play the Crucifixion backwards, and reverse the Logos – in the beginning was the flesh, and the flesh became Word? Celluloid the only recourse – moving pictures, presenting between Action! and Cut!, the seven ages of lechery. The pimply schoolboy creeping willingly into his sex-instruction classes; then the youthful, zestful sex-instructed lover. After him, the grown man, bearded like the pard, twin-slitted coat, motel habitué, with contraceptives to hand, stoking up nature's fires with bottled ones; followed by the seasoned veteran, round bellied, full of wise saws and modern instances culled from his Bond, his Clockwork Orange, his Last Tango. Finally, the lean and slippered pantaloon, with spectacles on nose, squinting into his TV screen; and last scene of all, a second childishness and mere oblivion, sans teeth, sans taste, sans everything; even – the ultimate desolation – sans telly.

Moore disliked the views I expressed in my leaders no less than Wordsworth did. So it was a great relief to us all three when it was decided that I should go to Simla and represent the paper during the summer months when the Government of India functioned there. My four friends saw me off at Calcutta Station; we were never to be all five together again.

The train pulling out of the station, gave me an enormous sense of relief. For most of the fifteen months I had spent in Calcutta, I felt ill, dispirited, melancholy. Apart from somehow staggering through the Butler book, my time had been wasted and my mind vacuous. At last I was on the move again; and movement can seem a substitute for being. Like tops, we spin ever faster in order to be still. I stopped off in Delhi for a couple of days. India's new capital was then still in process of construction; the only deliberate architectural monument the Raj left behind it. The foundation-stone was laid by King George V in a cemetery by mistake, and Clemenceau provided the perfect benediction when he said that, of the six ruined capitals round about the same site, the Raj's would provide the most magnificent ruin of all. Even this is doubtful. The princes were never to take their places in the splendid Chamber of Princes designed for them, and it was in the garden of the Commander-in-Chief's residence that, two decades later, smelling the roses still blooming there, I waited to record a television interview with Jawaharlal Nehru, ruler over an independent India.

It was exhilarating to be in the little train climbing up into the mountains to Simla; the air getting appreciably cooler and fresher all the time, and bringing the travelling Sahibs visibly to life. To the handful of English who manned the highest administrative posts, it seemed, even at this late hour, the most natural thing in the world that the government of some four hundred million souls should thus be transferred to a little mountain eyrie, so far away and so inaccessible. They found the hot weather oppressive in the plains; therefore, the whole lumbering administration must follow them to higher altitudes where they would be more comfortable. It was like moving a general headquarters in a war. Whole convoys of lorries carrying files and other documents, whole train-loads of clerks and minor personnel; then the heads of departments, the staff-officers, and finally the Viceroy himself, at this time Lord Willingdon, and his Vicereine, along with their little court – their Comptroller-of-the-Household, their ADC's and secretaries, valets and maids – to take up their residence in Viceregal Lodge, a hill-station version of an English country house.

Simla, at any rate, was an authentic English production; designed by Sahibs for Sahibs, without reference to any other consideration – not even Maharajahs. If, in the future, it is desired (something extremely improbable) to preserve some genuine memorial of British rule in India, then Simla is the place which really conveys what it was like; and, mysteriously, still does. The church, whose dilapidated state is not apparent in the distance; the Mall, along which the Sahibs and their ladies took an airing on Sunday afternoons, with a band-stand where an army band entertained them with appropriate music as they strolled up and down, the ladies with parasols, the gentlemen in large white topees. There were separate houses for the more important officials, allotted in accordance with their status, their name and department indicated on a board at the gate, so that everyone knew who and what everyone was, from members of the Viceroy's Council downwards. On the Mall, a little theatre where plays were produced, and Kipling once acted – Gilbert and Sullivan, Pinero, Barrie, and, more daringly, Noël Coward. Then Viceregal Lodge itself, with a special guard of Sikhs, their black curly beards in nets to keep them tidy, and Wildflower Hall, built by Lord Kitchener when he was Commander-in-Chief, some little distance away from Simla, just far enough to make a pleasant ride and to feel like a rival seat of authority.

Journalists follow authority as sharks do a liner, hoping to feed off the waste it discharges, with perhaps someone occasionally falling overboard to make a meal, and once in a way the whole ship going down and providing a positive feast. There was a little band of us swimming along in the wake of the Government of India – Sandy Inglis, representing *The Times*, and Jim Barnes, Reuter's man, as well, of course, as any number of representatives of Indian newspapers and news-agencies. Public relations, as we know it today, was in its infancy, but already the Government of India had its spokesman, whom we constantly pursued for hand-outs and leakages, and to arrange interviews. Among other useful services, he made a point of mastering the first names of Indians who were going to be knighted, so that on the very day the Honours List came out, he had them pat – Sir Shrinivasa, Sir Rahimtoolah, Sir Girja. It was, in any case, a glad day for one and all. Indian politicians and civil servants were even more avid for honours than their English opposite numbers, and the distribution of knighthoods and lesser decorations, down to MBE's, was followed with breathless interest; so much so, that equivalent post-Raj honours have had to be devised.

Sandy Inglis and his wife Jean became great friends of mine. He was a shrewd, hard-working Scot, who toiled away at producing turn-over articles and news stories about the Reforms, packed tight with information, and full of sober hope for the future. Naturally, he deplored my disparagement of the very idea that the Raj could reform itself in any way that would be acceptable to the Swarajists. The Raj, I vociferously insisted, would either have to re-establish itself on an authoritarian basis – which was virtually inconceivable – or wind itself up, while pretending that power was being gradually and lawfully transferred to Indian hands with a view to creating an All-India democracy on Westminster lines.

We often argued about this, mostly good-naturedly, but sometimes acrimoniously. I have never really been able to understand how anyone can believe in the possibility of compromise in matters of power, which is an absolutist passion, and felt the same incredulity in Simla about the proposed constitutional reforms as I did in Geneva about the League and the ILO as instruments for promoting international and industrial peace. Sandy, on the other hand, faithfully read and digested all the relevant documents, and patiently listened to the various officials concerned as they interminably explained what they were at and what they hoped to achieve. Extreme attitudes are often an excuse for laziness; if the apocalypse is just round the corner, why bother with what is to be done today or tomorrow? All the same, in this particular case it would seem that I lost nothing by avoiding an avalanche of irrelevant words, written and spoken, and that Sandy's heroic labours to reduce them to some sort of sense were a barren pursuit. There never was to be any genuine constitutional reform; only a constitutional debacle, celebrated by Mr Attlee, the Prime Minister responsible, by a visit to the cinema. Or so his then Press Officer, Philip Jordan, told me. I like to think of the little man sitting in the three-and-six-pennies on the day the Bill making India and Pakistan independent states became law, and the Raj was finally wound up. Poor Sandy deserved better than that.

Jim Barnes, the other English journalist in Simla, was the exact antithesis of Sandy – a fanatical admirer of Mussolini and pro-Fascist. A man with a violent temperament, to the point at times of seeming a little mad. He had just come from reporting the Italian conquest of Abyssinia for Reuter's. I never read any of his by-lined dispatches, but it would surprise me if they were notable for impartiality and objectivity. He used to stride up and down the room gesticulating and bellowing about Eden, and the rottenness of British policy, and the feebleness of the Raj. Sometimes I went riding with him; he sat heavily on his horse, and on one occasion, when it persistently refused to canter, I heard him shouting into its ear: 'You're my slave, you've got to do what I say!' His Italian wife was more measured in her attitude to Mussolini than he was, and just accepted her husband's tantrums as an incidental affliction. Once I went to Mass with her, and on the way back, à propos of nothing, she said to me: 'Perhaps one day God will

take pity on you.' Barnes's father had been in the ICS, finishing up as
Governor of Burma; his mother had died when quite young in Quetta,
and was buried in the cemetery there, like many other Sahib's wives,
and he was brought up by his Strachey grandmother in Italy. The poor
fellow never managed to sort himself out, and spent the 1939–45 war in
Italy, where, like Ezra Pound, he broadcast anti-Allied propaganda,
though, unlike Pound, he had no admirers or defenders in the victor's
camp. After the war, he hid in a monastery, where it would be nice to
think he found the peace which had hitherto eluded him. Through his
brother, George Barnes, for a while Broadcasting House's Director of
the Spoken Word (that inimitable title which only a Sir William Haley
could have invented), and then Director of BBC Television, I was about
to get a friendly message to him. Later, I heard that he had died.

I doubt if any government has ever existed so cut off from the
governed as the Government of India nestling among the Himalayas in
Simla. Up there, we might read of rioting, or famines in the plains
below, or – as happened when I was in Simla – of a ferocious earth-
quake in Quetta but these disasters were far, far away, and scarcely
impinged on us. For researchers into the nature of government, Simla
provided a unique opportunity for studying one in isolation; examining
it, as it were, under the microscope; without any confusing involvement
in side issues, such as people, or demagogy, or armed forces, or taxes.
It was government pure and undefiled; endlessly minuting and circulating files, which, like time itself, had neither beginning nor end, but
just were. I grew familiar with the various government departments,
trudging, as I had to, from one to the other to find out what, if anything,
they were at. All housed in identical wooden structures, with broad
verandahs, it was impossible to distinguish Finance from Home, or
Political from Defence, except that, in the case of the last, instead of a
peon in red and gold dozing at each office door, there would be a
sepoy in khaki drill. Typewriters hard at work, Indian clerks and minor
officials clustered together like bees in a hive, the senior officials still
mostly Sahibs, and, at the centre of it all, the Queen Bee, or member of
the Viceroy's Council, responsible for the department in question.

Mooning about in these departments, waiting to see someone I didn't
want to see in order to ask him questions I didn't want answered, I used
sometimes to think of India as I knew it. The dusty roads, the teeming
bazaars, the lurid paddy fields, the sluggish rivers, the women carrying
water from the well in pitchers on their heads, the brown bodies sweating
in the sun as they followed behind the lumbering oxen and steered their

wooden ploughs; the innumerable villages, and feet endlessly padding – little processions, a man leading, then a woman with a baby on her back, and a child barely able to walk, clutching her hand, other children trailing behind. Everywhere people; washing, sleeping, chanting, buying, selling, giving birth, suckling, living, dying. Where was the connection between them and this typewriter fusilade, these dozing peons, the clerks, the Sahibs, the Members of the Viceroy's Council? Power only exists in so far as it connects the government and the governed; the gap between them has to be spanned, whether by demagogy, or the long lashes of whips and barrels of guns, or lies shouted or borne on the waves of sound and light, or magical incantations and emanations, or, as is more commonly the case, by some combination of all or some of them. In the case of Anglo-India, the gap had widened to the point that it was no longer spannable. Governors and governed were like two jagged coastlines, with a torrential sea running between them, and no ferry-boats plying, overhead telephone lines all down, under-water cables all broken; the machinery of government still ostensibly functioning, but like a main-line station with no passengers, a supermarket with no customers.

The focus of all attention in Simla, political, social, administrative, was, of course, Viceregal Lodge; whether ladies aspiring to appear, suitably arrayed, in the highest circles, or their spouses with an eye on promotion and the increments and honours that went therewith, or just anyone, white, brown or mottled, buzzing round the honey-pot of authority in the vague expectation that something sweet-tasting might be sucked out of it. Those embossed invitation cards – Their Excellencies request the pleasure . . . – how precious and sought-after they were! Their Excellencies never, or only rarely, in very exceptional circumstances, requested in vain. My turn came round. Encased in starched shirt and tails, conscious of lines being crossed at the back of my white waistcoat, embossed card in hand, I sat in a rickshaw propelled by four coolies trotting along like ponies, two in front and two behind; knowing, but trying to forget, that Simla rickshaw coolies all die young from enlarged hearts through trotting up and down hills at so high an altitude.

Anyway, there was no alternative; only the Viceroy and the Commander-in-Chief being allowed motor-cars in Simla. Who, in his senses, would care to arrive on foot, hot and dishevelled, for a dinner party at Viceregal Lodge? Certainly not I. So, on we trot, past the turbaned, bearded sentries, who spring to attention, and up to the main entrance where ADC's are waiting to speed guests on their way to join the glittering throng. Unglittering myself, without one single tiny medal, I fall into conversation with a resplendent Guards officer named Codrington, lightly ginger, with pale eyes, who has been trying, he tells me, to upgrade the military music provided by adding a touch of Purcel and summer a'coming in to the usual Colonel Bogey-ish repertoire.

The ADC's shepherded us into some sort of a line, the band struck up the National Anthem, two folding doors were ceremonially opened, and in came Their Excellencies, who proceeded slowly down the line to greet their guests; the names of any doubtful ones whispered into their ears, the ladies courtseying, and the gentlemen bowing low. When my turn came, I, too, bowed: 'I've heard of you,' the Viceroy said, a touch of grimness in his voice. It seemed better than nothing. The Vicereine, a large, zestful lady with a red sash, wore a permanent unvarying smile which beamed upon one and all. He, on the other hand, was slight and frail, like a Max Beerbohm drawing, and studded with gleaming stars and orders. I examined him closely. After all, at any rate in theory, he was one of the world's great potentates; absolute ruler over more souls than any other ruler extant. Even so, he gave out no emanation of authority, but might have been, at a casual glance, a chairman of some board or other, or a City Alderman, or, for that matter, what he really was – an amiable back-bench Conservative MP. Even a Maharajah in his train, with a great jewel in his turban and a self-indulgent face, seemed more like a ruler than the Viceroy. Should I have felt the same if it had been Curzon instead of Willingdon? I asked myself. Probably not. But then Curzon's power over his hundreds of millions of subjects was, to some extent at any rate, real, whereas Willingdon's existed only to the degree that he didn't exercise it. This office, the Viceroyalty, the only one under the British Crown carrying with it the trappings and pomp and circumstance of a Sultan or Caliph, aspired after by so many politicians, drab little men in black coats and spongebag trousers who saw themselves in those splendid robes, seated on a silver throne and presiding over Durbars of inconceivable magnificence – its glory had already departed.

We dined to music which bore little trace of Captain Codrington's efforts to amend it, and afterwards waited to be summoned to Their Excellencies. I was guided first to Lady Willingdon, where she sat giving out waves of energy and enthusiasm. She wished, she said, that they were staying on for another ten years. I put on an expression, I hoped convincingly, of one who wished likewise. What about our successors? she asked. I murmured 'Linlithgow,' with as much journalistic knowingness as I could summon up. 'He's terribly pompous,' she said. I agreed heartily. 'Look at John Anderson,' she went on, 'and how he's changed!' How? I wanted to ask, but at this point an ADC hove in sight to take me away and over to the Viceroy. It was somewhat unusual, I was given to understand afterwards, to be moved straight from her square to his, and was duly flattered.

Willingdon, when I got to him, looked tremendously like an old beau in a Restoration comedy; I half expected him to take a pinch of snuff and flick his handkerchief. People were inclined to think that India was difficult to govern, he began, but he'd found it almost ridiculously easy. You just had to be nice to these fellers, and they responded. Such, at least, had been his experience. He doubted if there was in all the world an easier country to govern than India. In the circumstances, it was a pretty extraordinary statement, and, while I was digesting it, he went on to say that he believed in Providence; otherwise, he'd never have been able to carry on. Then, looking sidelong at me, he added: 'You won't believe in that, I suppose.' Before I could elucidate my own attitude to Providence, my replacement had arrived; a man with a goatee beard who had some sort of connection with the *Round Table* and South Africa. I saw the Viceroy moistening his lips from a glass of water in preparation for another conversation.

Walking back to the Cecil Hotel where I was staying – I was happy not to need a rickshaw for the return journey – I kept going over in my mind what the Viceroy had said about India being so easy a country to govern, and those fellers (meaning, presumably, Indian politicians of one sort and another, from Gandhi and Nehru to the latest batch of Indian knights and CIE's) being so responsive to niceness. It was one of the little vignettes which mark out history like a surveyor's white posts; the last Viceroy but three, up there in the Raj's mountain re-treat, his guests around him, his ADC's at his elbow, his rumbustious lady within hailing distance, the band playing Elgar by way of a com-promise between Captain Codrington and Colonel Bogey – this grey fragile-looking old gentleman telling me how easy he had found govern-ing India and managing those fellers within so short a time of the Raj's total collapse.

I had several other meetings with Willingdon in his office in the way of duty as the *Statesman*'s man in Simla. His amiability, and a certain shrewdness acquired through the years as a politician and proconsul (he had been Governor-General in Canada in addition to his service in India), made him easy to talk to, but he never really said anything about anything. As Viceroy, he was content just to coast along. Indeed, there was nothing much else he could do. The only matter that cropped up about which he seemed to have strong feelings was the reputation of his predecessor, Lord Irwin – later Lord Halifax, and Chamberlain's Foreign Secretary. It annoyed him to think that, though Irwin's Viceroyalty had been full of trouble and violence, including the incursion of Afridi tribesmen, he passed in the public estimation for being the better man of the two of them. His method of denigrating Irwin was to begin by flattering him; he was, he said, a very great and high-minded gentleman (something, incidentally, that no one was likely to say of Willingdon, however admirable he might otherwise seem), but he had not found India, as Willingdon had, an easy country to govern; nor had he managed to get along with those fellers despite his sanctimonious exchanges with Gandhi. Why, then, such a high reputation?

To comfort him I developed on the spur of the moment a theory, often propounded subsequently – that to succeed pre-eminently in English public life it is necessary to conform either to the popular image of a bookie or of a clergyman; Churchill being a perfect example of the former, Halifax of the latter. Willingdon liked this notion, and we successfully applied it to a number of other public personages. As a matter of fact, I felt very much on Willingdon's side in his attitude to his predecessor; sentimentally virtuous people like Lord Halifax and Mrs Roosevelt do far more harm in the world than recognisable villains. Solzhenitsyn has provided the perfect parable on this theme with his description of Mrs Roosevelt's conducted visit to a labour camp where he was doing time. The estimable lady, who spawned the moral platitudes of the contemporary liberal wisdom as effortlessly and plenteously as the most prolific salmon, was easily persuaded that the camp in question was a humanely conducted institution for curing the criminally inclined. A truly wicked woman would have been ashamed to be so callous and so gullible.

The only member of Willingdon's Government I got to know well and like was P. J. Grigg, the Finance Member. We began – as almost everyone did in dealing with P.J. – with a ferocious row; in my case, over some articles I had written in the *Statesman* about India's fiscal policy, which, I argued at some length, was subordinated to British interests. After a slanging match between the two of us, we became friends, and remained so to the end of P.J.'s life. He was a strange, irascible, infinitely kind man, who from humble origins had risen to be a senior civil servant, and then was sent to India, where he had political responsibilities for which he had little aptitude, and administrative ones at which he was superbly competent. Life induced in him a more or less permanent condition or irritation, which he vented on anyone who happened to be around; especially his wife Gertrude, a stately lady, daughter of a bishop, who loved him dearly and proudly, and accepted his strictures with equanimity, while quietly working away at translating books into braille. She looked rather like a pantomime dame herself, and together they put up a wonderful comic turn. To P.J.'s great credit, the various prizes he had worked for – his professional advancement, his KGB, his familiarity with the great (he had been private secretary to both Lloyd George and Churchill), his easy financial circumstances, his directorships, his wine cellar and library and other such amenities – failed to give him any lasting satisfaction. To the end of his days he was looking for something else, but never, I think, found it; anyway, dying still irascible. Thinking of him – and of myself, for that matter – I draw comfort from Pascal's saying that to look for God is to find Him. In the Indian Legislature P.J. sat on the Government front bench in the style of the masters he had served in Whitehall; red-faced, feet up, ostentatiously sleeping through vituperative sessions – a second-string touring company performance.

After a spurt with the articles on fiscal policy which had so enraged P.J., I soon lost interest in the Simla scene, of which I was supposed to provide the *Statesman* with a day-by-day report. My communications to the Calcutta office grew ever shorter and more occasional, as did my responses to queries from London, where I had one or two stringer connections. One, I remember, asked for the reactions of Indians to the announcement of Linlithgow's appointment as Viceroy. It reminded me of the time in Moscow when I was asked for the reactions of the Soviet toiling masses to the lavish scale of entertaining in USSR embassies, and I had replied that the only ascertainable reaction was a desire to get near the buffet. In the case of Indian reactions to Linlithgow's appointment, there just weren't any; not even imaginable ones. So there was nothing for it but to fall back on quotations from the English-language Press, culling a few sentences where I could – 'If the New Viceroy will but see the need to speed up drastically progress to Indian self-government, then Indians, we are sure, will take him to their hearts . . .' Somehow, the idea of Indians taking Linlithgow to their hearts appealed to me.

My detachment from news-gatherings in Simla became total when I got to know Amrita Sher-Gil, an artist now generally considered to be the outstanding one of modern India. There is a room in the Delhi Art Gallery dedicated to her work, including a portrait she did of me. It was one of those obsessive relationships which for a while occupy one's whole being; then come to an end as suddenly as they begin. In the context of a life, a sort of play within a play. Her father was a Sikh nobleman, Sardar Umrai Singh, and her mother a red-haired solidly built Hungarian lady named Antoinette. I have no idea how they met, but their union gave an impression of being discrodant; he, Tolstoyan in his views and ways, ascetic, aloof, scholarly, and she a somewhat earthy person, who, when she played the piano – which she did a lot – seemed to be tearing greedily at the notes with her short, stubby fingers, the many rings on them knocking against the keyboard. Usually she wore European clothes – what used to be called gowns rather than dresses, with flounces and frills and billowing skirts; but when she appeared in a sari, as she sometimes did, she looked ungainly, her bare feet splaying out like trotters. They lived in a house at Summer Hill, just outside Simla, where I was a constant visitor. Amrita had her studio there, and I sat for her; or rather lolled on a sofa, sometimes reading, or just watching with fascination the animal intensity of her concentration, making her short of breath, with beads of sweat appearing on the faint moustache on her upper lip. It was this animality which she somehow transferred to the colours as she mixed them and splashed them on her canvas.

She was ten years younger than I, born in Budapest in 1913, and when she was seven came with her parents and her younger sister, Indira, to Simla, where she went to school. Then she studied art in Paris. When she spoke English, it had the Anglo-Indian lilt (called chee-chee in the days of the Raj); when French, it came straight from the *Ecole des Beaux Arts*. She habitually wore richly coloured saris with heavy gold or silver edging; and her face was Indian in its perfect symmetry, which she accentuated by painting – quite gratuitously, of course – a caste-mark in the centre of her forehead. The expression, however, lacked the characteristic softness of an Indian woman's face; Heavily made up, the lips loaded with red as her person was with jewellery – ear-rings, bangles, bracelets, necklaces, like gilded manacles – it was hard, self-contained, at times arrogant.

Even more than in my four friends in Calcutta, I sensed in her an inner conflict, which in her case was manifested in the disharmony of her parents. Her father, though smaller, more shrivelled, than Tolstoy, actually looked like him, with a similar beard and loose belted shirt, and displaying the same sort of petulance when assailed by distaste for what he considered to be the unduly luxurious manner in which the household was conducted. If, say, he were offered a pastry at tea-time, he would reject it with positive disgust, muttering: 'No, I won't take, I won't take!' Mme Sher-Gil's whole style of living – bourgeois Viennese in the days of the Austro-Hungarian Empire, transplanted to Simla, of all unlikely places – was displeasing to him. If the Sardar's displeasure became too marked, she resorted to her piano, getting going on a Richard Strauss or Liszt number; pounding away at the keyboard, head nodding, foot furiously pressing and releasing the pedal. He would then withdraw to the roof, where he spent much of his time engaged in abstruse calculations, and, by night, assiduously studying the stars through a telescope. I occasionally joined him there. Up on the roof by night, he was a wild-looking figure; hair and beard dishevelled in the wind, peering intently through his telescope as though he hoped thereby to get nearer to the stars and their celestial music, and further away from the Hungarian Dances whose strains reached him even there.

A similar disharmony was apparent in Amrita's painting. Her subjects were nearly all Indian; many of them peasants working in the fields, executed in the destructive twentieth-century style of the west – a mixture of something faint and dying and rather beautiful, and something furiously disintegrating. Rosewater and raw spirit. In the former mood, she sometimes seemed infinitely sad; in the latter, self-assertive, morally vacuous, even rather vulgar. Despite all the time I passed in her company, and our ostensible intimacy, I never felt that I got to know her. Or was it that there was really no one to know? In any case, she had built a wall between herself and the world, behind which she lurked, brooding on some secret of her own, or perhaps despairing; her sensuality being just fire signals that she sent up from her solitude to indicate where she was to any passing stranger. She often dined with me at the Cecil Hotel, where her appearance in the dining-room always created a marked impression. This I liked. In relations between the sexes, there is a strong element of exhibitionism. The pleasure of her company – and also at times the fatigue – lay in her vivid, forceful, direct reactions to life; the moral equivalent of her taste for steaks that were almost raw, and curries that were almost on fire. When she achieved, as she sometimes did, some sort of weird amalgam of the bearded Tolstoyan star-gazer and the red-haired pianist pounding away at her keyboard, she was very appealing. Often we talked on and on, with her rickshaw waiting outside the hotel – a smart yellow-painted one, with four coolies in a sort of livery to match; a characteristic Mme Sher-Gil touch. Then, at last, I would see her to it, and, rather than separate, walk beside it for a mile or so, still going on talking against the padding of the coolies' bare feet. Afterwards, walking back alone, smelling the pine trees and breathing in the cold mountain air.

As I had more or less severed all communication with the *Statesman*, and never went to any press-conferences or put in an appearance at any of the Government Departments, my position in Simla became rather ridiculous. Salvation came in the shape of a telegram out of the blue from Percy Cudlipp, editor of the *Evening Standard*, offering me a job on the Londoner's Diary at twenty pounds a week. I at once wired off accepting the offer, sent a letter of resignation to Moore in Calcutta, and with great thankfulness let Kitty know that I was coming home. Amrita saw me off at Simla Station in the very early morning – a great concession on her part, she being a late riser. We walked up and down the platform until the little mountain train blew its whistle to indicate it was starting, when I got in. Through the window she said we'd had some *beaux moments* together, which was true. I waved as long as she was in sight, knowing I should never see her again. In 1941, when she was still only 27, she died suddenly in Lahore. Then I heard that her mother had committed suicide. Somehow, neither Mme Sher-Gil's suicide nor Amrita's early death surprised me; I had always been aware of an aura of tragedy hanging over them.

Thirty years later, I was in Simla again with Kevin Billington when we were filming *Twilight of Empire*. By an extraordinary coincidence, Viceregal Lodge was just then being emptied of its contents – furniture, carpets, pictures, all loaded into vans to be taken away. So, in a sense, I saw with my own eyes the final dismantling of the Raj. When we came to film, little remained in the big reception hall except three silver thrones on which the Viceroy, the Vicereine and the Governor of the Punjab used to sit on ceremonial occasions. I sat on the Viceroy's throne, and tried to reconstruct the scene there as it had existed, and as I had known it, so short a while ago in time, yet already so infinitely remote – the bustling throng, the frail Viceroy in his grey frock-coat, the resplendent Indian Princes, the bearded Sikhs and sly old Dewans, and officers in all their regimental glory. All over now, and almost forgotten; soon to be wholly so. In the evening I went for a walk to Summer Hill, and looked for the Sher-Gil's house, but couldn't find it. It, too, seemed to have disappeared.

*

Back in London, I soon got in the way of going each day to and from the *Evening Standard* office in Shoe Lane, off Fleet Street. I have invariably felt about everything I have had to do for a living that I have been doing it always, and, equally, that I shall stop doing it tomorrow. Two seemingly incompatible states of mind – like free will and determinism – which nonetheless, in my experience, easily co-exist. I travelled up each morning by tram, from Kentish Town, via Gray's Inn Road, to Holborn; a form of urban transport that appealed to me, perhaps because of childhood memories of the virtues of municipal enterprise, and of similar tram rides to the Old Vic for the special matinees of Shakespeare productions put on for elementary schoolchildren.

The *Evening Standard*, a Beaverbrook newspaper, was produced in a single large room, the idea being that thereby the whole operation of bringing it out would be integrated and co-operative. Whether this aim was realised is doubtful, but at least the arrangement accustomed me to working in conditions of noise and disorder. The only person missing was the most essential – Beaverbrook himself, who never came to the office, but nonetheless managed to maintain from afar his close control of how the paper was run, and of everything that went into it. The single department which resisted the process of *gleichshaltung* was the Women's Page, which fought a last-ditch battle to maintain its seclusion, and obstinately went on functioning in what looked like a little hut amidst the encircling chaos. Inside it, two stern unbending ladies continued to deal magisterially with readers' queries about such matters as too large pores and the appearance of hair in untoward places. Their resistance was finally broken when one night, in their absence, their little hut was razed to the ground. Arriving the next morning and finding it gone, they had no recourse but to sit among us, which they surlily did.

In our Londoner's Diary corner, Bruce Lockhart reigned as a quasi-independent satrap. Having a direct line to Beaverbrook, he could treat with the editor, Percy Cudlipp, more or less as an equal; as well as with Captain Wardell, Beaverbrook's man on the premises. I once heard Bruce, on the telephone to Beaverbrook, call him 'Tich'; but the word was pronounced so softly and respectfully that it might have been some honorific title like 'Your Eminence' or 'Your Grace'. In matters of sycophancy, as of virtue, it is the spirit, not the letter, that counts. The Captain, as we all called Wardell, had an office upstairs, though what his precise functions were I never knew. He had a patch over one eye and high social connections, and as one of Beaverbrook's familiars was treated with considerable awe and respect. His eye, it seemed, had been injured in a hunting accident, and in his day paragraphs about hunting and related matters were frequent in the Diary. In his upstairs office he gave regular luncheon parties, to which I was occasionally invited. At them, one would meet such figures as Brendan Bracken, Beverley Baxter, Bob Boothby, and other such kulaks of journalism, politics and finance.

Bruce Lockhart himself was a cheerful, amiable Scot, who had been the first unofficial British agent in the USSR; an adventurous time for him, described in his book *Memoirs of a British Agent*. In the end, he was exchanged for Litvinov; a swap which might be considered, in worldly terms, advantageous to the Soviet side, but humanly speaking, I should have said we were the gainers. Bruce was on good terms with the Soviet Embassy, perhaps as the *de facto* donor of their Commissar for Foreign Affairs, and drolly complained on one occasion that paragraphs I put in the paper led to the discontinuance of his annual present of caviare. He and Lord Castlerosse were the two wild ones, *avec peur et avec reproche*, in Beaverbrook's little court, who brought to it a flavour of high living and society gossip; as Aneurin Bevan and Michael Foot did of Radical thinking and political gossip, enabling Beaverbrook to enjoy vicariously the sensation of being a rake and a rebel without jeopardising either his social or financial standing. When, as sometimes happened, the money-lenders closed in on Bruce and Castlerosse, they turned to their master for help. It was accorded with some ostensible grumbling, but, I suspect, much inward satisfaction. Beaverbrook felt he was subsidising their lubricity and general extravagance, in the same sort of way that Balzac's miser, Père Goriot, delighted in setting up his fashionable daughters in luxurious circumstances. Giving money away was a means of attaching people to himself; a kind of Devil's sacrament – 'This is my money . . .' At Christmas-time his smart lady friends could count on receiving a cheque, and Lord Ismay told me that when, in the 1939–45 war, he joined Churchill's *apparat*, the first thing Beaverbrook did was to offer him money, which, however, he prudently declined, realising instinctively that it would involve a dangerous servitude. Aneurin Bevan, too, told me that at one point Beaverbrook wanted to take him on to his payroll at a large figure, but, like Ismay, he saw the danger, and turned the offer down, contenting himself with drinking champagne at Beaverbrook's table and enjoying the company he met there – a strange taste for so fervid and sharp a mind. Money was really the only thing Beaverbrook believed in or cared about; it was the source of such power as he exercised, both within the organisation of his newspapers and in the larger world of politics. It was also the reason that, in the end, despite the huge circulations he commanded, and his intimacies with the leading politicians of his time, his influence was negligible. Money is a fragile power base to operate from, and can no more procure lasting influence than sensual pleasure can lasting affection.

Even *in absentia*, Beaverbrook's presence hung over the *Evening Standard* office as intensively as C. P. Scott's had over the *Guardian* office in Manchester. It was not just that he telephoned directives to particular individuals – though this, of course, happened; in the case, for instance, of the ill-starred leader-writer. One would see this unfortunate with the receiver glued to his ear, and a look of anguish on his face, desperately trying to grasp and stamp on his mind each word Beaverbrook uttered. Even when Cudlipp installed some sort of primitive dictaphone, things were not much easier. Out of curiosity, I listened to one or two of these recordings, and all one could hear distinctly was a raucous Canadian voice saying at regular intervals: 'You've gotta say.' When I left the *Evening Standard* I tried to take a few specimens away with me; I thought they would be nice to play over at one of those gatherings – like the Newspaper Proprietors' Association, or the English-Speaking Union – when *Areopagitica* is quoted, and our free press extolled. Alas, I found that, on Beaverbrook's orders, they had all been destroyed. After all, he was not a fool. More effective than such direct interventions was the mood he managed to create in his staff, whereby, instinctively or deliberately, they angled everything they wrote to please him; echoing what they took as being his thoughts, views and prejudices. This applied to correspondents abroad working for Beaverbrook newspapers just as much as to the home staff. Once I asked Milton Shulman what public he had in mind when he wrote his theatre and television criticism for the *Evening Standard*. He replied with singular honesty that he wrote with one little old reader in mind – Beaverbrook.

The essential difference between Scott's control of the *Guardian* and Beaverbrook's of his papers was that Scott had views and attitudes which, however distasteful, were fairly consistent, and could be cogently expounded; whereas Beaverbrook, when you got down to it, really had no views at all, but only prejudices, moods, sudden likes and dislikes, which his newspapers had to keep abreast of and reflect; in their news columns, as in their features and editorials. Overnight, he might reverse a previously held position as a result of a conversation, or of something he had read or heard. Or he might have a row with one of his children, and in the heat of it start a campaign for higher death-duties; or fail to ingratiate himself with some high-born lady and, to work off his irritation, mount a ferocious attack on class distinctions. Equally, if the approach proved successful, we might find ourselves adulating the lady in question, as being notable for beauty, wit and concern for the commonweal. Working for Scott was like waltzing with some sedate old dowager at a mayoral reception in Manchester; for Beaverbrook, like taking the floor in a night-club in the early hours of the morning, when everyone is more or less drunk.

Beaverbrook's affections were as unstable as his views, and he greatly enjoyed playing off one of his familiars against another. He might, for instance, instruct Bruce Lockart to review adversely a novel by his friend Arnold Bennett, and then, when Bennett complained, shake his head over the impossibility of controlling his subordinates. One of his best coups in this *genre* – which, I must say, I greatly enjoyed – was to punish Rothermere's *Daily Mail* for having acquired at great expense exclusive rights in Dickens's *Life of Christ* by publishing Thomas Wright's disclosures about Dickens's affair with Ellen Ternan. His pet aversions – for instance, in those days, John Reith and the BBC – were relatively steady; it was as much as anyone's job was worth to let a favourable word about them get into the paper. In other cases, his feelings fluctuated, and one had to make sure, before going into print, how the barometer stood. Happily for me, I was not considered of sufficient standing or reliability to be entrusted with promoting any of his political campaigns, and so was spared the humiliating task of trying to make sense of intrinsic absurdities like Empire Free Trade. On the Diary we were concerned more with personalities than politics, and there are few in public life at whom it is not a pleasure to take an occasional swipe. In this respect, the job suited me well enough.

Underneath Beaverbrook's vagaries and inconsistencies, however, one soon came to detect a strain of cunning and self-interest. Thus, our policy was to be cheerful and hopeful; everything was going well, prosperity reigned, and would steadily expand; the war that everyone was talking about and expecting, just wasn't going to happen. Such a view, of course, was good for advertising, and reassuring for Beaverbrook himself. He read and believed his own papers, even though they were fashioned specifically to convey all his favourite fantasies. When they told him there was not going to be a war, he having instructed them so to do, he felt reassured, and assumed, I daresay with reason, that advertisers would react likewise. The true doom of the Media barons at all levels is to believe the Media, thereby infallibly encompassing their own ultimate destruction.

Another strand in the web of fantasy we wove on Beaverbrook's behalf was religiosity. Something of his early Calvinist upbringing lingered about him; he was not quite sure that there might not be such a thing as everlasting damnation, and if there should be, then, clearly, he would be a likely candidate. An evening with his cronies was liable to end with a hymn-singing session, and his book about Christ – *The Divine Propagandist* – is another essay in reassurance; this time against hell fire rather than another war. Jesus, he concludes, was a cheerful, sociable soul, who, as the parable of the talents shows, believed in investing money shrewdly and making a killing on the Stock Exchange when a good opportunity presented itself. Any suggestion that he was inclined to take a poor view of man's earthly circumstances represents, Beaverbrook insists, a distortion of his teaching; as does the literal interpretation of those parts of the Sermon on the Mount which deal with non-resistance, the suffering of persecution gladly, and the doctrine of turning the other cheek. An antidote to such error was provided in the *Evening Standard* by Dean Inge's weekly articles which, Beaverbrook considered, took a decently realistic view of the Christian message, while upholding something he clung to with particular tenacity – the sure hope of immortality. One of Inge's articles on this theme was advertised on our vans with the bill: IS THERE AN AFTER-LIFE? SEE TOMORROW'S EVENING STANDARD. Beaverbrook, as it seemed to me, was a perfect example of the validity of the Faust myth; he really did believe he had sold his soul to the Devil, and was terrified of having to settle the account.

The basic policy laid down for us was to write always on the assumption that our readers were a notch or two higher in the social scale than was actually the case. In the columns of the Londoner's Diary, they had all been to public schools, played rugby football rather than soccer, changed for dinner, went to the Private Showing of the Royal Academy and to gala occasions at Covent Garden, read the novels of Evelyn Waugh, and liked Shaw's plays for serious theatre-going and Noel Coward's for relaxation, attended the better-known race-meetings, especially Ascot, ski-ed, motored, and knew their way about the Riviera and the Rue de Rivoli. They might even hunt – but this was a shade beyond our reach, and only included out of deference to the Captain. Such a picture of themselves was comforting as they commuted between Purley and London Bridge, and alleviated the tedium of trimming their privet hedges on Saturday afternoons, or holidaying *en famille* at the seaside in the summer.

Working on the Diary, we divided the various portfolios between us. Thus, Bruce Lockhart handled diplomats and diplomacy – ambassadorial postings, Excellencies turning up in London from distant places looking bronzed and fit, anecdotes about diplomatic bags and linguistic misunderstandings; anything like that. He also had the first bite at the Honours' List, when it appeared, speculating on such matters as what titles the ennobled were going to take, and what coats-of-arms they might be expected to adopt. Here, Garter or one of his underlings at the College of Arms was invaluable. Bruce would arrive in the morning bursting with what he had heard the evening before at this or that party – so-and-so tipped for such a job – and had a quick eye for pointers in the morning papers. As when he spotted in *The Times* Personal Columns that a dog had been lost near Churt. Could it be Lloyd George's? A few telephone calls – we all spent most of our time telephoning – elicited the fact that it was, and Bruce, his eyes sparkling, led that day's Diary with the story of how the self-same littler terrier which had once disgraced itself by biting the Italian Prime Minister, Sr Orlando, during negotiations at Rapallo, was now at large in Surrey.

Politics rested largely in the hands of Randolph Churchill, who, to the considerable awe of the rest of us, could telephone almost anyone without fear of a rebuff. That you, Bobbity? Duff? Fruity? Bob? Rab? There was also, of course, his father, to whom he could always turn, and who contributed a highly paid weekly article to the *Evening Standard*; in those days, very much out of things, and, I thought from a fleeting glimpse I had of him, showing it. I have always been fascinated to note how indelibly worldly success and failure write themselves in a person's appearance; the one keeping the trousers pressed, linen fresh, shaves clean, and the other, almost over-night, bagging the trousers, fraying cuffs, leaving tufts of hair and dried gobbets of blood on the chin. Randolph still had about him some of the glow of his youthful promise, when he was called – alas, only by the first Lord Rothermere – England's young man of destiny. In the succeeding years I saw him from time to time, and so was able to observe his rogue-elephant course; growing obese and grey and feebly thunderous, though never quite losing some quality of, if not originality, unexpectedness, which almost amounted to it. Perhaps it was fitting that his days should end enmeshed in what was to be an interminable biography of the father whom he had so assiduously emulated, and even copied, and in whose shadow he had been fated always to live. I wrote his obituary in *The Times* – the only one I have ever done, or been asked to do. It would have seemed an unlikely eventuality in our Diary days.

The portfolio of cultural affairs was in the hands of Patrick Balfour, son of a Scottish judge and peer; a versatile writer who, in the course of many assignments, collaborated with the Duke of Windsor, which at one point involved their sharing a forlorn Thermos of tea on the steps of the Duke's sometime residence, Fort Belvedere. It was he who attended art shows, went to the ballet, knew Beverley Nichols, Somerset Maugham and Evelyn Waugh, and even frequented publishers' cocktail parties – the equivalent, in gossip-writing terms, of slumming. John Betjeman, the film critic when I first joined the paper, helped out with architectural and ecclesiastical news, especially clerical appointments. There was also a strange, red-faced, rather tragic figure with dyed black hair named Philip Page who had been in his day a well-known theatre critic, but now just sat around contributing occasional paragraphs to the Diary. His harmless vanity was to have known everyone intimately, but it was noticeable that, whenever this knowledge was put to the test of providing a paragraph, it needed heavy reinforcement from the cuttings – those envelopes, bulky or scanty according to the estimated eminence of the subject, containing whatever fragments of information had appeared about them in the press. Footprints of a kind in the sands of time. When the subject died, the word 'dead' was scrawled across the envelope; a necessary precaution, in Page's case particularly; he was all too prone to turn in a paragraph about having run into Beerbohm Tree, or Lily Langtry looking prettier than ever, at the Trocadero.

Page had one of those rich, port wine voices you seldom hear nowadays, and in all weathers wore a bowler hat and an overcoat with a velvet collar. He alone of us all believed in what we were doing; seeing each Diary paragraph as a sacrificial offering laid on the altar of social rectitude. When King George V died, I found him in tears, staring at a half-crown piece, which, as he said, was the man's picture. It was a testing time for us all, instructions having been handed down by the Captain from Beaverbrook that until the royal funeral had taken place every paragraph in the Diary must deal with the nation's bereavement. This meant, in all, some 120 paragraphs. I remember wrestling with a couple myself about a tapestry that Queen Mary had been working on at the time of her husband's death. It was heavy going – for me, I mean; though doubtless for her, too.

Literary paragraphs were turned in by Howard Spring, the book critic; a former *Guardian* star-reporter, with an adoring wife whose praises of him, Neville Cardus once remarked, would have been excessive even if he had been Shakespeare. In the course of reporting an Empire Free Trade meeting in Manchester for the *Guardian*, Spring referred to Beaverbrook as a pedlar of nightmares. Crozier, ever timid, thought this rather strong, and altered 'nightmares' to 'dreams', thereby procuring Spring an immediate offer of a job on the *Evening Standard* at a greatly increased salary, which he accepted. Later, as a successful popular novelist, he became a pedlar of dreams on his own account.

The real pillar of the Diary, and, to me, far the most sympathetic person connected with it, was Leslie Marsh, who, in effect, edited it. He was a strange, sad, infinitely lovable man who had drifted into journalism, like so many others, because it seemed to be vaguely connected with writing, and, at the same time, offered regular wages. Like an aspiring actress who joins the Bluebell Girls. At one point he tried to break away, and turned to hedging and ditching for a living, but family responsibilities brought him back to Shoe Lane. His distaste for the Diary was very great. If one asked him whether he had enough paragraphs, he would never admit to more than: 'I can fill'; if one sought his help in finding a subject, more often than not his only response would be: 'Have you looked at the stiffs?' I used to say that he was like Augustus Moddle in *Martin Chuzzlewit*, who spoke for all the poetically disappointed when he wrote to Miss Pecksniff: 'I love another. She is Another's. Everything appears to be somebody else's.' When I went to *Punch*, the first thing I did was to ask Leslie to join the staff, which, to my great joy, he did. When I left, he was still there; the only truly useful contribution I made to the magazine's well-being.

My own role in the production of the Diary, as the latest arrival, was to deal with unconsidered trifles like sudden deaths, a book that needed to be hurriedly gutted for some morsel of gossip, or the appointment of a new headmaster at one of the lesser public schools like Lancing or Repton. Also, I was considered as something of an expert on the Labour Party alternative Establishment that was taking shape, and whose gossip potentialities were beginning to be apparent. Kitty's family – Stafford Cripps, the Webbs, the Booths, Lord Parmoor – were an important element in this. Windsor, Eton and King's contributed Dr Dalton; Winchester's offering – Crossman, Gaitskell, Jay – were already in the pipe-line. At the London School of Economics they were gathering for the harvest; from the high-tables and senior common rooms the word was passed down that Labour could wear a mortar-board as well as a cap. Nor was the Church behind-hand, with Archbishop Temple ready to add an eight-hour day and public ownership of the means of production to the other Beatitudes, and his Dean in Canterbury, Dr Hewlett Johnson, already preaching in the Cathedral that Stalin was busily engaged in building the Kingdom of Christ. The Services and the Law likewise offered their quota, and as for literature – with Shaw, Wells, Bertrand Russell and a large Bloomsbury contingent to the fore, why should lesser pens hold back? Well might an old-timer like George Lansbury rub his eyes over so gilt-edged a recruitment, but from a gossip-writer's point of view, it was gravy.

My political prognostications were less fortunate. For instance, I remember writing a paragraph when Major Attlee (as he was then always called) was elected leader of the Labour Parliamentary party, to the effect that the appointment must be considered purely a stop-gap arrangement. So obscure and light-weight a figure, I contended, would never make an effective leader of the Opposition, let alone a Prime Minister. I thought of this when I happened to run into him in the lavatory of the Reform Club shortly before he died. He was on his way to some sort of banquet, in full evening dress, every inch an earl, his tiny frame borne down by the weight of hardware upon it, his eyes glazed, his face skull-like; but indubitably no stop-gap. Our paths vaguely crossed in the sense that we had the same lecture agent in America – the redoubtable Mr Colston Leigh, and were liable to pass one another like ships in the night at Cincinnati, Ohio, or Denver, Colorado. His form, I was told, was splendid except for his propensity to fall asleep; the local worthy collecting him at his hotel was quite likely to find the Earl tucked up and fast asleep in bed, and even when delivered onto the platform he sometimes dropped off during the chairman's intro-ductory remarks. Once awakened, however, he would advance to the podium, and deliver a flawless, if somewhat abbreviated, address on the ardours and practice of government.

Our hours on the Diary were short. We were expected to arrive round about ten o'clock; the Diary went to press at half past twelve, and in those days was seldom changed between the afternoon editions. With so many of us working on it, two, or at most three, paragraphs was our daily stint. Quite often one made no contribution at all. Every Friday, at the accountant's office on the ground floor, we collected our pay in cash, mine being four white, crinkly five-pound notes. It was, on any showing, good money for very little work. In theory, it is true, we were expected to spend our afternoons and evenings roaming the town, making contacts, picking up useful information, attending social occasions – cocktail parties, dinner parties, receptions, first nights, even hunt balls. Randolph, of course, was in great demand among hostesses, and Patrick Balfour had his own special milieu where paragraph-fodder was plentiful; but I personally never sallied forth or attended anything on the Diary's behalf. Appearing in it was considered in those days very good publicity, and all sorts of people, from debutantes to authors and Intelligence agents (in the last category, one who used to bring two mastiffs with him when he visited the office) were after us in the hope of planting something, or, at any rate, just getting a mention.

The easier course, from my point of view, was to rely on the cuttings and my own inventiveness. I found that no objections were ever raised so long as what appeared in the Diary ministered to the subject's self-esteem; not even to purported quotations given in direct speech. Dr Johnson had the same experience when he was producing reports of parliamentary debates without ever going near the Houses of Parliament. Indeed, he gave the job up when he discovered that the fictitious speeches he attributed to Noble Lords and Honourable Members were being taken as true. Journalism has moved a long way since his time, and I must say it never occurred to me to feel any qualms when my imaginary conversations passed unchallenged. At times there might be carping over trivialities; as when, as a matter of routine, I said of a newly ennobled Scottish peer that his grandfather had been a poor crofter, and he wrote in to deny that this was so. Honour was satisfied when I made the necessary correction by stating in a subsequent paragraph that his grandfather had been a rich crofter. On another occasion I chanced my arm by remarking of an up-and-coming politician that he was very fond of music, and never missed a symphony concert if he could help it. Afterwards, I heard from someone who knew him that he was tone-deaf, but by that time my paragraph had got into the cuttings, and a lover of music he will now remain for all time.

Occasionally, a Beaverbrook-sponsored paragraph would come my way, marked with the word 'must'. One, I remember, consisted of a scribbled, garbled quotation about many aspiring but few succeeding, which was to be applied to animadverting upon how rarely politicians who move over from Westminster to the City make good there. The point was clear enough; Beaverbrook had acquired a huge fortune, but been a relative failure in politics, and so wanted to read in the Londoner's Diary – a favourite feature – that making money was a more difficult pursuit than politics. My own researches, such as they were, failed to provide much support for this proposition; and I turned to what was for all of us in all circumstances a last resort – Bonar Law, who had made no particular mark either as Prime Minister or tycoon, and could therefore be said to have tipped the balance either way. What was more important, he was highly esteemed by Beaverbrook, who, when Bonar Law was on his death bed and worrying over some falling copper shares, is said to have bought them in to keep the price up, thereby enabling his friend to die in piece. Another 'must' paragraph entrusted to me was to point out that the bronchial complaint of which Sir James Barrie was reported to be dying, was known as 'old man's friend' because it was so painless. Again, the reason was clear; Beaverbrook an asthmatic, expected to die of a similar complaint, and wanted to be reassured that it made for an easy death by reading it in the Diary. Harley Street was unresponsive when asked to provide confirmation, but the Diary nevertheless made the point, and kept its little old reader happy.

This well-paid and unexacting servitude to Beaverbrook's wayward fancies and malign purposes was more spiritually burdensome than might have been supposed. There was a steady and insiduous process of corruption going on all the time, which I could observe working in others, and, in moments of candour, in myself. Underneath all the buffoonery, I detected a whiff of sulphur; a transposing of values, whereby whatever was most base was elevated, and the only acceptable measure of anyone and anything was money, the only pursuit worth considering, worldly success. My own part in the Beaverbrook circus was, happily for me, only a minor and insignificant one. Even so, it became increasingly distasteful, and I decided to take a chance, and spend the remaining time before the next war began engaged in my own pursuits rather than Beaverbrook's.

Almost the last two tasks I was given on the *Evening Standard* might have been specially designed to confirm me in taking this decision. The first was to provide some copy for a page of advertisements on behalf of various charities, the editorial space available being carefully marked out to correspond exactly with the amount of advertising space taken. Thus, Distressed Gentlefolk might have three lines, the Salvation Army five, Dr Barnado's Homes eight, and so on. The other task was to take note of a book called *Metropolitan Man* by Robert Sinclair without distressing our readers by drawing their attention to disagreeable data about their urban environment. As the book consisted almost entirely of such data, it was a difficult if not impossible, assignment.

When I pointed this out to Percy Cudlipp, he quite agreed, but still insisted that the Beaverbrook directive to keep everyone cheerful must stand. It seemed time to hand in my notice, which I did, knowing I should miss the four five-pound notes on Fridays, but nothing else.

As it happens, I was employed by the *Evening Standard* again some twenty-five years later, when Charles Wintour was editor, to write a weekly book article. This arrangement was terminated, and my place taken by Michael Foot, when an, I must admit unsympathetic, account by me of the Beaverbrook cult in New Brunswick appeared in the Canadian magazine *Maclean's*. This is the only occasion in my life when I have been actually fired. In the course of my visit to Fredericton, New Brunswick's capital, I ran into the Captain, who has a suite in the Lord Beaverbrook Hotel where I was staying. We spent an evening together, in the course of which he described to me how, on Beaverbrook's advice, he had taken over the local newspaper, the *Gleaner*, whose publisher and editor-in-chief he now was. For some reason, spread about his room, he had a lot of new camera equipment, including a lens, which from time to time he extended, until it reached a truly enormous length; then appeared to be squinting at me through it. After dinner, we stepped across to take a look at an exhibition of ultra-modern art – Beaverbrook's latest benefaction to Fredericton. The Captain, I could see, cared as little for the pictures as I did, but he characteristically comforted himself by observing that, if experts like Kenneth Clark approved of them and millionaires like Beaverbrook bought them, they must be good. It seemed a *non sequitur* to me.

Strolling about in Fredericton, and surveying all the different intimations of Beaverbrook's connection with the place – the bronze statue in the centre of the town, the Beaverbrook Art Gallery, the Beaverbrook Birdbath, the Beaverbrook Theatre, the Beaverbrook Reading Room, the Lord Beaverbrook Hotel – I wondered what would be the outcome of this deliberate pre-humous creation of a shrine and a cult. Would it, perhaps, be oblivion just the same? – and this not so much because of Beaverbrook's intrinsic insignificance, as the insignificance, as it would turn out, of the historical setting in which he had gone to such pains and expense to make a place for himself. After buying up all those papers – Bonar Law's, Lloyd George's, H. G. Wells's even; after all that suborning of people, and faking of the record; after piecing it all so carefully together – then to find that, after all, it signified nothing. Deserving, at most, one tiny little footnote rather than large tomes – would not that be something?

We found a house in the country at Whatlington, near Battle, which cost eight hundred pounds – a sum that we could just manage with the aid of a mortgage. It was quite large, and had been unoccupied for some considerable time. As we discovered after we had moved in, it had quite recently been the scene of a rather disagreeable suicide; and this, added to the fact that it had once been a village shop, reduced its desirability, and so brought down the price. The suicide didn't trouble us, any more than the shop. In fact, as far as the latter was concerned, if it had been practicable we might well have opened up business again. Having disposed of our house in London, we moved in with our, now, four children – our youngest son, Charles, having lately arrived on the scene. It was a fairly austere existence; water came from a well which had to be pumped by hand, and drinking water from a spring some little distance away. Each day I fetched two bucketsful. Bathing was done in a small metal bath in front of the kitchen stove; there was no heating apart from fires, and, of course, we had no car. The nearest shopping-centre was Battle, some two miles away; and we would usually walk or cycle in and out.

My only regular income was five guineas a week for doing a weekly column on novels in the *Daily Telegraph*. A parcel of five would arrive on Mondays, and my copy had to be sent off on the following Friday. It gave me a distaste for new novels in dust-jackets which I feel to this day – for Mr A who can spin a rollicking yarn, for Miss B who so subtly explores the relationship between a housemaster's wife and one of the prefects, Mr C who writes with a fine zestful bawdiness reminiscent of *Tom Jones*. I used to put off opening the parcel when it came as long as I dared, and even then it took me quite a time before I could nerve myself to read even the blurbs – as far as I got in some cases, I regret to say; but then I would comfort myself by remembering Dr Johnson's saying about the novels of Congreve, that he would sooner praise them than read them. Gerald Gould, who had been in the business much longer than I, had reached the point that his weekly quota of volumes used to be passed to him through a hatch; after which he could be heard groaning and beating his head against the wall. Other odd jobs turned up. For instance, I ghosted part of the translation of Caulaincourt's *Memoirs* at thirty shillings a thousand words, and contributed two items, at fifteen guineas each, to a book of Fifty Famous Crimes given away by the *Daily Herald* to boost circulation. My subjects were a French maniac who murdered his entire family for the insurance money, and a sordid affair of poisoning in Penge. Kingsmill, who also contributed two items, with singular obstinacy tried to get hold of a copy of the book, but was finally defeated, even though he tracked down a barge loaded with them on its way to Manchester.

I also did quite a lot of work for Lady Rhondda's *Time & Tide*; a feminist organ, largely staffed and written by women. Lady Rhondda, plump and curly, was the daughter of a coal magnate who had been Food-Controller in the 1914–18 war. She and her father were on the *Lusitania* when it was torpedoed in 1915, and she wrote a very good description of the adventure. It appears that she found herself in the water holding onto a spar, at the other end of which there was a man likewise holding on. She says that she and this man looked at one another, whereupon he unaccountably disappeared. Somehow, I understood why; working for *Time & Tide* was rather like holding onto a spar with Lady Rhondda at the other end. All the same, she was very kind to me, and let me write what I liked. I particularly appreciated her literary editor and friend, Theodora Bosanquet, who had been Henry James's secretary when he was living in Rye; a salty, hearty lady who wore well-cut tweed suits and good shoes with flat heels. She and Lady Rhondda shared a house in Surrey and a flat overlooking St James's Park; both establishments being so luxurious that they were almost uncomfortable – the cream too rich to eat, the peaches too soft and large to bite into, the beds too downy to fall asleep in.

The three years I spent in Whatlington waiting for the war, despite financial anxieties and stringencies, were the happiest I had known. Our children were beginning to emerge as separate people whom I could get to know; Kitty was well content, as she always is when they are near, and the ardours of house-keeping are heavy. When we are staying in France I have the greatest difficulty in stopping her joining the women at the communal village washing place, scrubbing away in cold water. The routine of my day was the one that has best suited me always; waking up early, working through the morning, walking or gardening in the afternoon, working again in the early evening, and lolling about and talking until bedtime; with no contractural job to bother about, no fixed obligations to fulfil, no forms to public entertainment to sit through – least of all the cinema, about which I have always nourished a secret distaste and dread, today amply justified. Above all, the scene I looked out on as I worked was the one I most love – the English countryside.

The happiness of this time was enormously enhanced by my friendship with Hugh Kingsmill, who lived nearby in Hastings with his wife Dorothy and their three children. Most weeks we met two or three times, either in Hastings or Whatlington, and often had long conversations on the telephone. It is impossible for me to convey the delight his companionship gave me, or what I owe to him for the enormous enhancement of living I derived from the stimulation of his mind and imagination. There is scarcely a book I care about which is not, as I turn over its pages, evocative of him, to the point that even now, a quarter of a century since his death, I positively hear his voice commenting on it, and feel, welling up in me, the wonderful laughter that was never far out of reach, whatever the matter under consideration might be. For someone like myself, among the walking-wounded from the ideological conflicts of the age, he was the perfect physician, simply because he was himself totally uninvolved in them. In some mysterious way, he managed to remain uncontaminated and unbrainwashed in an age that specialised in both processes. When, under financial stress – a chronic condition with him – he took on doing a book about D. H. Lawrence, he used to read aloud to me with a kind of wonder dialogue from Lawrence's novels (for instance, the exchange between Mellors and Lady Chatterley's father, Sir Malcolm Reid, the Royal Academician – 'Sir Malcolm gave a little squirting laugh, and became Scotch and lewd . . . ! "How was the going, eh? Good, my boy, what? . . . My daughter, chip off the old block, what? . . . You warmed her up, oh, you warmed her up, I can see that. . . . A gamekeeper, eh, my boy! Bloody good poacher, if you ask me. Ha-ha!" '), as though asking: is it conceivable that this should be regarded as human speech arising out of a human relationship? It was very refreshing and very funny.

Similarly, he never for one second entertained any hope or expectation that the various political prospectuses, from Left to Right, for making an earthly paradise, were realisable, or conducive to any lasting good for mankind. All such expectations he dismissed as Dawnism; and no one has ever stated more clearly than he the fallacy of the collective remedies for our ills that Dawnists so ardently recommend, when he wrote in his Introduction to *The Poisoned Crown*: 'What is divine in man is elusive and impalpable, and he is easily tempted to embody it in a concrete form – a church, a country, a social system, a leader – so that he may realise it with less effort and serve it with more profit. Yet the attempt to externalise the kingdom of heaven in a temporal shape must end in disaster. It cannot be created by charters or constitutions nor established by arms. Those who seek for it alone will reach it together, and those who seek it in company will perish by themselves.' Such an attitude struck Orwell, with his mania for categories, as Neo-Toryism; and in his 'Notes on Nationalism' he worked out a Neo-Tory *apparat* which included, as well as Kingsmill, Wyndham Lewis, T. S. Eliot, Evelyn Waugh and myself. After the war, I brought Kingsmill and Orwell together, and they got on quite well. Recalling the meeting, Kingsmill said that Orwell reminded him of a gate swinging on a rusty hinge. I saw what he meant.

Either I would bicycle into Hastings to see Kingsmill, or he would take the bus to Battle, and I would set out to meet him along the road from Battle to Whatlington, delighted when I first caught a glimpse of his solid figure in the distance and heard his shouted greetings: 'Hullo! old man! Hullo!' He walked with a rolling gait, rather like a sailor's; always hatless, his head exceptionally large, his already grey hair (he was fourteen years older than I was), sparse and dishevelled, his complexion ruddy. Even when he was full of troubles – as was all too often the case – he invariably gave an impression of immense cheerfulness. All his complaints were addressed to the phenomenal world, which he saw as only the shadow of another greater reality. 'Poor old mankind,' I would sometimes hear him mutter, as he might affectionately about some friend who had run into a lamp-post or fallen down a man-hole. Even his money difficulties, pressing though they were, came into the category of the phenomenal world; and when there was no post, as on a Sunday or Bank Holiday, to bring him bills or solicitor's letters, ceased to worry him. It was only a surface worry, though a persistent one. He had the foolish habit, based on his incorrigible hopefulness, of sending post-dated cheques in settlement of bills, and was very amused when the recipient of one of these wrote back asking for 'something liquid'. Another time, we noticed, in a grocer's shop in Hastings that the ham was recommended as being 'mild and cured'. It was, Kingsmill said, the condition we should all aspire after.

Sometimes, when he just had to lay hands on some ready money, he would make a foray on London, travelling up grandly from Hastings in a first-class carriage with the pass Sir Henry Lunn, his father, still had from his tourist-tycoon days. This pass, I may add, was in pretty constant use one way and another; I was even given an occasional run with it myself. Once in London, Kingsmill would survey the possibilities; like a general looking over the terrain for an attack on enemy positions. He might decide to descend upon some unwary publisher with a proposal for an anthology; he always had ideas for several floating about in his mind, and could knock them off in no time, without recourse to libraries, from his well-stocked, retentive memory. Or there was the office of the *New English Review*, edited by his friend Douglas Jerrold, whose literary editor Kingsmill then was. There would surely be some review copies of books lying about there, which could be glanced over, and then disposed of to our friend and benefactor, Thomas Gaston, in the Strand. On one heroic occasion, nothing else offering, he made his way into Bernard Shaw's flat in Whitehall Court – he had a faint acquaintanceship with him – and said boldly that he needed money. As Kingsmill described the scene to me, Shaw was sitting there, bolt upright, and giving an odd impression of being made of cotton-wool. He just leant forward stiffly, took out his cheque-book, and gave Kingsmill a cheque for ten pounds; as it were, in full and complete settlement of his obligations as an affluent author to an impecunious one. Kingsmill wished afterwards that he had stood out for fifteen.

A joint venture we were involved in was to describe a series of literary pilgrimages for a short-lived *New Yorker*-type magazine, *Night & Day*, at the suggestion of Graham Greene, its literary editor. The two I remember best were to Paris to see Wordsworth's great-great-granddaughter, Mme Blanchet, a direct descendent of his illegitimate daughter, Caroline, by Annette Vallon; and to Wimpole Street at dawn to commemorate Tennyson's dawn visit to No 67, where, shortly before Hallam died, the two of them had spent a happy time together. Mme Blanchet showed us a copy of the *Lyrical Ballads* sent to Annette by Wordsworth, and a number of documents in which Wordsworth's name occurred – for instance, Caroline's birth and marriage certificates – usually as M. Williams of Rydalmount near Kendal. As usual, the legend proved to be the exact antithesis of the truth; far from Annette being a revolutionary influence against which Wordsworth turned when he became respectable and Poet Laureate, she was a strong royalist, decorated for her services by Louis XVIII after the restoration of the monarchy, and greatly concerned to get Caroline respectably married, which she succeeded in doing, without, I regret to say, any substantial help from M. Williams of Rydalmount. We spent the night before our dawn visit to Wimpole Street at a nearby Turkish Bath, talking about Tennyson as we sweated on adjoining stone slabs, and then were kneaded, thumped, soaped and sluiced under the masseur's hands. The scene in Wimpole Street, when we got there, all too exactly fitted the lines from *In Memoriam* that Kingsmill quoted:

He is not here; but far away,
The noise of life begins again,
And ghastly thro' the drizzling rain
On the bald street breaks the blank day.

I also did a joint piece for *Night & Day* with Graham Greene – on a one-day trip to the Continent. We took off from Margate, where we spent some time in Dreamland, being particularly struck with the easy way some Air Force cadets picked up girls.

Once, in the British Museum (a place I always pass with a shudder, remembering the hours I have spent in the Library looking up things I didn't want to know) Kingsmill and I overheard a conversation between two attendants in blue uniforms. One asked the other where so-and-so – obviously another attendant – was; and the first replied; 'Oh, he's in the Illuminated', meaning, of course, the Illuminated Manuscripts Room. Thenceforth, we adopted the term, the Illuminated being the world of the imagination, as Wordsworth's Sunless Land was the world of the will. Kingsmill saw the imagination and the will as contending impulses, and he liked to recall an inscription on a stone found in North Africa: 'I, the Captain of a Legion of Rome, serving in the desert of Libya, have learnt and pondered this truth: "There are in life but two things, Love and Power, and no one has both." ' The will was the dynamo of action and the fuel of lust; the imagination, the way to ecstasy and the fount of love. To live in the will was to be imprisoned in the dark dungeon of the ego; the imagination was a window, to look out of, and dream of escaping. On the one hand, the men of the will – Caesar, Cromwell, Napoleon, Hitler and Stalin; on the other, the men of the imagination – Jesus, St Francis, Blake, Bonhoeffer and Solzhenitzyn. The will belongs to time, the imagination projects time into eternity. When Jesus rejected the Devil's offer of the kingdoms of the earth, he turned away from the will; on the Cross he died in the will; the Resurrection was his rebirth in the imagination.

All this is worked out very beautifully in Kingsmill's too little known novel, *The Fall*, in which his hero, having fallen and cracked his skull, comes to in the Illuminated. Thus, this Fall is the opposite of the one in *Genesis* – from the will into the imagination, rather than the other way round. A sort of Paradise Regained. The original of Kingsmill's hero was his younger brother, Brian, who also lived in Hastings, and who actually did fall from the top of a bus and crack his skull, afterwards giving intimations of being in the Illuminated, as well as, from time to time, having rather violent spasms. He was a highly eccentric, lovable character who lodged with the widow of a naval petty officer named Mrs Pitcher, in a house that had formerly belonged to an undertaker and monumental mason, and still had tombstones and immortelles lying about in the garden. One of the local sights was to see him early every morning run down to the sea for a swim, wearing the white shorts of the late Petty Officer Pitcher. After his accident he went for a time into the local hospital, where Kingsmill and I visited him. In view of his occasional violent spasms two male nurses sat with him, one on each side of his bed. Our arrival was the signal for them to go for a break, and Kingsmill and I were left looking at one another rather uneasily across Brian's inert body, which, to our great relief, continued to be inert until the male nurses returned. When he came out of hospital, Brian had an enormous piece of plaster down the middle of his large bald dome of a head where it had been cracked. The effect, when he suddenly took off his hat, as he frequently did, especially in saloon bars, was sensational.

It was at this time, doubtless owing to my companionship with Kingsmill, that I began consciously to have mystical experiences, and have gone on having them ever since, though sometimes, when I have been particularly caught up in egotistic or sensual pursuits, only at very long intervals. The first intimation is, quite simply, that time stops, or rather one escapes from time. Then all creation is seen in its oneness; with each part of it, from the tiniest insect or blade of grass, to the vastnesses of space, with the stars and comets riding through them, visibly related to every other part. One sublime harmony, with no place for the discordancies of hatred and the ego's shrill demands; the death of death, since each note in the harmony exists harmoniously for ever. Peace that is no one else's strife, sufficiency that is no one else's famine, well-being that is no one else's sickness. Flesh still, mind still, leaving the soul free to experience the inconceivable joy of seeing beyond the Iron Gates, to where the Creator watches over his creation.

I can remember three such experiences during my time in Whatlington. On the first occasion I was standing with Kingsmill on the cliffs, just outside Hastings, and looking down on the Old Town. It was an autumn evening, slightly misty and very still, with a sharp chill in the air. From the chimneys below, wreaths of smoke were rising into the sky; from each particular chimney, pale smoke, briefly separate, then becoming indistinct, and, finally, lost to view; merging into the grey, gathering evening. I was suddenly spellbound, as though this was a vision of the Last Day, and the wreaths of smoke, souls, leaving their bodies to rise heavenwards and become part of eternity. At the same time,

I felt full of an inexpressible tenderness for these fellow-humans, sending up smoke-signals to me from their separate hearths, and an inexpressible joy at sharing with them a common destiny.

The second occasion was at harvest-time, and I was standing on a little hill that overlooked our house. It was quite late – about eleven o'clock; there was a full moon, and the fields' abundance filled the air, almost visibly, like a mist of fruitfulness. Behind me stood Whatlington Church, small and very ancient, making a shadow in the moonlight, beyond which there was a massive yew tree, and grave-stones all around standing in lush grass. I suppose for a thousand years and more past, anyone standing on that little hill would have surveyed the self-same scene. I felt myself being incorporated into it, until I no longer existed, except as a voice in a choir of innumerable voices, swelling a chorus of gratitude for the gift of life, of sharing in its plentitude, of experiencing its joys and its afflictions, and treading its ordained path, from the womb where I was shaped, to a grave under that yew tree where I hoped to lie. Some ancestral memory formed on my lips the words *Gloria in excelsis Deo.*

The third experience was the most dramatic, and made the deepest impression. Kitty was in hospital, on the danger-list, and I was told by the surgeon who had operated on her that she had only a very small chance of surviving. It was a cruelly anxious time from every point of view. Each day, arranging for someone to be with the children, I went and sat with her. She was fighting to live, her face pared down to a skull, her body a yellow skeleton. Whilst I was there, the doctor came in and said that in the night she had lost a lot of blood, and desperately needed a blood-transfusion – it was before the days of bottled plasma. Wouldn't I do for a donor? I asked, with a sudden access of hope. My blood-count was taken, and to my infinite relief proved satisfactory; and there and then, by a procedure that would seem grotesquely primitive nowadays, I was joined to her by a tube with a pump in the middle, so that I could actually watch the blood being pumped out of me into her. 'Don't stint yourself for blood,' I said to the pathologist, a man named Barlow, perhaps partly to be theatrical, but also feeling it. Never in all our life together, had I so completely and perfectly and joyously experienced love's fulfilment as on that moment. As my blood, systematically, to the pump's rhythm, pumped into Kitty's veins, bringing life visibly into her face, my blood pouring into her to keep her alive, my life reinforcing hers, for the first time I truly understood what love meant.

I tried to put some of the fruit of these experiences into a short book I wrote at this time called *In A Valley of This Restless Mind*, but failed to make myself clear, at any rate to reviewers. A gratifying exception was Evelyn Waugh, who wrote a long and perceptive review in the *Spectator*. Otherwise, the book was a total failure. My main occupation during the period of waiting for the war to begin was writing *The Thirties*, a survey of the decade now coming to an end, commissioned by Hamish Hamilton. I managed to acquire *The Times* for the whole ten-year period, and stacked the issues in piles on the floor of my study, so that I was, literally, walled in by my material. In addition, I carried in my head echoes and memories of the events I had reported or commented on as a journalist; while, at the same time, of course, the drama was unfolding from day to day – the Spanish Civil War ending, the Abdication, the Anschluss, the invasion of Czechoslovakia, and Chamberlain's grotesque essays in international statesmanship. I wrote the book knowing what the end would be; from Ramsay MacDonald's formation of a National Government, everything happened with the inevitability of a play – the tragi-comedy of our time. Each character had his part, and came on the stage precisely on cue; scene followed scene, moving towards a pre-ordained climax, which was to fall exactly pat, some two months before the decade's end.

The summer of 1939 happened to be an unusually beautiful one, and I somehow knew – I think we all did – that the passing hours were particularly precious; golden hours unlikely to recur. Kingsmill and I went on meeting as often as possible. Sometimes, when he came to Whatlington, I would walk with him to catch his bus at Battle, and then he would decide to walk part of the way back to Whatlington with me. So we would perambulate up and down the road, talking and laughing into the night, as though the talk and the laughter might soon be running out, and we must grab them while we might. Often Hesketh Pearson, a close friend of Kingsmill who became a friend of mine, was with us on these occasions.

When news came of the conclusion of the Nazi–Soviet Pact, I knew, of course, that the waiting was over. In a way, I had been expecting such a development; never losing an opportunity to say that Bolshevism and National Socialism were the same thing, except that one was a Slav version and the other Teutonic. Why should they not come together, then? My first reaction to the actual line-up between them was a fearful joy. I thought with glee of the confusion in the office of the *Daily Worker*, where they had to get out a leader saying that the holy war against Hitler they had been demanding so vociferously must now be regarded as an imperialist one, and at all costs prevented from happening. Of the distress in Cross Street, Bouverie Street and Long Acre, that there should now be so mighty a hole in the common front against Fascism they had been advocating. Of the sadness in Printing House Square that, after all, Stalin was not going to come forward as civilisation's resolute defender, and take the Houses of Parliament, the Bank of England, Black Rod, and for that matter *The Times* itself, all under his wing. Of the desolation in Great Turnstile; of the Left Book Club volumes in their yellow dust-jackets being silently removed from windows in Henrietta Street, and, perhaps, even the Dean of Canterbury having a momentary doubt as to whether Stalin really would go on building the Kingdom of Christ now that he had aligned himself with Hitler. For a minute, in my delight, I thought that apologists for the Soviet regime among the Western intelligentsia were confounded for ever; and then, of course, I realised – not so. In a little while, they would recover their breath at the *Daily Worker*; in Cross Street, Bouverie Street and Long Acre, be tapping away again as confidently as ever; joy returning to Great Turnstile, the Dean recovering his nerve, and the Henrietta Street windows filling again. Like alcoholics after taking the cure – never another drop; well, just a taste perhaps, and then, before you could say knife, back on the meths. Meanwhile, there was the war.

2 *Grinning Honour*

Soft! Who are you? Sir Walter Blunt:- there's honour for you! . . .
I like not such grinning honour as Sir Walter hath: give me life;
which I can save, so; if not, honour came unlook'd for, and there's
an end. — Falstaff

Even wars, then, are waged with peace as their object, even when
they are waged by those who are concerned to exercise their warlike
prowess, either in command or in the actual fighting. Hence it is an
established fact that peace is the desired end of war. For every man is
in quest of peace even in waging war, whereas no one is in quest of
war when making peace. In fact, even when men wish a present state
of peace to be disturbed they do so not because they hate peace, but
because they desire the present peace to be exchanged for one that suits
their wishes. Thus their desire is not that there should not be peace
but that it should be the kind of peace they wish for.
— Augustine's *City of God*

AS NEARLY ALWAYS HAPPENS with long-awaited excitements, war,
when at last it came, proved an anticlimax. After all the apocalyptic
warnings delivered on so many solemn occasions from so many solemn
throats, we confidently expected the sky to darken, Big Ben to be silenced,
and destruction to fall about us with sheets of flame and mighty roarings
as of a tempest. It was all to come, but not yet. What happened immediately was that, on a bright September Sunday morning, an old man's
quavering, angry voice was heard on the radio, rising to shrill heights as
he told us that we were at war fighting against all the evil things in the
world and for all the good ones. Through the open window we saw our
stand-in parson, the Rev. Browell, making his way along the road with

great deliberation, and repeating at intervals, to no one in particular: 'We're in God's hands, we're in God's hands.' He had a bustling, purposeful air about him, like a teacher marshalling his charges. Alas, it seemed as though we were in Neville Chamberlain's hands rather than in God's, or even the Rev. Browell's. In my mind's eye I saw Chamberlain at the microphone, in black cutaway coat, with winged collar, and adam's apple throbbing convulsively above it; as forlorn at this moment of defeat as he had been vainglorious at his corresponding moment of triumph, waving in the air his piece of paper signed by Hitler, and prattling of peace with honour.

As Chamberlain's tremulous words died away, the sirens sounded, and the silver barrage balloons rose into the clear sky, riding on the wings of this most unmelodious melody which was to be our theme song for some years to come. I saw Kitty look round with her special vigilant air to take stock of where the children were and what they were at. I myself tried, without much conviction, to summon up a suitable expression of *gravitas*; as of a man resolved to do his duty come what might. As I have invariably found on occasions of public drama, I felt nothing more than a sense of suppressed excitement; I was curious about what was going to happen rather than appalled. Some deficiency in my mental make-up or metabolism prevents me from reacting otherwise; but for that very reason I feel bound to look preternaturally solemn, and strike an attitude of overwhelming concern. Just as, at a funeral, the mourners who care least about the deceased put on an outward appearance of being the most stricken.

We had all been talking about war for, literally, years past. It would be the end of civilisation – this without considering whether any civilisation still existed to be ended. Our cities would be razed to the ground in the twinkling of an eye; the bombers must always get through, there being no defence against aerial bombardment. Many thus held forth with great vigour and authority at dinner tables, in clubs and railway carriages; as did leading articles, sermons in St Martin's-in-the-Fields and other enlightened pulpits, after-dinner speeches at gatherings like the League of Nations Union and the Peace Pledge Union; wherever two or more were gathered together who felt they had the true interests of mankind at heart. Books appeared interminably on the subject, with lurid blurbs – usually in yellow dust-jackets; films were made about it, garden fêtes dedicated to it, tiny tots lisped out rhymes about it. All agreed that another war was unthinkable, unspeakable, inconceivable, and must at all costs be averted; coming forward in large numbers to vote against it in a Peace Ballot – resolved, and carried unanimously: That we will not countenance another war.

Well, now this other war had come. The sirens had sounded, the barrage balloons had risen, the hospitals had been cleared for the hosts of expected casualties, and the cardboard coffins manufactured in bulk in view of the anticipated shortage of wooden ones. We awaited the apocalypse, and nothing happened; like children shutting our eyes after a lightning flash in the expectation of a big bang to follow, and then cautiously opening them again to find everything precisely as it had been before. It was oddly exasperating. Not just to retired colonels irritably mowing their lawns in the Home Counties, and dreaming of adding to their campaign medals; of taking out their Sam Brownes once more, polishing them up and adjusting them to their enlarged girths. Not just to men of my generation who had missed out on the 1914–18 war, and saw a chance of getting into this one by the skin of their teeth; catching up on all the excitement, danger and fun that had eluded them on the previous occasion – the war books they hadn't written, the girls they hadn't slept with on some hilariously desperate forty-eight hours' leave from the trenches, the shell-shock they hadn't had, the decorations for valour they hadn't received and then contemptuously returned to show how they despised decorations and those who awarded them. Even the conscientious objectors had been looking forward eagerly to conscientiously objecting. Now it looked as though this so often predicted war to end all peace was going to prove as illusory as the peace to end all war.

On the Monday following the declaration of war I announced to Kitty that I was off to join the army. She did not, as I half expected she would, reproach me, but just accepted what was, given my age, circumstances and family responsibilities, an intrinsically imprudent, foolish and egotistic thing to do. The inducement was certainly not an access of patriotism; neither then, nor at any time subsequently, did I suppose that the war, however it turned out, could have other than ruinous consequences for all concerned, especially for England. The alternative to Hitler, as I well knew, was Stalin; and it was impossible to damage Hitler without helping Stalin, or *vice-versa*. So all the evil things which, according to Chamberlain, we were to fight against – dictatorship, bad faith, intolerance, persecution of the weak etc., etc. – must, whatever happened, get a boost. As, indeed, it has turned out.

The nearest recruiting office was at Maidstone, and when I got there I found quite a queue had already formed, consisting mostly of aspiring combatants, like myself, well on the way to middle-age. Conscription was already in force, so there was no occasion for the real cannon-fodder – between eighteen and twenty-one – to come along. The scene was very different from the beginning of the 1914–18 war, with all its hysteria, frantic outbursts of patriotism and distribution of white feathers. Everything was noticeably subdued; more in the style of a Labour Exchange in a period of economic depression than of a recruiting office at the beginning of a war. No A. E. Housman-esque bucolic sergeant with ribbons in his cap, all agog to inveigle a likely lad into accepting the King's Shilling. No likely lads, for that matter, or silver shillings; no band playing or flags flying. Just the eternal questionnaire – name, age, address, married or single, educational qualifications, religion, any record of VD, epilepsy or other disability? These the ice-floes, from one to the other of which we must nowadays jump; whether in seeking employment, getting married, exercising the franchise, or going to war.

There was only one man in the queue who seemed outwardly excited. He was, I should say, in his fifties; with snow-white hair, a battered rubicund face and broken teeth. Suddenly he began to gesticulate, and shout that he wanted to do something with his life. He may well have been drunk, but anyway was quite beside himself, to the point that a policeman who was keeping an eye on the queue led him gently away, still gesticulating and shouting. Did he, I wonder, manage to do some-thing with his life as a result of participating in the war? Or, for that matter, with his death? I rather doubt it; this particular war offering few possibilities of the kind in either case. The rest of us kept our thoughts to ourselves; remaining silent, if not morose, as we moved slowly forward with the queue. When my turn came, I filled in my form, and learnt that only specialists were being called up for the moment, and that, anyway, journalists of my age-group were classified as in a reserved occupation. So, wouldn't I do better at my typewriter?

I returned home feeling rather foolish, more particularly as I had taken a small suitcase with me of essential requirements with the idea that I might be sent straight off to a military depot. To relieve my feel-ings I wrote to Lord Lloyd, whom I vaguely knew, to ask if he would exert his influence to get me taken on as an Air Force pilot or rear-gunner; and when Beaverbrook and Brendan Bracken became Ministers, I likewise applied to them in the same sense. Needless to say, in each case I got only a polite brush-off. One or two middle-aged men disposing of more influence than I did – Sir Arnold Wilson, for instance – managed to get taken on as rear-gunners, and were duly killed; but there was no possible basis for my expecting such preferential treatment. I cannot pretend that it was heroism which prompted me in making these appeals; though possibly a desire to *seem* a hero – a very different thing – played its part. The armed forces, as I subsequently discovered, were over-flowing with aspiring 1914–18 war heroes – mute inglorious T. E. Lawrences, meticulously scruffy and insubordinate; Rupert Brookes with beautiful profiles, and poems scribbled down on army memo-pads with indelible pencils; Siegfried Sassoons ready at the drop of a hat to canter off the hunting field and into battle; clergymen who had become padres, damning God under their breath as they booked a double-room at the Regent Palace Hotel; HELLO, TO ALL THAT! from up and coming Robert Graveses.

The first days of the war were, for me, full of discontent and irrita-bility. Everything that was supposed to come to an end when hostilities began looked like going on for ever. I had to get off my review of five novels as usual, posting it at the very last moment in the same old way; my overdraft still stood, and the piles of copies of *The Times* in my study reminded me that there was still some way to go yet if I was to finish my survey of the Thirties by the end of the year. The siren-trumpet had sounded, but the walls of Jericho, shaky as they were, refused to fall down. Moreover, such outward manifestations of war as there were had a decided air of *déjà vu*; with the old sets, the old lines, and the old cast, most of whom were decidedly shaky and creaky by this time, but could still manage to get through their parts – just. So tatty a show, to be kept going, required a truly seasoned and outstand-ing impresario. Before long, one would be coming along, equipped with funny hats, siren suit, cigar, and, above all, rhetoric to fill the empty spaces of our hopes and resolution with portentous words – a blended brew of Macaulay, Gibbon, and the Authorised Version of the Bible, which, like Horlicks, could be taken at bed time to ward off night starvation.

About this time, I got a request from a publisher to undertake a new version of Ian Hay's *The First Hundred Thousand*, published in 1915, about the British Expeditionary Force in France. He must have meant pounds, Kingsmill said when I told him. Thinking about it – the advance proposed was substantial – I could not bring myself to relish the project. It would inevitably mean dishing the war up as some sort of a crusade, whereas I saw it as an act of self-destructive desperation on the part of all concerned. Even the most resourceful columnists and leader-writers had run into grave difficulties in avoiding, as they clearly felt they must, the semantics of the 1914-18 war. Thus, an article in the *News Chronicle* was headed: 'Making the World Safe for Go-Aheads to Live In'. 'Go-Aheads' seemed a shabby synonym for 'heroes'. How could I expect to do better? Turning over a few pages of Ian Hay's book convinced me of the hopelessness of the task. *The Last Hundred Thousand* would be more in my style, I decided, and declined the offer. The only basis I could discover for my own zeal to participate in the war was the sort of consideration which induced the Russian anarchist, Bakunin, when he saw some men setting fire to a house, to leap out of his carriage and lend a hand, without bothering to find out who they were and what was their purpose. When, after the war, I was a member of the Garrick Club for some years, I used sometimes to see Ian Hay there; a tall, lantern-jawed, elusive-looking man. I never managed to summon up the courage to tell him that I had been chosen, but declined, to pick up in the second world war the torch he had carried in the first. I felt it might upset him.

My distress at having to go on reviewing novels was relieved when I received a note from the literary editor of the *Daily Telegraph* saying that, in the light of the war situation, it was unlikely that sufficient works of fiction would be forthcoming to support a weekly feature, and that in any case the space would be required for copy relating to the national emergency. My joy at this deliverance was very great. Bunyan's Pilgrim did not climb out of the Slough of Despond more eagerly than I did out of this fictional slough in which I had been immersed, resolved never to fall into anything of the kind again. It is one of the few resolutions I have approximately kept.

By the same post as the letter telling me that my weekly column of novel reviews was no longer wanted, came another offering me a post in the newly established Ministry of Information. I felt bound to accept this, having now no regular income of any kind. It meant being in London during the week, and only coming home for week-ends. As things turned out, I was not to live with my family again, except for odd week-ends and periods of leave, till the end of the war; leaving Kitty to keep our home together, look after the children and see to their schooling in very difficult circumstances. I did this, not under compulsion, not from any genuine sense of duty, but just out of vanity and foolish bravado; ultimately, I suppose, because I wanted to get away on my own, and behave as I liked. Something that wars make permissible, practicable and even praiseworthy.

The hurriedly improvised Ministry of Information had been set up in the new London University building in Bloomsbury, where there were still intimations of its academic function; scientific formulae scrawled on blackboards, the whiff of chemicals and dead dog-fish in the laboratories, and even a tattered old gown hanging in one of the lavatories. When I presented myself, I found the place teeming with people, all moving about energetically and purposefully; like an airport. Some were in uniform, most carried brief-cases; dispatch-riders roared up to the entrance on their motor-cycles, and then, after a brief wait, roared away again, the only familiar sight being the commissionaires in blue, who spring up from an apparently inexhaustible supply whenever and wherever a new Ministry is instituted.

The department I was attached to was responsible for producing, for use all over the world, feature articles calculated to raise enthusiasm for the Allied cause. Leader-writing on the *Guardian*, the counterfeit words with which I was required to juggle – like 'freedom', 'democracy', 'self-determination' – had died on me.

Resurrecting them now into some sort of pallid existence for use as counters in a war that persistently refused to begin, was an uninspiring task. As it happens, under the auspices of the BBC, Orwell was similarly engaged, his special territory being India and South-East Asia. We often used to talk about this when I got to know him. From a studio deep under Oxford Street, he beamed at listeners in Cawnpore, Kuala Lumpur and Rangoon – assuming, of course, that there were any – *Areopagitica*, *The Wasteland* read by the author in person, and other gems of Western culture, with a view to enthusing them for the Allied cause. When I delicately suggested that this may well have failed to hit its target, the absurdity of the enterprise struck him anew, and he began to chuckle; a dry, rusty, growly sort of chuckle, deep in his throat, very characteristic of him and very endearing.

Graham Greene, who had also joined the Ministry of Information wartime staff, as characteristically took a highly professional view of what was expected of us, coolly exploring the possibility of throwing stigmata and other miraculous occurrences into the battle for the mind in Latin America to sway it in our favour. In the way of duty, he also had access to a file of letters from successful writers like Hugh Walpole, Michael Arlen and Godfrey Winn offering their pens for King and Country. Dipping into this gave us much pleasure. He was staying near the Ministry in a little mews flat where I spent an occasional evening with him, the invariable supper dish being sausages, then still available. Whatever his circumstances, he has this facility for seeming always to be in lodgings, and living from hand to mouth. Spiritually, and even physically, he is one of nature's displaced persons. Soon after his house on Clapham Common had been totally demolished in the Blitz, I happened to run into him. There was no one in the house at the time, his family having moved into the country, and he gave an impression of being well content with its disappearance. Now, at last, he seemed to be saying, he was homeless, *de facto* as well as *de jure*.

At the Ministry I was given a desk in a room for two, with, on the door, the word 'Editorial'. No one was ever able to explain what, if anything, this signified. My stable-companion was a pale, staid figure named Palmer from the League of Nations Secretariat. We neither of us had much to do, but when I girded against this, Palmer gently rebuked me. Such, he said, had been his lot on the League Secretariat for years past. He had grown used to it, and saw no reason why I should not in time come to do likewise. It was a perfectly permissible and acceptable way of life. Palmer had, indeed, as I saw, developed in himself a sort of Buddhistic power of contemplation as he sat at his desk staring in front of him; expenditure of energy being reserved for things like getting stationery, paper-clips and other clerical impedimenta together, taking control of the opening and shutting of our window, and seeing that his blotter was changed from time to time, and supplies of ink replenished. What thoughts and aspirations were in his mind during these protracted periods of contemplation I had no means of knowing, but he had, I gathered, a special interest in Eng. Lit., and had written a book or two in that field. He also collaborated with another League official, Hilary St George Saunders, in writing thrillers under a joint pseudonym.

Sometimes he spoke of Saunders, whom I vaguely knew, and saw occasionally after the war when he had become librarian at the House of Commons; executing his responsibilities as provider and distributor of books to Hon. Members with great aplomb. Palmer clearly held Saunders in considerable awe as a man with sparkling gifts born to shine in a world to which he, Palmer, could not aspire. Mixed with his veneration, I thought I detected a strain of envy, and perhaps resentment. The relationship between the two, yoked so strangely in the production of thrillers, fascinated me, and I tried to explore it in a novel of my own (*Affairs of the Heart*), in which two similarly dissimilar collaborators devise a plot whose only possible outcome is for one of them to murder the other, which he duly does, the single clue being the manuscript of the last novel they were working on together. The result, alas, was unsatisfactory, though published, and, for some inscrutable reason,

translated into Italian and Mexican. I came across the Italian edition –
Affari di Cuore – once in a Milan bookshop, standing, blameless, on a
shelf of porn; on the cover of the Mexican edition – *Deseo Y Muerte* – I
am described as '*el genio del Humor Negro*', an undeserved compliment.

The days passed at the Ministry of Information very much as they
had at the International Labour Office. There were even tea trolleys
and biscuits, but not stamped MOI as the others had been BIT.
R. H. S. Crossman was in an adjoining office, and we spent much time
talking together. It was then that for the first time I became acquainted
with one of the most versatile, engaging, and irresponsible of contemporary minds. My impressions at the time were only confirmed when,
years later, we were together, along with Peter Thorneycroft, on a weekly
television programme which involved endless talk on and off the screen.
Whatever position Crossman took up was defended with vigour and
panache, though he was quite likely, on another occasion, to demolish it
with equal vigour and panache. He left the Ministry of Information at
about the same time as I did, moving over to a secret organisation where
he found himself more sympathetically engaged in devising and disseminating Black Propaganda to Germany, using for the purpose admitted lies instead of, as at the Ministry, disguised ones. His great ambition
in life, he told me once, had been to become editor of the *New Statesman*
or Foreign Secretary; the first of these objectives he, somewhat belatedly,
achieved, but his performance at it suggests that it is just as well for all
of us that the other has eluded him.

Apart from the barrage balloons, which had now become part of the
London skyline, and posters exhorting us, among other things, to Save
for the Brave, the only evident sign of the war was the black-out. As
the winter came on, by the afternoon when it was time to leave the
Ministry and my communings with Palmer and Crossman, darkness had
fallen over London, unrelieved by street lamps. Buses and cars crept
silently along with only two tiny points of light to mark their extremities;
the people in the streets no more than passing shadows, everything
hushed and subdued, like Moscow when the snow had fallen. I preferred
to grope my way on foot through the black-out to Chelsea, where I was
staying in a house in Bramerton Street, rather than trying to get onto
public transport. From Gower Street via St Martin's Lane, to Trafalgar
Square, up the Mall by Buckingham Palace, past the tall houses in
Eaton Square, and on to Sloane Square, King's Road, and Chelsea
Town Hall – these were my land-marks, but I often lost my way,
suddenly finding myself by the Embankment, and once almost walking

into the Albert Hall. Muffled in an overcoat, umbrella up when it was
raining, sometimes choking over yellow fog, I had a wonderful sense of
being cut off and alone in a lost world. Along King's Road the prostitutes
signalled with torches, little quick flashes indicating their presence;
rather sweetly, as I thought. Thus groping my way about blacked-out
London, a phrase took shape in my mind: Lost in the darkness of change.
I said it over and over to myself, like some incantation momentarily
crystallising our human condition.

The house in Bramerton Street had been kindly lent me by Gerald
Reitlinger, who had managed to get into an anti-aircraft battery manned
almost entirely by Twenties figures like himself. It must have been one
of the most bizarre British Army units ever to be mustered, whose
personnel were trapanned, not, like the early East India Company's
troops, in the back streets and stews of Bristol and Liverpool, but in
the Café Royal, the Gargoyle Club, the Cave of Harmony and the
Fitzroy Tavern. In his private's uniform, especially fitted in Savile
Row, Gerald at last realised his lifelong dream of merging himself in
the English social scene, instead of, like Satan, going solitarily to and fro
in the world and up and down in it. Never can there have been so ardent
and battle-worthy a recruit. If Hitler had only struck then and there,
without a doubt his euphoria would have carried him into performing
deeds of valour deserving of the highest praise and decorations. Alas,
during the period of the phoney war, his morale gradually subsided, and
he finished up going round lecturing to the troops, a civilian again.
When, once, I asked him what he lectured about, he was evasive, and
I was never fortunate enough to come across anyone who had heard
him. His Bramerton Street establishment was littered with Twenties
bric-à-brac; his easel stood in its place with a half-finished Impression-
istic canvas still on it, the *Week-End Book* was placed by the bedside,
and, over supper, his housekeeper, Mrs Gray, provided anecdotes of
glittering figures like Constant Lambert, and even Augustus John, who
had at different times visited the house. Outside, the darkness of change,
inside the past; but where was the present? It eluded me then, and still
does. Perhaps there is no such thing; an imaginary point where the past
and future intersect. Or, as Pascal puts it: *'Le passé et le présent sont
nos moyens; le seul avenir est nôtre fin.'*

The Ministry was presided over during the first months of the war by
a Scottish judge, Lord Macmillan; a man with a thin, precise face and
judicial style of speaking, who seemed as far removed from his opposite
number on the enemy side, Dr Goebbels, as any run-of-the-mill

Archbishop of Canterbury from John the Baptist. We were required to take a similarly judicial attitude in our articles, eschewing bellicosity, and appealing rather to reason and enlightened self-interest. Germany's shortage of molybdenum, we argued, would infallibly bring the Nazi hordes to a halt; their supplies of rubber and petroleum products were running out, with no possibility of replenishing them, so their cause could be considered as good as lost. Towards putative allies of Germany whom we wished to coax over to our side, we were likewise supple and conciliatory. The Turkey of Kemal Ataturk might not be, in the technical sense, a one-man-one-vote democracy, but it was unquestionably progressive, and responsive to majority opinion; and even the USSR, despite having carved up Poland with Hitler, and mounted an unprovoked attack on Finland, might be considered as forward-looking, and so on the side of peace and freedom.

My *Guardian* training held me in good stead in meeting these requirements. At times, it almost seemed as though I were back in Cross Street, so reminiscent of my time there were the editorial specifications, as well as the earnest, sometimes heated, talk in the canteen about war strategy and aims, and the problems peace would pose when it came. Not to mention the people – those unmistakable voices, eager, throaty, tumultuous; that untidy hair, those keen, ardent, somehow ravening, eyes, with a core of calculation, like a drunk pulling himself together to count his change. How reminiscent they were of old *Guardian* colleagues! Indeed, many of them *were* old *Guardian* colleagues. Then the knowingness about this and that, and here and there – how things were up on the Burmese frontier, how the tribesmen were feeling in the Upper Nile, what they were at in the shanty towns of Brazil or on the shores of Lake Chad. A stage army of the just; in and out of Broadcasting House, on and off the campuses, marching triumphantly down Cross Street, fanning out through the USSR's wide open spaces, massing for the duration in the Ministry of Information, with ABCA (the Army Bureau of Current Affairs) to take the overspill, and, when the war was over, UNESCO providing a home from home, Chatham House a sanctuary. Indestructible, inexorable, sometimes reported missing, possibly dead, but always reappearing sooner or later behind the microphones, before the cameras. Do the panel think . . . ? They do, they do! Thinkers all!

The only tangible evidence I saw that any of the pieces I wrote while at the Ministry ever got published was a smudgy cutting from a Ceylon newspaper of an article under my by-line, headed 'Eternal Vigilance', and animadverting upon the cost and uses of liberty. Otherwise, it may be assumed that my offerings, though doubtless circulated to press attachés in the relevant countries, found no takers. Meanwhile, the Ministry visibly grew and grew; new departments being born almost daily, and old ones expanded. For instance, the religious department, with which I had occasional transactions, gathered in ever more personnel, including a miscellaneous collection of Roman Catholic lay intellectuals, a Jesuit or two, as well as a representative atheist. Palmer and I continued in the the seclusion of our office; he working steadily, I gathered, at some literary study, and I, fitfully, at the closing chapters of *The Thirties*. It was in these circumstances that I received a paper calling upon me to present myself at Mytchett Hutments, Ash Vale, with a view to joining the Field Security Police. I had almost forgotten that, after my abortive attempt to join up, I wrote a short satirical account in the *Daily Telegraph* of how, in this war, unlike the last, places in the armed forces were as difficult to come by as tickets for the Royal Enclosure at Ascot or invitations to the Lord Mayor's Banquet. It drew a rejoinder from a Lt-Colonel asking me whether I was bluffing or seriously wanted to join the army; if the latter, what was the matter with this new formation, the FSP, which had been advertising for linguists in the daily press? I replied that I was not bluffing, and asked nothing better than to be called to the colours in any capacity. The summons to Mytchett was the delayed response.

It was, I confess, with a sinking heart that I turned in my railway warrant at Waterloo station, and got in return a ticket to Ash Vale; especially as, the day before, I had been offered a higher post at the Ministry, which would have meant a substantial rise in salary and allowances. As usual, I inwardly equivocated, half hoping that I might be turned down for the FSP on health grounds, or because of my atrocious accent when I spoke French, the only foreign language I could claim to know; and then, thinking of the Ministry, its thronging corridors, its fraudulent output, the resonant voices prophesying peace against the rat-tat-tat of typewriters; Bloomsbury within and all about me – thinking of all this, I longed to make my escape, even though only into a barrack-square.

As the train approached Ash Vale I became aware of the Aldershot countryside, with its air of having been endlessly tramped over in heavy boots; like a chicken run, denuded of vegetation, bare and untidy. Mytchett Hutments, too, when I reached them, stood out bleakly among pine trees, very much recalling the picture I had formed in my mind of a Soviet labour camp. I might even then, I thought, turn tail and run back to my typewriter. In the end, I just surrendered myself to the process of becoming a soldier; filled in yet another prodigious form, stripped for the purpose of being medically examined, wandered about naked holding a phial of my urine; then swore on a dog-eared Bible to fight loyally for King and Country as and when required. Thus the matter was settled; the Ministry of Information knew me no more, and I became a private, acting unpaid lance-corporal, in the shortly-to-be-formed Intelligence Corps.

My medical category was low, C3, but I was subsequently able to persuade a drunken MO in a lax moment to alter this to A1, which I considered, I really think correctly, to be a truer description of my physical condition. Had the category stood, I should never have been sent abroad, and probably have remained at the depot for the rest of the war – a fate almost more awful than staying at the Ministry of Information. Battle-dress was still not on issue, and we were provided with riding breeches, puttees, peaked caps, and tunics with high collars and brass buttons; gear that I found it difficult to manage and to muster. On the first evening, when I arrayed myself in it as best I could, having acquired a bed in a barrack hut – one of fifteen – I felt, as I so often have, that I had acted impulsively, and landed myself in a ridiculous position. There were still some final pages of *The Thirties* to write; my pay and family allowances as an unpaid lance-corporal would make Kitty's circumstances even more straitened than heretofore, and I saw little prospect of shining in my new profession of arms. I thought with positive nostalgia of the room in the Ministry I shared with Palmer. Ah! if only I could get back there, would I not throw myself with renewed fervour into an appeal, even to the islanders of Fiji, or the head-hunters of Borneo, to rally to the Allied cause in defence of freedom and democracy. Alas, there was no escape route from Mytchett back to Bloomsbury now; once again I had kicked down the ladder on which I might have made a getaway. In the event, I managed to get the last pages of *The Thirties* written, seated on my bed in the barrack hut, with a pad in my lap, and they were by no means the poorest in the book. In the barrack hut, too, I got the news that *The Thirties* was a Book Society choice, and autographed the requisite number of title-pages in an edition on special paper, to the accompaniment of much good-natured derision on the part of my fellow-occupants.

Mytchett, the depot of the Corps of Military Police, or Red Caps, was run on very strict lines. Smartness was called for, saluting was vigorous and imperative, any carelessness in dress or slouching or lounging was anathema. The NCO's, and particularly the warrant officers, yelled out orders with thunderous emphasis, tucked their swagger-sticks under their arms, pounded the pavement with their boots, and larded their speech with swear-words and obscenities like any sociologist, underground newspaper, or alternative culture exponent today. When for a short while I became a warrant officer myself, I found, rather to my surprise, that I could emulate these old pros in volume of voice if nothing else; shouting out 'Squad, Abbbbout turn!', or 'Staand eas . . . . . . y!' as to the manner born. My performance was so unexpected that it attracted attention; a little crowd would gather to hear me at it, drawn, I suppose, by the ludicrous disparity between what I looked like, and perhaps was, and what I was doing. Or did my accomplishment in this field, like Dr Johnson's in emulating a bargee's vocabulary of abuse, which so dazzled Boswell, point to a potential loud-mouthed bully under my skin? I have sometimes thought so.

It was while I was putting up this impersonation of an old-style warrant officer that an incident occurred which, once and for all, demolished any military fantasies I may have entertained. It seemed that an important officer from the War Office was coming to Mytchett on some undisclosed but urgent mission, and I was instructed to meet him at Ash Vale station. It was, I felt, an important occasion. I pressed my tunic and trousers with loving care, polished up the crown on my sleeve till it shone like the morning sun, worked on the toes of my army boots with a hot spoon to give them a comparable glory. Thus resplendent, I awaited the officer's arrival on the station platform, and, when I saw him get down from a first-class carriage, gave him a thunderous salute, which he nonchalantly returned. Then I took his bag and saw him into an army car, seating myself beside the driver. In the driving mirror I studied the face of our distinguished visitor. He was young, I decided, to be so important a personage, with a sensitive, vaguely melancholic countenance. As I went on looking at him, it struck me that there was something familiar about his features, and all at once it dawned on me that I knew him. He was Edward Crankshaw, a neighbour of ours in the country, whom we had seen occasionally and liked; a gifted writer, and subsequently the *Observer's* Kremlinologist – the equivalent in our time of a Delphic Oracle, deducing our present fortunes and future prospects, not from a chicken's entrails, but from the turgid columns of *Pravda, Izvestia* and other Soviet publications.

Crankshaw, as he told me afterwards, had been going through the same motions of penetrating my disguise, and our mutual recognition was instantaneous. We began to laugh long and helplessly. He had been thinking that, after all, the old depot sweats like this sergeant-major who had met him at Ash Vale Station so smartly turned out, were still the fine flower of the regular army, and I that this brilliant young captain from the War Office was really more like an intellectual in uniform than the conventional notion of a staff officer. We laughed and laughed at the deception we had all unconsciously practiced on one another. Somehow, thenceforth, I was never again able to take my military duties, such as they were, quite seriously; like other exercises of the will, they required dressing up and histrionic skills to be convincing. The learned judge in his ermine, the erudite professor in his gown, the holy priest in his vestments, the anointed monarch with his crown and orbs, and I, impersonating a sergeant-major with shining boots and buttons.

The FSP were an alien element at Mytchett, and regarded by the native Red Caps with an implacable detestation. An advertisement for linguists such as had brought us together there, was calculated to assemble as sorry a company in their eyes as could possibly be imagined; ranging between carpet-sellers from Baghdad and modern language teachers in grammar schools and colleges, with a stray expert on Bengali or Sanskrit, or pimp from Marseilles or Beirut; as well as tourist agency men, unfrocked priests who had lived irregularly in Venice and Rome, and contraceptive salesmen who had roamed the world. Our appearance in uniform was even more derisory than when we first arrived among them as civilians; trimming and tidying us up only served to accentuate our disorderly bearing and ways. To add to the comedy, our own reaction to the situation in which we found ourselves tended to become. more military than the MP's themselves. We saluted on all possible occasions, we polished our buttons and our boots with an obsessive assiduity, we dropped out 'Sirs' when talking to officers and NCO's in wild profusion, and when called upon to step forward to receive our pay or a leave-pass we made such a clatter that the very floor-boards groaned. All this, far from endearing us to the Mytchett regulars, made us even more repellent, especially as promotion came to us, from their point of view, with dazzling rapidity. We moved up from being unpaid lance-corporals, to sergeants and sergeant-majors, almost overnight, as more and more Field Security sections were mustered. I well remember with what distaste the MP's looked at me on the first day I walked between the hutments with a crown on my arm. Then, when I became an officer some months later, all was changed. Hostility turned into amiability; I found myself quite a favourite when I condescended to visit the sergeants' mess, being regarded as a card, an odd fellow who said preposterous things but needed to be cherished and protected.

Apart from the drill, being given injections, assembling and setting out our kit in accordance with a set pattern (something I never properly mastered), and keeping our quarters spick and span, to the point of polishing the floor until it was like a skating-rink, and arranging the pebbles outside our hut into an elegant mosaic, there was the course in Security Intelligence. This consisted of a series of lectures given by officers and NCO Instructors on how Intelligence was collected, and how those collecting it on behalf of the enemy might be circumvented. The syllabus was based exclusively on 1914–18 War practice, and even to our inexpert minds had an air of irrelevance. For instance, there was the *Dames Blanches* organisation set up in Brussels, which consisted of Belgian ladies who counted the carriages of troop trains rumbling past as they knitted at their windows, thus providing material for making an estimate of the forces the Germans were moving up to the front. Another theme was how to set up an informer network, taking account of the fact that barbers and taxi-drivers were normally garrulous by nature, and could be tapped for information, which, however, must be accepted with some reserve. We were expected to follow the scripts provided with scrupulous exactitude, which, when I became an instructor, I faithfully did, in the process becoming quite attached to them, as I had when I was at Cambridge to the Latin grace in hall and other ceremonial incantations. To the best of my knowledge, they continued to serve right through the war. Whenever I ran into anyone from Field Security I always asked if the *Dames Blanches* were still going strong at the depot, and learnt with relief that they were. Also that the playlet about how an enemy agent was detected by finding among his toilet accessories a tell-tale ball-pointed pen for writing in invisible ink, was still being performed with great panache for successive courses.

The war itself seemed even more remote at Mytchett than it had at the Ministry of Information, despite our drilling, our uniforms, our military status, and the blood-curdling tales we were regaled with about the dreadful things that happened to Intelligence personnel who fell into enemy hands. We seldom spoke about the war, and our training soon became an end in itself rather than a preparation for subsequent action in the field. Occasionally, an officer or other rank who had been in France with the British Expeditionary Force visited us and spoke about trench life, and the unsympathetic attitude of the French civilian population; the general assumption being that the Maginot Line was impregnable, and that the Germans, with their dwindling supplies of essential war material, were bound to collapse and surrender before so very long. When I asked once what would happen if the attack came, not on the Maginot Line, but on some other relatively undefended part of the Franco-Belgian frontier, the question was brushed aside. Military expertise, I soon discovered, was even more dogmatic and immune to criticism than other kinds. Later on in the war, when I was on an Intelligence course at Matlock Hydro, an officer came especially from the War Office to give us an account of the defences of Singapore. He unrolled a map of the Malay Peninsula, and, waving his pointer about over it, demonstrated conclusively that no land force would ever be able to make its way through such jungle terrain. At that very moment, while he was speaking, the Japanese were moving swiftly down the peninsula to Singapore, which fell a few days later. The Hydro seemed a perfect shrine for such outmoded military lore; with its odour of hot baths, hot drinks and decaying flesh. A nearby chemist told me that when the inmates were evacuated to make way for our Intelligence courses, several of them died on the way to the station, and, subsequently, an occasional corpse of someone left behind was found in one of the remoter rooms.

Our life at Mytchett was really rather a happy one; we were cut off, alike, from civilian responsibilities and from the hazards of war. Our chief preoccupations were to keep our buttons and boots bright, our tunics pressed so that we made a good show on parade; to climb the ladder of promotion as expeditiously as possible, and to ingratiate ourselves with the CO and his officers in whose hands lay our future posting; as well as with the NCO's who allocated fatigues and handed out leave passes and stores. I, as an instructor, had also the lectures to consider, including one of my own on propaganda, in which I drew on journalistic experience, trying to present myself as an old, hard-boiled Fleet Street hand. Delivering them, I sometimes imagined myself back in Alwaye, and looking out of the window, half expected to see paddy fields and brown figures chanting as they trod round their bamboo irrigation wheels; instead, a squad being drilled on asphalt – 'Left, right! Left, right! Abbbbout turn!' It seems as though all my life I have been holding forth and looking out of windows; though, I venture to hope, rarely quite as irrelevantly as at Mytchett.

For those of my generation, it was a kind of charade of the war we had missed. We spent our evenings in local pubs, or made our way to Aldershot, clattering through its blacked-out streets; pushing open faintly lit doors into public bars, there to join other troops stoically drinking draught beer. The very songs we sang belonged to the last war – 'Pack Up Your Troubles', 'It's a Long Way to Tipperary'; the ENSA entertainers who occasionally visited us were getting on in years, and groaned over their dance routine as I did over my PT. Most week-ends I had a pass to go home, made out 'for the purpose of going to Battle', this being the nearest station to Whatlington; the only soldier in the British Army so bent, I used to boast. There, with Kitty and the children, I tried to play the part of a warrior taking his ease. It was not very convincing.

In the dark cavernous space of Waterloo Station, on my way back to Mytchett, I resumed my place as a member of the armed forces; a greying NCO somewhat abashed to be wearing a CMP badge pending the issue of a newly designed I Corps one. We were packed tight in railway compartments, dimly lit with blue electric bulbs, cigarettes glowing in the darkness; in our identical khaki, mostly silent and ruminative, except for an occasional snore or grunt. At Ash Vale, our contingent got off the train, and, in twos and threes, or solitarily, tramped to Mytchett; boots echoing up the hill, past the guard room and the sentry, on to my barrack hut, tiptoeing in, the other fourteen all tucked up and asleep. Undressing by torch-light, shining it across at my neighbours, their faces quite gentle, and even innocent, in repose, with the strange poignancy of sleeping men. One with part of a cigarette behind his ear, ready for the first morning puff; all the defensiveness and defiance dissolved in sleep, a rehearsal for death and its peace. I felt a great tenderness towards them; brothers-in-arms, except that we hadn't been issued with any arms.

I became an officer in May 1940. Having ordered a uniform and the necessary kit in Aldershot, I now went into the shop to put it on; entering as a company sergeant-major and emerging a lieutenant. As I arrayed myself, garment by garment, a feeling of melancholy, almost of despair, assailed me. It was rather like arriving at Montreux from Moscow; another imagined escape from bourgeois life had proved illusory, and I found myself infallibly back among the saloon-bar folk. I suppose everyone who has straddled the classes, moving from dinner to luncheon and from supper to dinner, from Saturday evening to daily morning bathing, from strong Indian to weak China tea, from weekly currency notes and coins in a little envelope to a monthly cheque paid into a bank account, is in some senses subject to such fantasies, which seem now to have quite taken possession of the middle- and upper-class young, who array themselves in tattered clothes, eschew bathing altogether, and live by Oscar Wilde's dictum that work is the curse of the drinking (in their case, pot-smoking) classes. Yet it is true that I greatly enjoyed the relationship of full and free equality which being an other rank involved, and regretted becoming an officer, having a batman, drinking too many pink gins in an ante-room before going to dine in a mess, and other intimations of commissioned status.

At Mytchett, depot life was, for us, the war. The nearest we got to being belligerents was to array ourselves in battle-dress, worn by officers and other ranks alike; the only outward sign of commissioned rank, apart from pips on the shoulder-straps, being the wearing of a collar and tie. I came in for some disapproving words in the mess when I developed the theory that we liked wearing battle-dress because, in case of a revolution or other upheaval, we could button up our tunics, take off our insignia of rank, and no one would know we were officers. In the event, it worked the other way round, as King George VI appears to have foreseen. P. J. Grigg told me that, when he was Secretary of State for War, the only point the King ever raised with him with any seriousness was the dangerous possibility that other ranks might take to wearing collars and ties with battle-dress; as, in due course, they did, thereby equalising upwards and all looking like officers.

Matters of dress, I found, loomed large at Mytchett, especially among the regulars. I was for a time in a barrack hut with several guardsmen, and marvelled at how prima-donnaish they were about their appearance, cavorting and twisting in front of a mirror when they had been issued with a new stripe or other embellishment, to see how it looked. They devoted as many hours to bulling themselves up as any society beauty, and felt very deprived if they missed their afternoon nap. They were like society beauties, too, in the attitude, humorous and at the same time complaisant, which they adopted to the amorous advances their splendid appearance brought them, whether from lonely females who, despite rationing, could produce a tasty supper, or – as, according to their own account, was more often the case – love-sick pederasts; this being a recognised hazard of guard duty at Buckingham Palace.

As spring turned to summer, the war suddenly began. Even in Mytchett we became aware of the Norwegian campaign, of Chamberlain's replacement by Churchill, and then of the triumphant sweep of the *Wehrmacht* through Holland and Belgium and on to Paris and the Channel ports, until it suddenly occurred to us that there seemed no particular reason why the momentum thus achieved should not carry them across the Channel. At our mess in the evenings we listened to the BBC's news bulletins, wearing grave faces at news of further German advances, and ardently discussing afterwards where a stand might be expected, and how the Allied disasters could be reversed. Mixed with the *angst* that news of disasters brought, was also a queer subterranean satisfaction; I think there is in most people, underlying their ostensible passion to win a war, a secret passion to lose it. The same thing applies to seduction. We also listened to Churchill's broadcasts, which, of course, had an electric effect, and were heard in an awed hush by one and all. I personally found the broadcasts somehow distasteful and embarrassing, especially as, from the beginning, they came to be imitated to a tiresome degree, so that practically everyone, in retailing any sort of anecdote or reminiscence about Churchill, copied his phraseology and tone of voice. I naturally hid these feelings, but sometimes they came out in some chance remark or derisory reference, which offended my fellow-officers. I think, on the whole, that their hostility was justified; it was necessary at that time to accept the validity of Churchillian rhetoric, which to me recalled the last sentences of Scott Fitzgerald's *The Great Gatsby* – a favourite novel – about beating on, 'boats against the current, borne back ceaselessly into the past'.

It was at this time that our depot was transferred from Mytchett to Sheerness, in the Isle of Sheppey, where, as it turned out, we constituted almost the only military force – if such we could be called – available to combat a German landing should one be attempted at what seemed to be, from a casual glance at the map, a rather vulnerable point in the Thames Estuary. To provide us with the means to carry out our role we were issued with rifles and twelve rounds of ammunition apiece, none of which, however, could be fired by way of practice to familiarise us with our weapons because of shortage of supplies. At night we prowled along the coast, steel-helmeted, battle-dressed, and shouldering our rifles; speaking only in whispers, looking out intently across the mud flats for signs of grey advancing figures, and to the estuary beyond for the dark shapes of approaching boats.

Our officer in charge was Captain Partridge, a bulky schoolmaster wearing 1914–18 campaign ribbons. He was carrying field-glasses, which in the circumstances could not be of much use, and a map-case which he occasionally examined by the light of a small torch. There were frequent alarms and alerts; once we thought we heard aircraft overhead, and Captain Partridge told us to throw ourselves on the ground, which we did with alacrity, my rifle, to my great shame, going off in the process. This caused near panic; everyone thought the invasion had begun. One lance-corporal insisted that he heard church bells ringing – the agreed signal that the invader had arrived – another that he clearly saw the outline of a boat approaching the shore. It was a case, Captain Partridge explained, of fighting to the last man and last round of ammunition; which in my case would now be the eleventh round instead of the twelfth.

While the troops prepared themselves for the desperate encounter which lay ahead, Captain Partridge spoke to me in whispers about the hopes he had entertained when, at the end of the last war, he had started on his teaching career. How he had tried to make the boys see the need for a kinder, juster way of life; Christian, but not in any narrow sectarian sense. And how he had really made some progress, getting, for instance, T. S. Eliot – later, he confidently expected, Dylan Thomas, and perhaps even D. H. Lawrence, but one had to proceed with discretion – included in the school syllabus, and birdwatching and country walks accepted as an alternative to compulsory games for those so minded. Such changes were not, he went on, in themselves particularly drastic, but all moves in the right direction. Now he felt that his work had all been undone; he did not think he would survive this second war in one lifetime, and was not even sure he wanted to. His voice droned on; I was conscious of his massive physical presence, the forlorn expanse of face under the steel helmet, so grieved and troubled. All I could do was murmur vague noises of agreement and understanding, hoping that the Germans would soon land and bring his anguish to a summary end. The night, however, was stiller than ever; no church bells were ringing, and the boat we had seen turned out to belong to a clandestine fisherman plying his trade despite security regulations. In the event, Captain Partridge lived on to continue after the war his work of enlightenment at one of the smaller public schools.

As it happened, the war did intrude visibly into Sheerness in the shape of French troops, fugitives from across the Channel, who arrived there in a state of great demoralisation. They were in all manner of uniforms, from all sorts of regiments; white and black and Moroccan. Some of them had weapons, which we took off them; all of them were exhausted, bewildered and disgruntled, grumbling and muttering about the absence of Allied air power to counteract the *Luftwaffe*, which, they said, dive-bombed them without respite. I felt very sorry for them so lost-looking and demoralised. Soldiers in such circumstances look particularly wretched, I suppose because one associates them with marching in formation and being smartly and identically attired; when their discipline breaks down they seem more disorderly than any civilian rabble. We looked at them with pity, and they looked at us surlily; as the ally who had failed them, whose immunity from attack had been procured at their expense, '*Où est le Royal Air Force?*' they kept asking savagely, rolling the 'R' in 'Royal', as though we had personally, for our own selfish ends, hidden it somewhere. Our first thought was to hand them cigarettes – that currency of the lost – which they looked at curiously; then lit, and gratefully sucked in the smoke.

As good security men, we had, of course, to take account of the possibility that enemy agents might have been infiltrated with them, and made a move to examine their documents, which, when they reluctantly produced them, turned out to be for the most part crumpled grubby bits of paper bearing a smudged photograph which told us nothing. Carried away, I even attempted to rally them with a sort of sub-Churchillian address in my bad French, about how the struggle against the Nazis had only just begun, and how the defeat we had suffered in France was but a minor set-back in a war in which the triumph of freedom, etc., etc., was assured. It got me back into an editorialising vein; I was, metaphorically speaking, tapping away at my typewriter again. In any case, my words notably failed to break the sullen discontent reflected in the faces of my audience, and I can only suppose that, fortunately for me and for them, they understood not a word of what I said. When I had finished, we marched them back to our depot, trying to maintain as jaunty a pace as possible, and on arrival sat them down for a meal. One of the French officers drew me aside to say that arrangements should be made for *les noirs* to eat and sleep and wash separately. I passed this embarrassing request to the camp commandant for him to deal with as he thought fit.

When, some months later, I had occasion to visit the French troops temporarily housed in Olympia, I found that some of them were from the Sheerness contingent. They had spruced up a bit, but still looked forlorn, despite a group of local girls who had gathered to stare appreciatively at them. I asked one or two about General de Gaulle, and whether they proposed to join the Free French, but they only shrugged and made non-committal remarks. Most of them, I heard afterwards, opted for repatriation. A thing I noticed about the war was how the lowlier participants usually seemed reluctant to join in if they could possibly avoid it; quite contrary to what might be supposed from the history books. The weapons collected at Sheerness made a sizeable pile, consisting of a great variety of guns and side-arms; some of them ancient enough to be regarded as antiques. I took for myself a small Belgian automatic, which thenceforth I always carried, fully loaded, in the breast-pocket of my tunic with a vague notion that in the times that lay ahead it might be as well to be armed. As things turned out, I never once fired it.

I had long been pressing to be posted to a unit, having wearied considerably of lecturing at the depot about the *Dames Blanches*. The CO, when I put this to him, said he could not sacrifice his tools, of which I was one; but at last he was persuaded, and I was posted to GHQ Home Forces, then located at Kneller Hall, in London, where military bands are trained. The last course in which I participated included an officer whose large soup-strainer moustache at once caught my eye. It was matched by Mongolian features which made him look rather like Maxim Gorky. I turned up his papers and found that he had been a classics don in Sydney, Australia, and that his name was Enoch Powell. The moustache, I subsequently learnt from him, was due to a passion he then had for Nietzsche, who had cultivated a similar one. I remembered noticing it in a picture I had seen of Nietzsche, painted in Venice when he was quite mad and on his death-bed; crying out on the last evening of his life, as he saw through his window the sun sinking in wild Turneresque colours into the Grand Canal: 'Good-bye sun! Good-bye, sun!' It was obvious at once that Powell was a very unusual man; isolated, as I later came to realise, in the terrible seriousness and intensity of a sense of destiny. This, for the time being, took the form of determining to be a brigadier in the Operations Branch, which he readily achieved, functioning with great success in this capacity at GHQ Middle-East in Cairo. Later, there were differences about Allied strategy which resulted in his withdrawing to India, where he discovered the British Raj just at the time of its final dissolution. He returned to London after the war resolved to become a Tory MP and save the Raj, succeeding brilliantly in the first objective, and inevitably failing in the other.

Kneller Hall, when I arrived there with my FS Section – myself and batman-driver in a small Austin car, the rest of the section on motor-cycles – was in a state of considerable confusion. Music-stands and other gear and regalia for training military bands were still about the place; a war-room had been hastily improvised, and arrangements generally made for the effective functioning of a supreme headquarters in a beleaguered country likely soon to be invaded. At the mess in the evening I was dazzled by the array of senior officers, booted and spurred, their leather all aglow, their breasts bright with decorations and campaign ribbons, their grizzled locks and white moustaches neatly trimmed. Never before had I consorted with such military eminence, and I felt very lowly, by contrast, in my sober tunic, ribbonless, with its general service buttons and meagre two pips. After dinner we listened to the nine o'clock news which told, in as unalarming a way as possible, of more Allied military reverses. I felt that the minds of the listeners were mostly far away from the silky voice of the news-reader; dreaming of their in-trays, of transport, of establishments and allowances and orders of the day. It was a Sunday evening, and so, after the news came the succession of national anthems of occupied countries, to which almost daily a new one seemed to be added. They caused a faint stirring in the mess; some of the officers, I daresay, had been military attachés, and had an instinctive impulse to rise to their feet; others put down their glasses and held their cigars or cigarettes out of sight. To me, this mustering of the defeated had a macabre fascination, and I was quite disappointed when it came to an end. Someone at Broadcasting House, it seemed, had the notion of including Abyssinia, about whose national anthem there was considerable uncertainty. After one false start which upset the exiled Emperor himself – at this time resident in Bath – it was decided to drop the whole procedure.

Feeling very out of things, I wandered about the Headquarters until I found an officer with red tabs and black buttons gloomily trying to plot the latest order of battle on a large survey-map spread out on a table. He had a collection of coloured wools which he stretched out between pins to mark enemy positions in accordance with the situation reports which a signals orderly brought in from time to time. I watched him, fascinated, for a while, and then was drawn into lending him a hand, and soon became quite absorbed, not so much with the war situation as such, as with the coloured wools; one colour indicating a Panzer Division, others Artillery batteries, reserve troops, observation posts, and so on. We worked away assiduously, only very occasionally exchanging a word or two. He plotted the positions and I arranged the wools. Things were moving at such a rate that I soon got left behind; so much so that, finally, he exploded at my ineptitude. What in the hell did I think I was doing? The whole thing was now in a frightful mess! I could find no better excuse than to blurt out: 'I'm sorry, sir, but there's no more wool'

– which was, as a matter of fact, true. We had used it all up, and there seemed as much chance of procuring a further supply as of stemming the German advance. I thought it the course of prudence to slip away, hoping that some more competent IO than I would appear on the scene; retiring, literally, to my tent.

It was the only time in all the war that I was under canvas. Owing to the shortage of accommodation in Kneller Hall, tents had been erected in the grounds, and I was allotted one of them. It gave me a great feeling of satisfaction to be thus accommodated – the grass floor, the canvas bed and wash-basin, the sound of the ropes straining in the wind, the fresh smell of the night. Shortly afterwards, the whole Headquarters moved to larger premises at St Paul's School, Hammersmith; a red brick, rather murky building evacuated by the school at the beginning of the war, and now demolished. My FS Section was accommodated in a semi-detached house nearby; we set up an office, with a telephone, a box covered with an army blanket for a desk, on the wall a map of Hammersmith and district, a file and other clerical accoutrements to hand. It was the invariable set-up for an army office; only the maps differed from place to place.

I was billetted myself in another semi-detached house in an adjoining street, along with an elderly major in the Ordnance Corps; a desiccated man with a sallow face who had served for some twenty years in India. Though the ordinary washing facilities were available, including a gas geyser, I was surprised to find that he used camp equipment in his own room. On my way back from the bathroom I would catch a glimpse of him crouching over a canvas wash-basin with a cut-throat razor in his hand. In this way, as I later discovered, he was able to claim field allowance, which otherwise, if he had made use of the house's facilities, would have been disallowed. The lady who ran the house, providing us with an ample breakfast each morning, joined me in finding the major's behaviour bizarre, but I think in her heart she preferred him to me. He conformed more to her notion of an officer and a gentleman, whereas my irregular, and sometimes dissolute ways, though she looked on them tolerantly at the time, induced in her a strong feeling of disapproval and resentment which later became apparent.

The excitement of expecting an imminent invasion soon wore off, and GHQ Home Forces, like Mytchett, developed its own routine and tranquillity. On warm afternoons the playing field at the back of the school buildings was littered with sun-bathing figures; in the smaller class-rooms, four majors would be sitting with in- and out-trays before

them, in the larger ones, two lieutenant-colonels, and in the more com-
modious staff-rooms and masters' studies, a single full colonel or
brigadier. I never penetrated to the Commander-in-Chief's office, but
probably he occupied the Headmaster's quarters. The laboratories and
lecture-theatres were turned over to Signals and squads of ATS pounding away at typewriters. Thus the Headquarters might be said to be in
full swing. My only personal part was being on the roster of duty officers,
which involved, when my turn came round, sleeping in a cubicle beside
a white telephone that would ring in the event of a German landing
anywhere. It would then be my responsibility to alert the Headquarters,
which would at once spring into action, dispatching a division here, a
division there, mounting special security guards on various key points
like Broadcasting House and the London Telephone Exchange, transferring essential personnel to a tunnel which had been specially dug
at Virginia Water to be an emergency operations centre, and generally
getting ready to cope with an invasion in accordance with a prepared
plan. Perhaps fortunately, these arrangements were never put to the test.
On my duty nights I always hoped the white telephone would ring, and
tucked up with a book, fully expecting that if it did ring I should hear
Churchill's voice at the other end. Alas, it remained obstinately silent;
except once, when to my great delight it rang. I rushed to pick it up,
only to hear a drunken voice asking for a taxi.

I find it difficult, looking back, to recall what regular duties I had, if
any. The administration of my FS section was in the capable hands of
my sergeant-major, a middle-aged man named Laversuch who had
spent a lot of his life in Africa. He subsequently became an officer, and
was instrumental, as I heard, in hijacking a German ship off the African
coast. Our section was supposed to be responsible for securing the
Headquarters from the incursions of enemy agents who might pry out
its secrets or subvert its personnel. This gave us a free hand to do almost
anything and go almost anywhere. If we went drinking in pubs, it was
to keep a look-out for suspicious characters; if we picked up girls, it was
to probe their intentions in frequenting the locality. A fellow-officer
told me of how, on a pub-crawl, ostensibly a security reconnaissance,
he got drunk, and, as was his way when in such a condition, pre-
tended to be a foreigner, using strange gestures and speaking with a
broken accent. The next day, badly hung over, he was sent a report of
the movements of a suspicious foreigner, and told to check up on them.
Tracing the suspect's movements from pub to pub, it slowly dawned on
him he was following himself the night before. When he told me of his

adventure, to comfort him I said that it was what we were all doing all the time – keeping ourselves under close surveillance. This was what security was all about. In a similar vein, another FS officer, idly thumbing over the Security List – a top-secret document containing the names of all subjects who were to be at once apprehended if they tried to get into or out of the country – found he was in it.

The officer at Headquarters to whom I had to report was Colonel Ross-Atkinson, an Irishman, I should say in his late fifties, with jet-black hair, a high colour, a large pointed nose, bandy legs from much sitting on a horse, and a kind heart. I grew very fond of him. He had been a regular soldier, and took a severely realistic view of his own and our side's prospects in the war. Occasionally, he lost his temper with my nihilistic views, and bawled me out, but something in him, despite his *Burke's Landed Gentry* credentials, responded to them. He had arrived in his own way at somewhat the same conclusion as I had about the future prospects of the British Empire, and his attitude to Churchill was well this side of idolatry. I ferried him about a lot in my little FS car, which saved him from getting one from the pool. He would ask me about things like homosexuality and Bernard Shaw and Stafford Cripps; in return, I learnt from him the bivouac attitude to army life that seasoned regular soldiers like himself had. How you must always, as it were, live off the land, taking advantage of every opportunity to scrounge and draw allowances. How the nearer you could get to the top command the better, because that was the fount of promotion and decorations; the dispenser of good billets of every kind.

Through driving him around and picking him up, I became familiar with his ways and circle of friends. His club was, of course, White's; he consorted with rich men, bankers and the like, and a certain number of fashionable ladies, somewhat faded and getting on in years. Also with racing people and old army cronies. When I called for him I used to be asked in, and had the feeling that I was being shown off; something, I regret to say, to which I have always been all too ready to respond; in life, as on the television screen. The high point of our relationship was reached in the Blitz, when the house of two of his lady friends was bombed so badly that they had to remove themselves, just as they were, in their night-dresses, to a nearby flat. The colonel was informed of their distress by telephone, and we went along together in my car to their bombed-out house to see what, if anything, could be salvaged. The fire-engines were there, and air-raid wardens and the police, but, with our GHQ Home Forces credentials, we were able to make our way in, and, groping about in the smoke and dust, managed to collect together an approximate wardrobe for the two ladies, including stockings, bras and underwear. Our emergence, bearing these various garments over our arms, obviously surprised and amused the onlookers; the more so as the colonel had thoughtlessly disposed of one of the ladies hats by putting it on his head.

Life at GHQ Home Forces was, if anything, more a matter of coasting along than at Mytchett, where at least I had drills and lectures to attend, buttons to clean, and various fatigues to undergo. The only occasion that Colonel Ross-Atkinson asked me to do anything that presented any serious complexities was quite early on, when he handed me a paper reporting how the car of the C-in-C, General Ironside, was often seen standing outside a house in Holland Park, some of whose occupants were alleged to have dubious political associations. Would I, he said, make an investigation; taking care, for obvious reasons, to be infinitely cautious and tactful. I, of course, realised that this was a potentially explosive assignment; the more so because Ironside was reputed to have had in the past associations with allegedly Fascist organisations. Such investigations as could be made, generally supported the original report, though it looked as though the general's interest in the house was personal rather than political. In any case, I felt vaguely shocked that, in the circumstances, he should be able to find time for his often quite lengthy expeditions to Holland Park. Though all too often irresponsible and self-indulgent myself, I have found it easy to be censorious about others.

What to do? It seemed to me quite futile to put in a report to Colonel Ross-Atkinson which would only embarrass him, and, anyway, was unlikely to result in any action being taken. The mere fact that he entrusted me with such a report suggested to me that he hoped I would do something about it on my own account; like one of those off-the-record confidential disclosures which are made to journalists with a view to their being leaked. I consulted my friend Bobby Barclay – we had been at Mytchett together – and he suggested we should pass on the story to his step-father, Sir Robert Vansittart, at the Foreign Office, to take whatever action he thought fit. After all, Bobby pointed out, it *was* the Commander-in-Chief who was concerned, and we *were* expecting to be invaded by the Nazis at any moment. With much trepidation I agreed, and an appointment was made with Vansittart for the following day. We went along to the Foreign Office together in the early afternoon, sent in our names, and sat on a bench on one of the landings on the large ornate stairway waiting to be summoned; rather conscious – at least I was – of being stared at by clerks and messengers passing to and fro with files in their hands. It must have been one of the very few places in London where there seemed to be no signs at all of war; everything, as far as I could judge, being just as it had always been.

Vansittart, when we were admitted to his presence, looked very much a part of the place; seasoned and solid himself, with gleaming brass fittings. Having quarrelled with Chamberlain over his Munich policy, he had been made special adviser on foreign affairs, which meant, of course, that no one took his advice, and he exerted no influence at all, while still having a large office and all the appurtenances of dignity and authority. When Churchill replaced Chamberlain, he fully expected to be brought into the Government to reward him for all the services he had performed for the new Prime Minister in his days in the wilderness; but the telephone did not ring for him. How many there were – John Reith among them – thus waiting for a call that never came!

I told Vansittart about the Holland Park affair, explaining to him why I considered it right to put the information in the hands of someone outside GHQ Home Forces who had personal access to the Government. Vansittart made no comment and took no note; just stared across his desk at us, a monocle in one eye; in his blank gaze all the past comprehended – Victorian–Edwardian, limited editions, epigrams fashioned, restaurant table looking out on the Danube and an orchestra playing Chopin and Richard Strauss, boots with trees in them, velvet smoking-jacket. A whole décor – embossed notepaper, 'My dearest love', leisure hours given over to literary pursuits: 'Lady Eleanor's boudoir. "The Count, my lady, left the flowers with a note." Opens, reads . . .' All this in a gaze directed at Bobby and me, not exactly vacant, but – how shall I put it? – stolid, wooden, impassive; like a heathen idol receiving the prayers and oblations of worshippers. On our way back to Hammersmith I felt uneasy, as though I had betrayed a confidence or behaved dishonourably. Bobby, on the other hand, seemed particularly cheerful; the more so the next day, when the evening paper had a banner-headline: IRONSIDE SACKED. I comforted myself by reflecting that it was inconceivable things should have moved so quickly just on the strength of our little scrap of information; that at most it would only have served to give an additional push to a position that was going to topple anyway, and that, however it was brought about, the replacement of Ironside by Sir Alan Brooke, who succeeded him, was on any showing advantageous to the war effort.

I never found out exactly what happened, and when after the war I saw Vansittart occasionally, I preferred not to question him further, I remember that it was a relief to read that Ironside had been made a field-marshal and raised to the peerage. When I went abroad in the war I left behind in a sealed package an account of the whole episode, imagining that it had some historical importance. Journalism conditions one to this magnification of transient occasions; rushing to the stone to get in a new lead – X RESIGNS, Y APPOINTED; bawling it down a telephone after an anguished wait for the connection; furiously tapping it out on a teleprinter, just in time, with luck, to make the edition. All expense of shame in a waste of spirit. So short a time afterwards – who was X, and what did he resign from? Who Y, and what was he appointed to? When he retired, Vansittart lived in a large house at Denham, where Kitty and I were occasionally invited to lunch. On winter days a large wood fire failed to keep the house warm, and the butler distributed rugs. We all sat under them, listening to Vansittart as he reminisced about his diplomatic days, which [also] seemed very far away and long ago.

Apart from thus helping to unseat the Commander-in-Chief, my days at GHQ Home Forces were uneventful. To while away the time I quite often played chess with one of my lance-corporals named Felix Fenston, who was partly Irish and partly Jewish; very quick-witted and eager to please. Once, while we were thus engaged, the telephone rang; it was another lance-corporal telephoning to say that he had caught a deserter, and what should he do with him? Without looking up from our game – which, incidentally, Fenston won, as he almost invariably did – I said: 'Let him go!' The episode got repeated and embroidered upon, and was thought to be rather funny. Recalling it now, it occurs to me that officers have been, perfectly properly, court-martialled for lesser misdemeanours than airily telling an NCO to release a deserter unconditionally. Nor can I claim, in justification, that I acted as I did out of sympathy with deserters, or because I considered the punishment liable to be meted out to them was excessive. It is just that I have always been prone, and am still, to what is called, I seem to remember from a court case I once followed, in psychiatric jargon, *la belle indifférence*. It would be comforting to relate this aberration to a preoccupation with spiritual considerations; to an awareness that, as Augustine puts it in *The City of God*, 'our good (whose end the philosophers jangled about) is nothing but to adhere to Him, and by his intellectual and incorporeal embrace our soul grows great with all virtue and perfection'. Alas, I fear it is primarily due to a sort of callousness and irresponsibility, more egotistic than other-worldly.

After I left GHQ Home Forces I heard from Fenston – he always addressed me as 'Muggers', which was another unofficerly procedure – from time to time. In one of his letters he told me of how he had been involved in a bad accident when he was riding his motor-cycle, which resulted in his having his leg amputated and being discharged from the army. Then I heard nothing more till after the war, when I got a note asking if I would dine with him one evening. It was from an address in Hill Street, and I vaguely wondered how Fenston came to be living in so select and expensive a neighbourhood, thinking perhaps it might be office premises, or even that he had a caretaker's job. When I went along, however, the mansion was in full swing, with waiters in tail-coats and white gloves on every landing, and pink champagne flowing freely. It seemed that it had been the Duke of Devonshire's residence, which Fenston had recently acquired. Later, when we sat talking, he explained how he had become a millionaire. It was terribly simple, he said, with noticeable irritation, as though this very simplicity was a mean trick, depriving him of the true satisfaction of acquiring riches. There he was in war-time London, with no job, a meagre disability pension, no prospects. All alone. Thus situated, an idea of dazzling, almost ridiculous, simplicity seized him. London was full of bombed-out sites which in the then circumstances had practically no value. If the war was won, they would recover their value anyway, and more; if lost, the question did not arise. In mundane terms, it recalled Pascal's famous wager. Why not, then, somehow raise some money and acquire a site or two? Then use them as collateral to raise more money, and so *ad infinitum*. By the war's end he was, like Gogol's hero in *Dead Souls*, on paper at any rate, a large property-owner. Thereafter, it was easy to become a property-developer and millionaire. By this stage in his recital he was almost shaking with rage to think that he, a sort of genius, should have had to bend to such paltry devices, when he could have done things so much more difficult, requiring so much greater audacity and imagination.

I saw him afterwards from time to time, but at very long intervals. He was always pressing for a meeting, almost embarrassingly. 'Muggers, I wish you'd promise to lunch with me every week', he'd say. I think my presence somehow comforted him; I being a fairly obscure journalist, by no means well off, and so reassuring him that, by comparison with me, he had scored by becoming a millionaire, and acquiring all the hangers-on, male and female, that went therewith. He was always trying to dazzle

me, too, with tales of big-game shooting in Kenya and India, of his
financial deals and his country estate. Or producing smart people at his
table. This culminated in a dinner party to meet Princess Alexandra and
her husband, Angus Ogilvy. Paul Getty, a lugubrious figure reputed to
be the richest man in the world, was another guest. After he had seen the
Princess off, Fenston did a strange thing; he went pounding down the
great stairway he had just come up, jumping ferociously from step to
step, until he got to the bottom, sweating and triumphant. With his
artificial leg and heavy build, the effect was frightening; he might so
easily have fallen and killed himself. I took it to be a demonstration,
primarily for my benefit, of his strength and virility despite his disability
and millionaire status. Some months later I read in the papers that he
had suffered a heart attack; then that he had died. It gave me a pang to
think I had only responded to his showing off by my own kind of showing off; not trying to meet him on some other basis – stretching out a
hand and receiving a hand.

The Blitz, when it came, gave a sort of focus to our existence at
GHQ Home Forces. It started on a bright summer's Sunday afternoon. I was standing on Camden Hill with Andreas Mayor, son of
Kitty's cousin, Beatrice Mayor, then serving with the Royal Fusiliers,
of whom I became very fond and saw often. He was tall and sallow,
with large, dark, molten eyes, full of a gentle, inert melancholy;
wonderfully aware of all the subtleties and delights of life and art and
literature, but also standing apart; aesthetically rather than spiritually
detached. An onlooker by temperament rather than by choice, a true
anchorite; but of the library, not the desert. There was a loud hum in the
clear sky, and we looked up to see a lot of planes in close formation
going by; not realising at first that they were enemy ones. Then came
explosions and the sound of ack-ack, and a thick cloud of smoke rising
in the East End, where the docks were. 'It has begun,' Andreas said in a
quiet, almost complacent, voice.

Thenceforth, the Blitz was a nightly occurrence. I nearly always
went out when it was on; often with Andreas, occasionally with Graham
Greene. This was not out of bravado, or a wish to be killed; just an
instinctive movement towards where the noise was loudest, as people on
a seaside beach gather where the throng is greatest. Also, there was
something rather wonderful about London in the Blitz, with no street
lights, no traffic and no pedestrians to speak of; just an empty, dark city,
torn with great explosions, racked with ack-ack fire, lit with lurid flames,
acrid smoke, its air full of the dust of fallen buildings. I remember

particularly Regent's Park on a moonlit night, full of the fragrance of the rose gardens; the Nash Terraces, perfectly blacked-out, not a sign of a light anywhere, white stately shapes waiting to be toppled over – as they duly were, crumbling into rubble like melting snow. Andreas and I watched the great fires in the City and Fleet Street from St James's Park. It was a great illumination, a mighty holocaust; the end of everything, surely. Threadneedle Street no more; likewise Cheapside and Moorgate which my father's feet had trodden day by day for forty years. The *Evening Standard*, the *Daily Express* – would they appear again? Even Printing House Square in jeopardy; even at Broadcasting House the suave recital of news interrupted by a muffled sound of an explosion in the building's very bowels. I felt a terrible joy and exaltation at the sight and sound and taste and smell of all this destruction; at the lurid sky, the pall of smoke, the faces of bystanders wildly lit in the flames. Goebbels, in one of his broadcasts, accused us of glorying obscenely in London's demolition. He had a point, but what he failed to understand was that we had destroyed our city already before the *Luftwaffe* delivered their bombs; what was burning was no more than the dry residual shell.

Andreas and I made our way to the Temple on foot, treading over firemen's hoses, and ducking when things fell about us; though he, noticing a fire bomb fall nearby, was liable to murmur in a disappointed voice: 'Oh, it's missed us!' Just as someone, looking out of a window, and seeing the postman pass without a rat-a-tat at the door, murmurs: 'Oh, there's nothing for us!' The Inner Temple was a smouldering ruin, the Round Church largely gone, but we managed to get into the Library, awash with water. The two of us all alone there, the sodden shelves at our disposal, a trolley of books ready loaded for distribution, but never to be distributed. Andreas mourned for the books, tenderly picking up one or two to see whether the damage was reparable, but I was thinking only of the lawyers; red-faced, heavy-jowled, with great beaks of noses, wigs on their heads or carried in boxes, gowns over their arms, their white bibs fluttering in the wind – 'I put it to you . . .', 'Tell My Lord what you were doing . . .' Forensic, otiose, watch-chains reposing on substantial stomachs; their haunts, too, laid low.

The Blitz was a kind of protracted debauch, with the shape of orderly living shattered, all restraints removed, barriers non-existent. It gave one the same feeling a debauch did, of, as it were, floating loose; of having slipped one's moorings. Once, in an access of folly, I drove round and round Piccadilly Circus the wrong way to celebrate the absence of all other traffic. Restaurants were often almost empty; it was possible, for instance, to dine at the Café Royal – still with marble-topped tables and red-plush seats – when there were no more than a dozen or so other patrons present, the five or six waiters on duty scurrying to and fro as though engaged in a game of musical chairs, and the music about to stop at any moment. From time to time, some shattering explosion nearby made the walls shake and the tables rattle and the windows crumble. Even at the much-boosted Windmill Theatre there would be just a handful of dedicated addicts in the auditorium, gazing balefully at the nudes; rather pinched and ravaged in the footlights' glare, yet still bound by law to keep absolutely still. Almost the only stillness to be found in all London those nights.

I went once with Graham Greene. The spectacle appealed to him for its tattiness and seediness; the guise in which he most likes the Devil's offerings to be presented. He explained how the *cognoscenti* knew just where to sit to get the best view, and how, as the front rows cleared, spectators at the back pressed forward to take their places; wave upon wave, like an attacking army. For expeditions in the Blitz, he made a special act of penitence and other appropriate liturgical preparations in case death came upon him unawares. It made me feel uneasy, and even envious; like travelling in a first-class railway carriage with a first-class ticket-holder when one only has a third-class ticket oneself. I imagined Graham being carried away to paradise, and I left behind in purgatory, or worse. Ever since I have known him, he has seemed to me to possess some special quality of aloofness and detachment from the passions he so concerns himself about in his novels, and, for that matter, in his life. If you come upon him unawares – as I sometimes have, catching a glimpse of him from the top of a bus, or walking in or out of Albany, where we both for a time resided – an expression in his face of isolation from everything and everyone around him, makes it seem almost as though he were blind. One almost expects him to have a white stick, and to need a friendly guiding hand to see him across the road. I once without thinking said of him that he was a saint trying unsuccessfully to be a sinner, and I a sinner trying equally unsuccessfully to be a saint. The remark, which was widely quoted, annoyed him, not so much because it credited him with being a saint (a role for which he has no taste), as because of my pretentions to be a sinner. What sort of sinner are you? he asked scornfully, as though I had claimed some quite undeserved achievement or beatitude.

By day, with my FS section, I explored the previous night's destruction, having somehow persuaded myself that this was one of our duties.

I doubt very much if it really was. The police reports of where the bombs had fallen came to Colonel Ross-Atkinson's office, and we plotted them on a map and checked on them; driving out to remote suburbs where whole rows of frail houses had been obliterated – Crescents and Avenues and Gardens reduced, literally, to handfuls of dust. Just vanishing overnight; their scanty remains, like cremated corpses, scattered to the wind. Jerry-built and Jerry-demolished. Or we would go to the main-line stations to see how they had fared, finding them often deserted and immobilised; great cavernous spaces with no trains, no passengers, no porters, no luggage; silent except for our own echoing footsteps. St Pancras, King's Cross, Euston – somehow, with all the hazards, these massive ungainly structures were surviving, seemingly indestructible. Contrary to the old song, echoed by T. S. Eliot, London Bridge was not yet falling down.

Waking in the night, it seemed as though the Book of Revelations had veritably come to pass. All the sky alight, and rent with furious sounds, the earth itself visibly shaking and groaning; missiles flying through the air, and occasional screams heard, followed by explosions. Then, momentarily, silence, as though for all eternity; actually, for a few seconds only. On one such turbulent evening Andreas took me to a party. So familiar a scene – glass in hand, hum of talk, eyes roving; in this case, mostly *Horizon* folk, like its editor, Cyril Connolly, unquiet in their graves. Nothing seemed changed, except that Stephen Spender, towering like a Snow King above the others, had a fireman's hat in his hand. Someone was playing a piano, the notes competing with the ack-ack din outside – 'Thank you, Natasha, for that beautiful music!' It was, it seemed, a new composition by Benjamin Britten, whose production, Raymond Mortimer said, was the most important event that had happened in the world for some considerable time. This was spoken *sotto voce*, and, at the same time, a little defiantly, as though uniformed men-at-arms like Andreas and me could scarcely be expected to understand; we no doubt supposed that the Battle of Britain, or Churchill's broadcasts, or the Atlantic Charter – some event of that kind – was what really mattered.

Another place Andreas took me to was a basement flat in Bentinck Street, belonging to Lord Rothschild, where Andreas's sister, Tess – who was subsequently to marry Rothschild – was then staying. Above was the office of the *Practitioner*, in whose boardroom we lingered, seated, lordly, on leather chairs, and staring at the magazine's splendidly bound volumes, before venturing below. There, we found another gathering of displaced intellectuals; but more prosperous, more socially secure and successful, than the *Horizon* ones – John Strachey, J. D. Bernal, Anthony Blunt, Guy Burgess, a whole revolutionary *Who's Who*. It was the only time I ever met Burgess; and he gave me a feeling, such as I have never had from anyone else, of being morally afflicted in some way. His very physical presence was, to me, malodorous and sinister; as though he had some consuming illness – like the galloping consumption whose symptoms I had seen in my father's brothers and cousins, or leprosy as I remembered it in India. The impression fitted in well enough with his subsequent adventures; as did this millionaire's nest altogether, so well set up, providing, among other amenities, special rubber bones to bite on if the stress of the Blitz became too hard to bear. Sheltering so distinguished a company – Cabinet Minister-to-be, honoured Guru of the Extreme Left-to-be, Connoisseur Extraordinary-to-be, and other notabilities, all in a sense grouped round Burgess; Etonian mudlark and sick toast of a sick society, as beloved along Foreign Office corridors, in the quads and the clubs, as in the pubs among the pimps and ponces and street pick-ups, with their high voices and peroxide hair. A true hero of our time, who was to end his days in Moscow; permitted even there, for services rendered, to find the male company he needed. Now gone to Stalin's bosom; hip before hipsters, Rolling before the Stones, acid-head before LSD. There was not so much a conspiracy gathered round him as just decay and dissolution. It was the end of a class, of a way of life; something that would be written about in history books, like Gibbon on Heliogabalus, with wonder and perhaps hilarity, but still tinged with sadness, as all endings are.

It was about this time that I attended, on Colonel Ross-Atkinson's instructions, the trial in camera at the Old Bailey on security charges of an American diplomat, Tyler Kent, and Anna Volkov, a Russian lady whose father, Admiral Volkov, had been the last naval attaché at the Imperial Russian Embassy. When the Revolution happened, the admiral stayed in London, and in due course he and his daughter ran a sort of tea-shop-cum-restaurant in Kensington which for a time enjoyed a certain vogue. There was no really valid reason for my presence at the Old Bailey, but each day I gave Colonel Ross-Atkinson a new thrilling instalment of how things were going, which he greatly appreciated; especially any episodes reflecting on MI5's handling of the case – of which there was no lack. I think at some point he must have been reprimanded for allowing me to attend the trial at all, for quite suddenly he became unusually insistent that any record I made of the proceedings should be scrupulously destroyed. As I made no record, there was nothing to destroy.

Anna Volkov, as I remember her in the dock, was short, compact, and, though still quite young, already white-haired; Kent, one of those intensely gentlemanly Americans who wear well-cut tailor-made suits, with waistcoat and watch-chain, drink wine instead of high-balls, and easily become furiously indignant. They always strike me as being somehow a little mad. A tour of duty in Moscow had given him a maniacally hostile attitude towards the Soviet regime, and an extra hatred of Roosevelt and his policies, besides fortifying his anti-semitism. Thus, between him and Anna there was much common ground; while her aristocratic origins doubtless gave her an extra glamour in his eyes. Kent, it appeared, had been removing whole suitcases-full of secret documents from the United States Embassy, then presided over by Ambassador Joseph Kennedy, founding-father of the clan. He showed some of them to Anna, who passed on any that seemed of interest, via the Roumanian Embassy, to Lord Haw-Haw (William Joyce) as material for his broadcasts from Berlin. The Italian and German Intelligence Services also got a sight of them. I became quite absorbed in the case, snatching a quick snack at a pub opposite the Old Bailey in order to be back in court in time to miss none of the proceedings. The fact that every now and again the sirens sounded, and one and all – Judge, Learned Counsel, prisoners, witnesses – repaired to underground cellars to await the All Clear, only added to the drama. Outside, such sound and fury; inside, the Judge with his wheezy dispassionateness, doodling or listening with closed eyes to interminable cross-examinations. A strange, remote, barely human figure; glasses on beaked nose, layers of wig and folds of cloth about his withered person, fingers tapping, or scribbling down a word or two.

At one point a whole contingent of internees under Regulation 18b were summoned from the Isle of Man to testify on behalf of the defence that they had no knowledge of the two defendants, or of what they were at. Distraught women in battered fur coats, blonde hair whitening and dishevelled, make-up running; men in tweed jackets to their knees, leather-patched, frayed club ties, suede shoes; Sir Oswald Mosley himself, bearded at this time, his suit crumpled, speaking with the vibrant voice of a wronged man who asked only to be allowed to join his regiment in the battle-line to fight for King and Country. Also, Captain Ramsay, a Scottish Member of Parliament – for Peebles – with a passing resemblance to Neville Chamberlain. A letter of his was read out in which he referred to 'those two lovely ships' (*Scharnhorst* and *Gneisenau*), and how sad it would be if anything untoward happened to them. This brought a prodding finger from the prosecuting Attorney General, Sir William Jowitt. Was this a way to speak about two enemy warships? With the benighted innocence of the crazed, Ramsay said that when he wrote the letter it still seemed possible that the war, though declared, would never get going; in which case the loss of the ships would have been a pity. It was part of Hitler's weird genius thus to be able to persuade a lost bourgeoisie and their treasonable clerks in attendance, that he intended them no ill. Stalin performed a similar feat with a lost intelligentsia. Ramsay and the others were a woebegone procession indeed, as, one after the other, they held up a Bible and swore to tell the truth, the whole truth and nothing but the truth, while outside their erstwhile heroes and putative allies tried to blow the Old Bailey, along with all the rest of London town, including them, to smithereens.

In the end, Anna Volkov got ten years' penal servitude and Tyler Kent seven. When his sentence had been pronounced, Kent made an indignant protest, pointing out that he had acted throughout as a patriotic American anxious to keep his country out of a ruinous war. This was doubtless genuine enough, and if his illicit disclosure of secret papers had been Leftwards instead of Rightwards directed, he would have found himself, like Daniel Ellsberg, numbered among the contemporary saints, and appeared on post-Christendom's most notable stained-glass window – the cover of *Time* magazine. In such circumstances, too, he would have had many vociferous champions, in the press and the legislatures and the pulpits, to denounce the harsh punishment meted out to him. Even at the court proceedings themselves, despite their being in camera, what had really troubled Kent was slurred over – the exchanges between Roosevelt and Churchill when he was First Lord of the Admiralty, sent via the United States Embassy, and by-passing Chamberlain, the Prime Minister, which conveyed such classified information as the siting of minefields and the clear lanes for Allied shipping; evidently designed, Kent considered, to manœuvre America into becoming a belligerent. He professed to be outraged by so devious and unconstitutional a procedure, which, he contended, entitled him to leak what was happening, even though, as it turned out, he thereby ensured that the Italian Government was made privy to the highly un-neutral relations subsisting between the President and the First Lord, and so was given an extra pretext, when the time came, for declaring war on the Allies. As we know from Ciano's *Diaries*, Mussolini had made up his mind to declare war anyway, and may be assumed to have decided exactly how and when, on a basis of calculations of his own. It is a favourite illusion that historical events would not have happened but for such and such a disclosure, or might have been prevented by some skilful *démarche* here or *pronunciamento* there. There never need have been a Nazi–Soviet Pact if only someone more important than Strang had gone to Moscow to negotiate with Stalin! Italy never would have joined in the war as a belligerent of sorts if only Tyler Kent and Anna Volkov between them had not let the Duce know that Roosevelt and Churchill were hand-in-glove! Journalists and diplomats, even historians, thrive on such fantasies; I have, in the exercise of my profession, aired many, not one of which had the slightest validity.

The Blitz became a sort of apocalyptic *son et lumière*; a nightly spectacle widely appreciated. When it began, with sirens sounding the alert, everyone scattered – to air-raid shelters if they had one, or to cellars and basements, or to special little nests under tables or stairs; wherever they might hope to have some sense of security, real or illusory. A few, in places like the Dorchester, tucked up in beds arranged in the basement, resplendent in dressing gowns and negligées; many others repaired to the nearest Underground station, where they bedded down on the platforms and along the draughty corridors, apparently oblivious to the roar of the trains, coming and going, and to the passengers passing. Then, surfacing at dawn; a strange sight – grey dishevelled figures carrying blankets, sometimes draped in them, emerging in the pale light from below ground. Like a Brueghel painting of Resurrection Day – predestinated souls rising from their graves. I saw them so on several occasions, when returning myself from hazily dissolute adventures; in that moment of rare lucidity between the end of the night and day's leaden hand on one's shoulder. Long after the Blitz was over, the night-time Underground habitués continued to sleep there, preferring these public beds to their private ones. Finally, they had to be dislodged by force; otherwise, they might be sleeping there still.

I drove about everywhere in the little camouflaged Austin car I had as a Field Security Officer. It gave me great immunity; no one ever asked me who I was, or what I was about. Once, by mistake, I attached myself to a procession of cars which turned out to be a Royal cavalcade, with King George VI leading in his Daimler. I came to just in time to avoid driving into Buckingham Palace. My car and my time at GHQ Home Forces, as it happened, came to an end simultaneously. On the evening of the day that Colonel Ross-Atkinson told me I had been transferred to

5 Corps Headquarters near Salisbury, I imprudently went on a round of night clubs with a fellow-officer. By about our third port-of-call I had lost track of where I was, and even of who I was. My companion at some point disappeared, and after what seemed like a long time I found myself at the wheel of my car trying to go somewhere. As I drove along I was aware that the dawn was breaking, and in its first light I glimpsed vaguely familiar buildings; like Admiralty Arch and the Houses of Parliament, some of which recurred as I proceeded on my way, still no nearer to my elusive destination. My progress was abruptly terminated when I ran into a lamp-post on a traffic island at Blackfriars Bridge. The shock brought me sufficiently to my senses to make me aware that I was in no condition to account for myself. Already the traffic over the bridge was beginning. I managed to extricate myself from the car, and, shaking some of the glass out of my hair, hailed a passing cab which delivered me at my billet in Hammersmith. There I had a bath and went to bed. I have Fenston to thank for never hearing anything further about the wrecked car. When its discovery was reported by the police to our FS office, Fenston took the call, and in a truly masterful way managed so to arrange matters that the wrecked machine was removed to a REME station, where it disappeared without trace forever. It has to be admitted that such debauches have occurred from time to time in my life. I look back on them now with distaste rather than remorse.

Five Corps HQ was situated in Longford Castle, the seat of the Earl of Radnor, a mile or so from Salisbury; a large mansion partitioned off into offices for the various branches of the Headquarters. I was given a perch in one of these under the heading I(b), or Security Intelligence. After St Paul's School, the scene was familiar enough; repeated in numerous other castles and mansions throughout the West country, including the seat of the Earl of Pembroke at nearby Wilton, hallowed in my eyes because Shakespeare was supposed to have played Adam in a production of *As You Like It* in the grounds. The war familiarised us with these stately homes, which, when it was over, were to become places of pilgrimage for Welfare State citizens and destinations for motorists with nowhere to go. It was almost like getting into Debrett.

On my arrival at Longford Castle I noticed displayed about the place curious notices asking: 'Are you 100% Full of Binge?' They represented, as it turned out, my first acquaintance with General Montgomery, or Monty as he was even then universally known, who had devised them, being at that time GOC 5 Corps. The use – or misuse – of the word 'binge' was highly characteristic. Even this initial whiff of his presence gave me strongly the feeling that he was the man of the hour. It is something at once detectable, to those accustomed to picking up the scent; an aptness of a particular ego or temperament for dealing with a particular set of circumstances. With his schoolboy mind and ebullience, his wierd idiom, his exhibitionism and love of dressing with punctilious informality, his flair for publicity and eye on the main chance, Monty seemed just right for the war we were engaged in. After one of our Corps exercises (which consisted, for me, in wandering about looking hopelessly for map references I never could find), we would all be assembled in the largest cinema in Bournemouth. Then, not exactly to the roll of drums, but with a spotlight playing upon him, Monty would appear on stage, pointer in hand; a tiny figure, ferret-faced, a huge map displayed behind him over which his shadow flitted. In a curious intonation, more schoolmasterish than military, with a touch of evangelical clergyman thrown in, he would go over the exercise, making jokes as he went along; obsequiously laughed at by the senior officers in the front rows, arousing ribald cries from the NCO's at the back, and in the middle regions, where the majors and the captains sat, myself among them, little response. It was in its way a brilliant performance, delivered without a note, ad-libbed throughout. When I became a television practitioner, I recalled the scene, realising that Monty was an instinctive camera-soldier; as was also Rommel, his opposite number. The Western Desert provided an ideal location up and down which the two of them could chase one another; like those much-trodden-over stretches of sand and battered rocks just outside Los Angeles where a thousand Westerns have been shot.

After the war, when I was working on the *Daily Telegraph*, I got to know Monty quite well through P. J. Grigg, the two having been closely associated when Grigg was Secretary of State for War. Despite his obvious faults – the showing off, the ungenerous attitude to fellow-generals like Eisenhower and Alexander – there was something engaging and very endearing about him. I don't understand warfare well enough to know if, in Liddell Hart terms, he must be considered a great general or not, but he certainly won victories – which is, after all, the essential qualification, as Lincoln remarked when someone complained to him about Grant's drunkenness. His way of looking at things was so entirely his own, even at times so comical, that his company could be highly enjoyable. There was a clown inside him struggling to be heard; his very overweening egotism being part of the act. I visited him once or twice at his Hampshire Mill, where he lives with his old Command Caravan to hand, just as it was, maps and all, when he directed operations from it in the Western Desert; as well as all his different trophies – the freedoms of cities, the honorary degrees, the portraits. One of these was by none other than General Eisenhower – no Valesquez, certainly, but recognisable. Such treasures displayed, like the rows and rows of ribbons on his army tunic; gaudy cankers of a troubled world.

Once, when I was on the point of leaving for Singapore to do some articles on the Communist insurrection in Malaya, he summoned me to Paris for a briefing, which, as a matter of fact, proved most useful. There was no time to pack a bag; I just rushed to the airport, caught a plane, and at Orly found a car waiting to take me out to Fontainebleau, where Monty had a chateau provided for him as NATO Deputy-Supreme Allied Commander, Europe. When I arrived at the chateau he was warming in front of a large open fire a pair of flannel pyjamas that he proposed to lend me. It was long past his bedtime, I knew, which made the scene all the more touching. Also, he had a drink ready, though, of course, he never took one himself. At once we began to talk about Malaya. Monty had a report on the situation there by the then Colonial Secretary, Oliver Lyttelton, not yet published, which he gave me to read when I went to bed. There must, I knew, be something particular on his mind, and it soon became clear that he was considering whether to go to Malaya himself and deal faithfully with the Communist guerrillas. I knew from Grigg that he had long entertained the fantasy of being called upon in the post-war years to become England's Man of Destiny – the politicians all shown up as having no capacity for real leadership, no master-plan. Then a cry going up: Monty! He saved us in the war, leading a victorious army from El Alamein to Berlin. Let Monty now take over on the home front, with equally beneficial results. Would Malaya, perhaps, prove a stepping-stone to the realisation of this dream? That's what was in his mind.

The dream never was going to be realised, of course; his glory had faded, along with the circumstances which brought it to pass. As phantom Deputy-Supremo of a phantom army, his strangely concocted phraseology – knocking them for six, a dog's breakfast; 'Over the Rhine, then, let us go, and good hunting to you all on the other side', no longer pulled. Nor did his black beret with its two badges, and other sartorial eccentricities. They were an old comedian's useless props. Better stay where he was in his chateau, with a plane to carry him to and from his Mill, along with bottles of wine and cheeses to regale his guests. Over

the Channel, then, let us go. . . . In the event, it was Templer who went to
Malaya. At breakfast the next morning a youthful ADC provided a
résumé of the news, which he did, blushing and stuttering, like a shy
sixth form boy reading the lessons in chapel. Before I left to catch my
plane to London, Monty took me for a stroll, delighted when anyone
seemed to recognise him – 'Vive Montgomery!'

I was on leave with Kitty and the children at Whatlington in June
1941, when Hitler invaded the USSR, and we listened together to
Churchill's speech announcing that all possible aid would be provided to
the Soviet Government. The following December, in the officers' mess
at 5 Corps, I heard a BBC announcer report that the Japanese had
attacked Pearl Harbor, automatically bringing the United States into
the war. 'That settles it; we're bound to win now,' an officer remarked
complacently. Each of these occasions gave me a leaden feeling of
apprehension rather than of jubilation; history, as it seemed to me, was a
ferocious current inexorably bearing us on to rapids whose roar could
already be heard. I thought of the men in the Kremlin as I remembered
them; the grey, hard faces grouped around Stalin, the greyest and hard-
est of all. They were now the liberators, bearing aloft the banner of
freedom and justice and enlightenment. Even so, I cannot claim to have
foreseen the wilder ironies – the Nuremburg judges, a Soviet one among
them, solemnly condemning the Germans for partitioning Poland and
making use of forced labour; that ribald trio, Churchill, his fur hat
awry, the dying Roosevelt in his cloak, Stalin inscrutable behind his
moustache and slit eyes, settling between them, as they supposed, the
world's future; Vyshinsky's venomous rhetoric translated from the
Moscow court-room, where it was directed against old Bolshevik
colleagues, to the vapid deliberations of the UN about national
sovereignty and the right of self-determination. All this lay ahead, but
still I envisaged already the awful perversion of words and meanings
that would soon be upon us. On sleepless nights read, and even wrote,
in my mind, the leaders in the *Guardian* and *The Times* about our great
ally with whom we looked forward to collaborating in making a just,
free, and above all peaceful, world in the years to come. Heard the
speeches at banquets; Churchillian rhetoric about his old comrade-in-
arms, Marshal Stalin, whose word was as good as his bond; generals
rising in their places, all a-glitter with medals, to toast the feats of the
great Red Army in defending European civilisation and its free institutions against the barbarian Nazi hordes. It was an unappetising but
inescapable prospect.

At 5 Corps I spent my time going from one office to another, turning over papers, initialling them, and speeding them on their way. Or getting on my motor-cycle and liaising with other headquarters – at Wilton, or Sherbone, or Blandford, or as far away as Taunton. Roaring across Salisbury Plain, and, on arrival, like a dispatch-rider with important papers to deliver, jumping off my machine; a little dazed from the wind and the sun, goggles removed. Then, opening the door of a Nissen hut, standing at attention, a tremendous salute, to find confronting me the identical scene I had left behind – officers seated at trestle-tables, ordnance maps covered with talcum and marked with coloured crayons, orderlies coming and going, antique typewriters tapping. How are things? Later, off to the mess for a drink; some idle chatter about anything that might be happening – promotions, transfers, gossip, even the war. In the evening light, roaring back across Salisbury Plain on the return journey; remembering Hazlitt lying on his back there, thinking how happy his life had been, despite *Libor Amoris* and other troubles. Mine, too, inexpressibly happy; even then, battle-dressed, on an army motor-cycle, the wind in my face, ostensibly engaged in a war. Back at 5 Corps, dutifully full of Monty's binge, I was in time to bath, change, and appear in the mess for dinner. Another day had passed.

Other officers at the Headquarters, including Intelligence officers like myself, were obviously busy and anxious; hurrying back to their offices when meals ended, impatient at being held in casual talk. From Monty downwards, there was a sense of urgency; of things to do and not enough time to get them done. What were they all at? I often wondered, but never properly discovered. There were, of course, a few specific duties. For instance, each week – a particular notion of Monty's – all the officers at the Headquarters were required to go on a run along a carefully marked-out course, with the Chaplain at the end to take our names to make sure there were no defaulters. Presumably, Monty chose the Chaplain for this task as being a man of integrity, with little to occupy his time. One or two of us found the run too strenuous for our years and training, and managed to join the runners at a later stage in the course, thereby arriving in relatively good shape at the finishing-post. It was remarkable to see some of the senior officers, too conscientious to adopt any such deception, puffing and blowing as though about to expire, all with a view to pleasing Monty, who occasionally joined the Chaplain to watch late arrivals.

Another task that fell to the Intelligence Branch, in which I participated, was to make a dummy of a German soldier with all the appropriate badges and insignia, and stand him outside the mess so that officers coming and going could familiarise themselves with him. Having set him up more or less correctly, I felt an irresistible impulse to make him wounded and bloody; with his arm in a home-made sling, and a blood-stained bandage round his head. Then, warming to the work, I put him on a crutch, and finally amputated one of his legs. It was another of the occasions when I did something which caused almost universal offence, without any deliberate intention, or even awareness, of so doing. It culminated in the BGS, Gerald Templer, shouting at me furiously: 'Take that horrible thing away', which I duly did. There was no high-minded intention, let me add, to express a loathing of war by drawing my fellow-officers' attention dramatically to what it signified; Templer and the others, in any case, knew much better than I what war was like. Doubtless, this was why they were so annoyed.

Templer was a dashing figure. He wore superbly polished boots, and a great-coat which almost swept the ground; had a sallow, lean face, with a moustache so thin as to be barely perceptible, and spoke in sharp, clipped words. Once, for no apparent reason, he showed me a letter he had received from Claire Luce, whom he had met in the early part of the war, when stationed in France with the BEF. I saw him as a character in *Le Rouge et le Noir* dedicated to the profession of arms, a d'Artagnan (my old hero) of the twentieth century, and found him correspondingly attractive. Though I received much kindness at his hands, he was unmistakably relieved when, in due course, I disappeared into the limbo of MI6, the wartime version of the Secret Service. Among his fellow-officers after dinner in the mess he would sometimes engage in the strange horse-play which often characterised these gatherings. I found it a curious spectacle – grizzled veterans who had served in distant parts of the Empire, tanned and scarred and covered with medals and decorations, now leaping and prancing about like undergraduates on Boat-race Night. Belabouring one another with rolls of paper: on one occasion, aiming potatoes through a cardboard partition, on the other side of which, all unknown to them, a number of valuable pictures had been stowed away, through one of which – a Romney – a potato passed, leaving a gash in the bottom of the canvas. This, as may be imagined, caused quite a rumpus, and an expert had to be fetched from London at considerable expense to repair the damage.

While I was at 5 Corps I did an attachment with a Motor Reconnaissance unit at Hinton St Mary nearby. They were nearly all young, eager officers, and I greatly enjoyed my time with them. The house where the unit was stationed belonged to G. H. L. Fox Pitt-Rivers who had been interned under Regulation 18b for his pro-Hitler attitudes, and in his library there was an elegantly bound presentation copy of *Mein Kampf*, which was occasionally taken out and looked at, almost reverentially; then put back, without ever being damaged or mutilated. I found this bizarre, but rather endearing. The house was in excellent condition, Pitt-Rivers being, as I gathered, very rich. Despite wartime stringencies, the extensive grounds were all maintained, and there was a neat little theatre which Pitt-Rivers had constructed for his wife, an actress. Someone told me that she used as her stage-name, Mary Hinton, after the place, and then I remembered with a pang that she had taken the part of one of the frustrated young women in my play, *Three Flats*, at its Stage Society production at the Prince of Wales Theatre in 1931.

When I got back to 5 Corps I wrote to the commanding officer at Hinton St Mary to say how happy I'd been there, and to ask if there was a chance of my joining the unit, which, of course, there wasn't. It was yet another of my fatuous endeavours to become a belligerent soldier. Soon after this futile *démarche*, I got a mysterious communication to the effect that I was to present myself at an address in London with a view to being considered for special Intelligence duties. The summons was a consequence of a plot long before hatched with Graham Greene, whose sister, Liza, worked for someone important in the Secret Service. We hoped that she would recommend us both to her boss as suitable overseas representatives, and be able to pull the requisite strings to get us accepted. I had almost forgotten we ever entertained such a plan when the summons came. When I reported the matter to Templer, he said he envied me, which might even have been true. Though he was so dyed-in-the-wool a regimental soldier, I think he had a secret taste for the more nefarious aspects of warfare. I went to London for my interview, which turned out to be with a writer of thrillers named Williams, whom I met at his club, the Savage; a man with bushy eyebrows, and, I seem to remember, like his best-known character, a club foot. His brother, Douglas Williams, was a colleague of mine on the *Daily Telegraph*. Writers of thrillers tend to gravitate to the Secret Service as surely as the mentally unstable become psychiatrists, or the impotent pornographers. Williams spoke darkly of the dangers involved in a service in which, by the nature of the case, a blown agent had to be discarded. After a year as IO at a corps headquarters, I said, this held no terrors for me. To my great satisfaction, shortly afterwards I heard that I had been accepted.

I might have said of my duties at 5 Corps, as Gibbon did of his as one of the Lords Commissioners of Trade, that they were not intolerably severe, but, unlike him, I was temperamentally incapable of enjoying the many days and weeks of repose that, as he mentions so complacently, they permitted. Thus, it was an enormous relief to be departing. What remained with me from the experience was the delight of travelling freely and pointlessly about one of the most beautiful parts of England, and visiting its ancient towns – Sherborne, Wincanton, Dorchester, Yeovil, Shaftesbury – all, in the war-time absence of traffic, tranquil and alluring. I particularly appreciated the different views of Salisbury Cathedral from whichever direction one approached the town, and, in moments of distress, have turned to the memory of its grey steeple reaching so exquisitely into the sky, never in vain. As, for instance, on an American lecture-tour, at some cinema on a week-day morning in the fastnesses of Oregon or North Dakota; several hundred chattering, perfumed, blue-rinsed ladies assembled before me. Or in Los Angeles, facing row upon row of tousled UCLA students, with only breasts or whiskers to signify their sex, and that sometimes indeterminately. On such grievous occasions, the cathedral and its steeple have delivered me from despair.

During most of my stay at 5 Corps I lodged with a number of other officers in an agreeable house, The Moat, about half way between Longford Castle and Salisbury. My room-mate, Victor Stiebel, our camouflage officer, was in private life an eminent dressmaker. His profession, as he explained to me, provided a natural training in camouflage; especially in coping with some of his more eminent clients. Sharing a room with him brought great advantages in the way of extra comforts. He managed, for instance, to ensure that in cold weather we always had a bright fire, and that our morning tea came punctually; and he even, on occasion, had a hot-water bottle put in his bed. His own appearance was magnificent – splendid pale riding breeches and top-boots that shone even more brightly than Templer's. He and the BGS, incidentally, were on excellent terms, and used to swop stories about Noel Coward. I began by regarding Stiebel as a somewhat ridiculous figure, but through our companionship and the long talks we had, I came to realise that he was a person of unusual sensitivity and perceptiveness; particularly apparent when he spoke about South Africa, where he had spent his childhood. In his later years he developed some sort of paralytic complaint, which he bore with great fortitude.

Our association at 5 Corps was brought to an end when the APM, a Northern Irishman named McNally, who was also Mess President, had me turned out of the house. It was my talk, he said, which had caused the trouble; there had been complaints. When I pressed him to tell me what particular things I'd said which were considered offensive, he refused to be drawn; it wasn't anything specific, he went on, just how I talked, the whole tenor. People couldn't stand it. I ought, I suppose, to have been annoyed, and even perhaps to have taken the matter to the Corps Commander; made an issue of it, demanded an explanation. But I knew I was leaving soon, and it didn't seem worth while. In any case, McNally looked so abashed and troubled himself that I felt quite sorry for him. He had drawn me aside to talk under the stairs where no one would see us or overhear us. I have never found any difficulty in understanding how irritating I can be to other people; perhaps because I so often irritate myself. So I affected to be magnanimous; in police terms – I imagine that he belonged to the Royal Ulster Constabulary – I agreed to go quietly, and moved over to the Castle for my short remaining time. That was the end of 5 Corps for me. I ran into them once or twice in Italy afterwards, recognising the Viking ship which was the Corps sign; but never with any particular cordiality.

3 *On Secret Service*

But vain the Sword and vain the Bow,
They never can work War's overthrow.
— Blake

Only when a man has become so unhappy, or has grasped the misery
of this existence so profoundly that he can truly say, 'For me life is
worthless;' only then can life have worth in the highest degree.
— Kierkegaard

MY INSTRUCTIONS were to present myself at an office in Broadway,
opposite St James's underground station, which I duly did. As a reader
of *Ashenden* I was naturally excited at the prospect of entering the
portals of the world-famous British Secret Service (or SIS as it was
usually called), though I assumed that at this first preliminary encounter
I should not be admitted to the actual headquarters, but only to some
shadow set-up, or façade, used to try out aspirants before definitely
taking them on. I may add that everyone I saw and everything that
happened seemed to support such an assumption. It was only later that
I came to realise I had been in contact, not with a hurriedly improvised
dummy, but the real thing. While I was awaiting my own clearance at
the main entrance, I was able to observe the people coming and going.
A good proportion of them were in the services, with the Navy pre-
ponderating. I only saw one, as I thought, false beard – a luxuriant
tangled growth, whose wearer turned out, on closer acquaintance, to be
a former trade-unionist and Marxist, allegedly from the boiler-makers'
union. He was responsible for providing expert guidance in industrial
matters; and his beard, he assured me, was genuine, though he admitted
that he had allowed it to proliferate since joining SIS, as he had also
his use of strong language, and tendency to bang the table to emphasise
a point. The last glimpse I had of him was towards the end of the war,

in the Athenaeum Club dining-room, where he was holding forth noisily to some abashed-looking Americans, including a three-star general.

My contact, to whose office I was led, turned out to be an agreeable man named Leslie Nicholson, who had been, I learnt afterwards, a Secret Service agent himself in Riga. His manner was gentle, amiable and helpful; more in the style of a Bertie Wooster, I decided, than of a spy-master as popularly conceived. He told me that various stations were being opened up in Africa, and that the intention was to send Graham Greene to Freetown and me to Lourenço Marques in Mozambique. I said that nothing could suit me better, implying that Lourenço Marques was a place I had always been interested in and wanted to visit, though in point of fact I had never before heard of it, and had no idea where it was. My ready acquiescence, I think, pleased Nicholson, who might otherwise have had to look up where Lourenço Marques was himself, and answer questions about its climatic conditions, port facilities, population, and so on. As it was, we could agree on my departure there without either of us being unduly troubled about the whys and wherefores. When, a few days later, we dined together at Boodles, Nicholson's club, we talked, as I recall, about everything under the sun except Mozambique. I did, in point of fact, read up the entry in the *Encyclopaedia Britannica* on Mozambique, and learnt – it is the solitary fact remaining with me – that Gladstone could have bought it off the Portuguese for a million pounds, but decided the price was too high. His parsimony was ill-judged; it would have been a good buy, Delagoa Bay providing an excellent harbour, which Durban notably lacks.

My first task, as now an MI6 officer, was to get myself, notionally, transformed into a civilian. For this purpose I was handed a passport stamped to indicate that I had lately landed in the UK, and giving my address as St Ermin's Hotel. To form some idea of my place of residence I dropped in there for a drink, finding the lounge dim and quiet, suggestive of conferences to promote world governments, family planning, or the practice of eurythmics. My instructions were to go with my passport to Caxton Hall, and apply for a civilian identity card, explaining, if asked why I had not got one, that I had recently arrived at Liverpool from extensive travels abroad, and was expecting to leave the UK again at any moment for further travels. I was also instructed to memorise the number in the left-hand top corner of the form of application for an identity card, and to apply for an emergency ration card. Waiting my turn in the queue, I was seized with anxiety. Supposing they asked me the name of the ship on which I had arrived at Liverpool, what should I say? Or questioned me about the places I had been to abroad, and how long I had stayed in them? Or asked for details of my projected departure and subsequent travels. My story, as it seemed to me, was full of obvious pitfalls. And how should I ever memorise that number in the left-hand top corner when I find it impossible to remember the registration number of a car, even when I have been driving about in it for years? By the time my turn came, I was in a state of nerves which must have seemed highly suspicious in the light of my threadbare story, tremulously recounted. To my great relief, no questions were asked, the man behind the *guichet* positively winking as he handed me my identity card and emergency ration book. As for the number I was supposed to memorise – I forgot all about it, and no one ever asked me for it.

It might well be wondered – as, indeed, I wondered at the time myself – what was the point of this exercise in mystery when it would have been as easy to procure an identity card and emergency ration card for me as it had been to procure a passport. To ask such a question is to fail to understand the whole character of secret Intelligence, one of whose basic precepts is that nothing should ever be done simply if there are devious ways of doing it. With old hands it becomes second nature, for instance, to communicate in code, and to use an accommodation address, for perfectly innocuous communications; to prefer a cache in a potting-shed to a normal letter-box, and a diplomatic bag to a suitcase for carrying blameless personal effects. Kim Philby's American wife, until she got used to it, and came to regard it as a harmless eccentricity, was astonished when he sent her loving messages on tiny fragments of tissue paper, which, as he explained, could comfortably be swallowed if this should be required in the interest of security. As it happened, the address of the Broadway office and the names of most of its leading occupants had been given out on the German radio quite early on in the war following an incident when two SIS representatives at The Hague fell into enemy hands. This made no difference to security arrangements; the Chief, at the time Sir Stuart Menzies, was still known as 'C' even in the internal telephone directory, and all other blown symbols and aliases were scrupulously maintained. Again, in coded messages, countries had always to be referred to by symbols – Germany, for instance, was 'Twelve-land'. The practice was scrupulously observed throughout the war even though, on one festive occasion at an Istanbul hotel, when the orchestra played the German national anthem, the staff of the German embassy stood to attention and sang as one man: '*Zwölfte-land, Zwölfte-land, uber alles!*' Outside 'C' 's office a blue light shone, like a dispensary or a police-station; the sense of secrecy was so great that, walking by it, one instinctively tiptoed. Secrecy is as essential to Intelligence as vestments and incense to a Mass, or darkness to a Spiritualist seance, and must at all costs be maintained, quite irrespective of whether or not it serves any purpose.

The two captured Secret Service men at The Hague – both slightly parodying what they purported to be; with monocle, trimmed grey moustache, club tie, touch of the Raj, whence, in fact they came – had imagined themselves to be in touch with a group of dissident Germans, including a general, who were anxious to get rid of Hitler and call off the war in return for an honourable peace. What excitement in Broadway as the messages from The Hague came in! Passed Most Secretly from hand to hand, until they reached the Prime Minister, Neville Chamberlain himself, and his Foreign Secretary, Lord Halifax. Full approval was given to keep the contact going; finally, for a meeting face to face at Venlo, a drab little place on the Dutch–German border. There, alas, it turned out that the so prized contact was not with a dissident general at all, but with the Gestapo; and one more dream that the doom which had come upon us could be averted – the last Munich – blew up in the faces of the dreamers. One of the captured men, Payne Best, was in custody for a time with Dietrich Bonhoeffer, and went with him on the last journey, in April 1945, to the East German village of Schonberg, participating on a bright Sunday morning in the service Bonhoeffer conducted there, which concluded with the singing of *Eine Feste Burg ist unser Gott*. Almost immediately afterwards, Bonhoeffer was taken away to be executed. Before leaving, he entrusted Best with a message for Dr Bell, the Bishop of Chichester, to tell him that the 'victory of our universal brotherhood, rising above all national interests, is certain'. Thus, for Best, from the total fantasy of Venlo to the total reality of Schonberg; from darkness to light – the full circle.

Becoming a civilian again, by means that struck me as grotesquely devious, after my so strenuous efforts to be a soldier; discarding my uniform when I had first put it on with such a sense of drama, was like washing off the make-up for the last time, turning in props and costume, when a play's run is ended. My MI6 indoctrination comprised visiting its various branches and affiliates. First, Section Five, responsible for counter-espionage abroad, under whose auspices I should largely be operating; located at that time at St Albans. It was here that I came across Kim Philby; not, as he recalled, for the first time. We had met before, when I was working on the *Evening Standard*, at the office of the

Review of Reviews, a magazine started by W. T. Stead, and subsequently reborn in De Witt Wallace's *Reader's Digest*; a golden Phoenix indeed. The then editor, Wilfrid Hindle, introduced me to Philby; a dark shy young man just down from Cambridge, and, as Hindle whispered, son of the well-known Arabist, St John Philby. Even on this brief encounter I noticed his stutter, which was liable to become truly agonising, his lips moving convulsively and his hands clawing the air as he tried to get words out. It was more like some kind of a fit than just a speech impediment. Shortly afterwards, the *Review of Reviews* finally collapsed, and Hindle, as I heard, went into the Foreign Office, which of course meant into SIS. Perhaps he was already in it when he tried, from a journalistic point of view very unconvincingly, to make a go of the *Review of Reviews*, and either recruited Philby or had him planted on him. Since Philby, according to his own account, had by this time started working for Soviet Intelligence, this would have meant that his career as a double-agent had already begun when I first met him.

Philby's was undoubtedly the dominating presence at St Albans. Felix Cowgill, the head of Section Five, a kindly, conscientious, nervous man, by comparison made only a dim impression. He had the sallow face and withdrawn tired air that came of long years of service in India – in his case, with the police. Quite a number of the senior personnel in MI5 and MI6 in the days of the Raj were similarly drawn from retired members of the equivalent Indian services, which provided, as it was considered, valuable experience in dealing with matters like espionage and subversion, which arose only rarely and exotically at home; men of the kind, incidentally, under whom Philby's namesake, Kipling's Kim, worked – and against the Russians. Philby, on the other hand, gave an impression of great energy and determination, which in some mysterious way his stutter only seemed to enhance. After his defection to Moscow many of those who had known him spoke of his irresistible charm and magnetism. The prevailing impression I had was of a kind of boyishness, even naïveté. As I think of him now, in Moscow, in what must be rather melancholy circumstances, no doubt turning to the vodka bottle for solace; studying cricket scores in old copies of *The Times*, managing to get supplies of Players cigarettes sent over from London, and listening clandestinely, whenever possible, to the Overseas Service at the BBC, I see him rather as a boy-scout who lost his way than as the cool, calculating player of a long-drawn-out traitor's role, which, I am sure, is how he would like to see himself.

In the office he habitually wore an old army officer's tunic of his father's in the 1914–18 war; an indication, I assumed, of how much he would have wished to be a combatant soldier, this being precluded, presumably, because of his stutter. Also, of his undoubted filial admiration for his father, at that time interned in the Isle of Man under Regulation 18b, along with some of the weird figures I had seen at the Tyler Kent–Anna Volkov trial. Philby senior's incarceration resulted from some, as it turned out, ill-considered advice he gave to his friend King Ibn Saud of Arabia to keep out of the war, which, he insisted, Hitler was bound to win. Had Philby succeeded in becoming a combatant soldier, he would almost certainly have got himself killed; the violence one sensed in his temperament would have found full expression in actual fighting and killing. As it was, he had to exercise this side of his nature through the often infantile plots and stratagems his Section Five work involved, as well as by his ultimate stupendous double-cross. In a letter I had from Ben Gurion after I had recorded a television interview with him at the kibbutz where he was living in retirement near Beersheba, he remarked of Philby: 'I knew his father; he was not a nice man. The father became a Moslem, so why should not the son become a Communist?' It summed the situation up neatly and succinctly, I thought.

Philby was not a person who, at the time, particularly interested me; but inevitably, when he became notorious and much written about, I found myself looking back meticulously on early impressions, refurbishing dim memories and resurrecting lost ones. The legend that emerged about him was of a patrician charmer who received advancement, and escaped retribution, because he had been to the right school and spoke with the right accent. A sort of espionage Raffles; a Bond in reverse, whose brilliance and audacity made him, at once, the Secret Service's favourite son and the master-spy of the age. As far as his accent was concerned, it was totally muffled by that appalling stutter; he might have been speaking broad cockney, Glaswegian Scottish or stage Yorkshire, but no one would ever have have known, so strangled and malformed were the words that finally emerged from his tormented mouth. His tastes, habits and attire might, I suppose, be regarded as characteristic of the wilder reaches of the contemporary public school product, though the drinking, on any showing, was excessive and indiscriminate. His friends and cronies, in so far as I met them, were far from being, in the conventional sense, upper-class, but rather oddities; often disreputable, like Burgess, about whom Philby always spoke in adulatory terms. There was, too, a Jewish antique-dealer who may have been as erudite and fascinating as Philby implied, but who by no stretch of the imagination could be considered as figuring in the old-boy network that was supposed to have operated so faithfully on his behalf. I should have said myself that he was as little in the style of a Steerforth of our time as is Chairman Mao or Germaine Greer.

Since Philby's defection became public, I have often tried to work out in my mind what were its origins. His own *Apologia Pro Defecto Suo* tells us less than nothing; in any case, emanating, as it did, from Moscow, and therefore requiring the Kremlin's imprimatur, it cannot but be as worthless as any similar recantation at the time of the Inquisition. Conversations with him, as far as I remember them, provide no clue. He rarely spoke about politics, though one assumed he took the vaguely Leftish position fashionable among the bourgeois intelligentsia of his generation. Far stronger in him than anything of this kind, as it seemed to me, was his romantic veneration for buccaneers and buccaneering, whatever the ideological basis – if any – might be. Boozers, womanisers, violence in all its manifestations, recklessness however directed, he found irresistible. Hence his, and many others', otherwise unaccountable love for Burgess, and tolerance of his preposterous and unlovely ways. On this showing, he would have been more at home among Nazi bully-boys than the pedantic terrorists of the USSR. He actually said to me once that Goebbels was someone he felt he could have worked with. At the time of his defection a group photograph in which he appeared was published; taken at a dinner given by one of those societies which existed in the thirties to promote Anglo-German fellowship – the Nazi equivalent of organisations like the Society for Promoting Cultural Relations with the USSR.

Philby at this dinner, we have been told, was building up his cover. But was he? I think it far more likely that he attended it as a genuine member. His admiration, if not veneration, for his father would have pointed in this direction. I have always myself believed that he joined up with the Soviet *apparat* at a much later date; when it was clear that the USSR was to be in the victor's camp. In other words, he and the other gilt-edged defectors, actual and potential, were more toadies than rebels; aware that a new giant had arisen in the world with whom they wished to make their number in good time. Another contingent was at the same time moving westwards across the Atlantic to shelter under America's wing. None of them had much regard for the displaced giant, our poor old Britannia, who had come staggering into the ring for one more round, mouthing old rhetoric, wearing old braid, flaunting old medals, waving old banners. Burgess at least had the honesty to admit that it was this very feebleness which induced him to offer his allegiance elsewhere. According to his friend Goronwy Rees, his rage, for instance, when the British Raj was abjectly wound up, knew no bounds. In any case, had Philby been a convinced Marxist or sentimental friend of the Soviet Union rather than just Old Kim looking for a better 'ole, he would, we may be sure, long ago have – as Mrs Webb would have put it – disappeared, along with Spanish Civil War veterans and other revolutionary heroes who made the mistake of returning to the Soviet Fatherland in Stalinist times.

My instructions at St Albans were to familiarise myself with the working of Section Five, and generally – a favourite expression at that time – put myself in the picture. This involved going from room to room and from desk to desk, and listening to particular officers explaining what they were at; whether directing and supervising the operations of agents in the field, devising and planting deception material, or co-operating with other counter-Intelligence agencies connected with the various Allied governments-in-exile like the Poles and the Czechs, or with the French, whether Pétainist, Gaullist or nondescript. They had obviously had occasion to do this explaining many times before, and had developed a standard dissertation; in the case of the service personnel, especially the military, delivered to a regular rhythm that runs right through the forces, from sergeant-instructors explaining the working of an internal combustion engine, to chiefs-of-staff respectfully putting a Secretary of State or Prime Minister into the picture of some impending offensive. The civilians were different; more like advertising executives (which some of them, in fact, were); persuasive and plausible in expounding a carefully prepared sales campaign with the aid of graphs and tables and coloured diagrams. My old facility for seeming to listen attentively without hearing anything, again held me in good stead. Though my thoughts were usually far away, I still managed to ask a question or two, betokening interest and attention, though, at the end of it all, I was little nearer putting myself in the picture, or even knowing what the picture was supposed to be.

There was also a fair amount of paper to look at, the prize exhibit here being the yield of cracked enemy ciphers; especially, in my case, material relating to Mozambique, which, I must say, held my rapt attention. These messages from enemy sources had the rarity value of Dead Sea Scrolls, and had to be handled accordingly. Their circulation was rigorously restricted; very few hands touched them or eyes rested upon them. By virtue of just knowing about them, I automatically came into the category of those who must in no circumstances fall into enemy hands for fear that, under interrogation or torture, I might be induced to disclose my knowledge, whereupon the enemy cipher would be changed, and all the work of cracking it need to be done again. Thus, henceforth it became a positive duty, rather than just a negative inclination, to keep well away from the enemy. At the same time, being privy to this source of high-grade and impeccable information about the enemy's plans and intentions gave me a new sense of importance. I might be a mere captain, but now I could look with condescension at brigadiers, and even generals, conscious that, as far as what was called 'the overall Intelligence picture' was concerned, I was likely to be more in it than they were. This sense of importance, of cherishing secrets beyond the ken of ordinary mortals, was characteristic of SIS personnel at all levels; particularly the females, who, however careless they might be about their chastity, guarded their security with implacable resolution. So much so that a party of them arriving in Cairo were unable to find anyone to whom they felt able to disclose the nature of their mission, and in the end had to be sent home.

Cracked cipher material was, indeed, as things turned out, the staple product of MI6, and provided the basis for most of its effective activities. The old procedures, like the setting up of agents, the suborning of informants, the sending of messages written in invisible ink, the masquerading, the dressing-up, the secret transmitters, and the examining of the contents of wastepaper-baskets, all turned out to be largely cover for this other source; as one might keep some old-established business in rare books going in order to be able, under cover of it, to do a thriving trade in pornography and erotica. As 'C' quickly saw, he never need fear criticism or cuts in his budget as long as he could drop in on the Prime Minister at breakfast time with some tasty item of Intelligence – the enemy's latest operational orders, say, or a full report of one of the meetings between Hitler and Mussolini immediately after it had happened – whose authenticity he could vouch for without being too particular as to its source.

The establishment which produced this precious material was located at Bletchley, in a manor house in which I spent some days familiarising myself with the place, its staff, its output and manner of working. As might be supposed, in view of the business in hand, the staff were a curious mixture of mathematicians, dons of various kinds, chess and crossword maestros, an odd musician or two, and numerous wireless telegraphy experts. Not surprisingly, Andreas joined them before the war was over, and proved one of their most capable practitioners. On a superficial glance, it might have been taken to be a Fabian summer-school, or – a more ancient model – one of those reading parties Victorians were so fond of organising in the long vacation, in the Lake District, or further afield, in Switzerland or Italy, when they all grew bored together over unreadable books instead of separately. Perhaps, even, some kind of public affairs forum or seminar of the kind which, in the post-war years, were to be clandestinely financed by the CIA; dealing, say, with Whither Europe? or: After Fascism, What? or: South-East Asia – a New Look?

Each day after luncheon when the weather was propitious the cipher-crackers played rounders on the manor house lawn, assuming the quasi-serious manner dons affect when engaged in activities likely to be regarded as frivolous or insignificant in comparison with their weightier studies. Thus they would dispute some point about the game with the same fervour as they might the question of free-will or determinism, or whether the world began with a big bang or a process of continuing creation. Shaking their heads ponderously, sucking air noisily into their noses between words – 'I thought mine was the surer stroke,' or: 'I can assert without fear of contradiction that my right foot was already . . .' The females, too, were mostly donnish; either dons' molls, with solemnly pretty faces, studiously amorous or amorously studious according to their temperaments or the exigencies of the occasion; or themselves academics, grey, untidy, rough and hairy and spluttering – Asia Minor excavators, experts on Beowulf and Anglo-Saxon, delvers into folklore and marriage customs. Instinctively, I relapsed into my Cambridge state of mind, and thought how long the afternoon was bound to be, how interminable the wait for tea. Intelligence services in wartime naturally look to senior common rooms and high tables for recruits, and not in vain; a don-watcher in any of the theatres of war might hope sooner or later, if he was patient enough, to catch a glimpse of a Major Trevor-Roper, a Captain Ayer, a Lt-Colonel Rothschild, and in far-off Washington, DC, of an Isaiah Berlin, a John Foster, among the numerous attachés.

My instructress at Bletchley was an elderly lady who had been ciphering all her life at different embassies throughout the world. I noticed she was suffering from codist's thumb, the thumb she used for turning over the pages of the code-book having become slightly deformed through the years, with a consequent protective thickening of the skin, like Koestler's midwife toad. In all her extensive travels, what she most vividly remembered was not famous sights like the Taj Mahal or the Chinese Wall, but occasions when ciphering changes had been introduced – at Teheran we started on one-time pads; at Kabul we tried out the new machines. Under her kind and patient guidance I was able to grasp more or less how I should cipher and de-cipher messages myself, but I never became proficient. I was billeted at another country house nearby, where technical staff resided. On the first evening, after dinner, a hunt was organised, led by a plump wing-commander blowing on a horn; we followed him up and down stairs, in and out of rooms, shouting Tally Ho! and other appropriate cries. What we were supposed to be hunting I never discovered; unless it was a pretty WAAF girl, who fell to our chief huntsman, the wing-commander.

My tour of instruction ended with a short course in invisible inks and their use. This took place in a house in Hans Crescent, so innocent-looking outside, with its trim curtains and array of milk bottles by the front door, that I thought I must have mistaken the address. However, when I rang the bell, sure enough a Signals NCO opened the door, and, when I had established my identity, took me upstairs to where my instructor awaited me. He was a sad-looking man with a large rubicund face, thinning black hair and short fingers. Another old SIS professional, as it turned out, who obviously felt he had come down in the world in being relegated to expounding the mysteries of writing in invisible inks to such as me – as though some county cricketer had been put to selling cricket bats in a toy shop. He had his array of ball-pointed pens, his various substances and liquids, a small collapsible stove for heating the paper, thereby bringing out any invisible writing on it, and other appropriate gear, amidst which he sat like some weird, doleful alchemist. My lesson went on through the afternoon and into the evening. First mixing my inks, the simplest being milk, and, at a pinch, wine; then solutions of various chemical substances, among them a well-known brand of headache tablets which had the advantage – besides being, as I discovered, an excellent hangover specific – that it could be carried in one's luggage without arousing suspicion. And, finally, what my instructor referred to primly as BS, meaning bird shit.

This last required some special explanation; it could, he said, be used when all else failed, and worked well, but procuring a supply was not as easy as might be supposed. For instance, he once had to fall back on it when he was stationed at The Hague, and had imagined that crumbs spread out on his little balcony would bring a goodly number of sparrows along that might be relied on to leave behind a supply of BS. Not so; the birds duly arrived and ate the crumbs, but, whether because they were constipated, or out of delicacy, there were no droppings. In the end, he explained to me, he had to take a walk in a public park – which, fortunately, was spacious – and when he saw traces of BS, he dropped his handkerchief as though by chance, and scooped the BS up. His dolefulness became almost unbearable as I pictured him walking mournfully about questing for BS, and I tried to cheer him up by expressing unbounded admiration for the brilliant stratagem he had devised, which, I said, I was sure would prove invaluable in Mozambique. He nodded, I thought without much conviction, and expressed some doubts as to whether the sort of birds found there would prove suitable donors.

Having dealt with the inks, we moved on to practise writing with them, using a ball-pointed pen very lightly so as not to mark the paper. I was very ham-fisted at this, and, holding up one of my productions to the light to show that the indentations I had made were clearly visible, my instructor shook his ponderous head over me, as much as to say: 'You'll never make a spy at this rate.' I tried again, this time with better results, and we then tackled the process of heating the paper to develop the writing on it. This, also, my instructor said, required great care; not using too much heat, which would burn up the paper before it could be read, or too little to bring out the writing at all. We toiled away, scarcely noticing that by this time it was dark outside. Maybe, I reflected, he had a family awaiting him. Or lived alone, feeding the birds for company, but now disinterestedly, without any thought of benefiting from their visitations. I'd come again, I said, if he was dissatisfied with the standard I had attained; no, he replied, I'd done well enough, though from the tone of his voice I felt he'd known better students. Sitting with him there and looking out on the still blacked-out square, not a light showing, the absurdity of what we had been doing struck me with such passionate intensity that I had great difficulty in not blurting it out to him.

What were we at? What was it all about? How had we been induced, two grown men not totally incapable of making some contribution, however lowly, to human existence – how had we been induced to spend our time thus? He and I, strangers, but also fellow-humans. And not just us. Bletchley, where those donnish heads were bent over ciphers, wrestling to get at their meaning as though they contained the key to life's secrets, instead of just the trivialities and fatuities which constitute far the greater part of all Intelligence traffic. 'C' in his office with his blue light shining, the Prime Minister in Downing Street, Hitler in his Chancellery, Stalin in his Kremlin; armies marching and counter-marching, maps earnestly studied, planes flying, bombs falling, U-boats prowling, convoys sailing. The whole vast panoply of war, down to this room in Hans Crescent where I had been learning how to fabricate and write in invisible ink. The intensity of my mood seemed to have spread to my instructor, for now he looked thoughtful, as though some urgent question were racking his mind, too – perhaps as to whether history itself might not be recorded in invisible ink; our very lives, not just, as Raleigh put it, writ on, but also with, water! As I went through the door I turned and shouted to him: 'I'll remember BS.' So, as it happens, I have; when I have forgotten so much else.

It now only remained to pay my respects to 'C' before venturing into the field on his behalf, and to shake the hand of the head of Passport Control, whose parish took in Section Five personnel posted to neutral countries in the same sort of way that the Bishop of Gibraltar's see takes in Siberia. There was also a man in the Foreign Office whose 'friends' we purported to be for the purpose of being allowed to make use of diplomatic bags to communicate with our headquarters in London. He, however, accepted us as friends without requiring, or even, I should suppose, wanting, to make our personal acquaintance. The head of Passport Control, I found, kept his office in a permanently twilit condition, with the curtains closely drawn, in order to counteract as far as possible the extraordinary colour of his face – a rich purple fading into pale blue, or thickening into a murky black, due, it was said, to his having been given the wrong injection by a doctor who combined attending to SIS's medical requirements with being on call at the Savoy Hotel. Despite this weird pigmentation, he turned out to be particularly agreeable, and, after an amicable chat, we duly shook hands, and I took my leave.

The visit to 'C' was more exacting. Just penetrating beyond the blue light that shone outside his room, required a special effort; I had a feeling that perhaps I ought to wait for it to turn amber before entering. Overcoming this hesitation, I made my way into an inner sanctum where I found two sedate, middle-aged secretaries who gave an immediate impression of being exceptionally well-bred. Readers of the Bond books will recognise the scene, but, of course, glamorised in Fleming's version; the secretaries more alluring, 'C' more steely, the office more daunting. I once, long after the war had ended, dined in a private room at the Garrick Club with a company that included both the then reigning

'C' and Fleming. It was like dining with Sherlock Holmes and Watson, or, perhaps better, with Don Quixote and Sancho Panza.

The 'C' of my day, Sir Stuart Menzies, was a regular officer in a Scottish regiment; sandy-haired, liable to be kilted, with a soft hand-shake and an air of indolence, belied by a glint of cunning in his brown eyes. His predecessor had been an admiral, the then practice being to alternate the office between the two services. We chatted together about Mozambique, he having obviously been briefed from the same source as I had acquired whatever knowledge I had of the place – the *Encyclopaedia Britannica*. On such occasions as this, I always find myself torn between a desire to please and resentment at so desiring, and have to confess to never having worked out a basis for harmonising the two states of mind. The interview with 'C' was brief; after a few desultory questions, he got up to indicate that it was over, and wished me well in Mozambique. I only saw him once again. This was in his hotel room in Paris shortly after the Liberation, when he was in full uniform as a major-general; booted and spurred. With us was Paiolle, head of the French *Securité Militaire*, whose liaison officer I had been. 'C' was much impressed by the punctilious way Paiolle packed cushions round the telephone in the room to counteract any possible listening device, even though – or perhaps because – his countrymen were again in charge in their capital city.

Before finally taking off, I had a few days' leave, which of course I spent at Whatlington with Kitty and the children. It was the only place I ever wanted to be, and the place I was constantly leaving; my heart was there, but my body was restless and nomadic. Kitty and the children were with me always, yet easily forgotten in the foolish, and often vainglorious, if not squalid, preoccupations of the moment. The saddest thing to me, in looking back on my life, has been to recall, not so much the wickedness I have been involved in, the cruel and selfish and egotistic things I have done, the hurt I have inflicted on those I loved – although all that's painful enough. What hurts most is the preference I have so often shown for what is inferior, tenth-rate, when the first-rate was there for the having. Like a man who goes shopping, and comes back with cardboard shoes when he might have had leather, with dried fruit when he might have had fresh, with processed cheese when he might have had cheddar, with paper flowers when the primroses were out. 'Nothing is so beautiful and wonderful, nothing is so continually fresh and surprising, so full of sweet and perpetual ecstasy as the good,' Simone Weil writes. 'No desert is so dreary, monotonous and boring as evil.' True; but, as she goes on to point out, with fantasy it is the other way round – 'Fictional good is boring and flat, while fictional evil is varied and intriguing, attractive, profound, and full of charm.' Alas, so much of my life has been spent pursuing this fictional good, and forgetful of the other, the real good, that is ever inspiring, ever renewed, making us, again to quote Simone Weil, 'grow wings to overcome gravity'.

The days at Whatlington passed quickly and happily, even though the situation was intrinsically absurd. Here was I, notionally, going to the wars, but actually to Lisbon; a destination I was not supposed to divulge. I could scarcely, in the circumstances, take a brave stance, gathering my wife and children to me, as I remembered my eldest brother doing to us when he went off to France in the 1914–18 war. The drama, in so far as there was one, was all on their side; if there was any danger, it was they, with the possibility of more daylight raids, who had to confront it, not I, who was making for a neutral country where there was neither rationing nor blackout. How, then, should I conduct myself? Though it was true that I was going away for an uncertain time to an uncertain future, that I was under orders, and even if I had wanted to, could not have remained with them, I still felt ill-at-ease, a deserter, running away from my responsibilities rather than to them. Looking back I feel this more than ever; the loss was inestimable, the gain, to me or to the war effort, negligible. All that I can be grateful for is that, despite my shallow departure, thanks to Kitty our little bark remained afloat, and remains so still.

Leaving for Lisbon in 1942 had a special character of its own, even for someone as departure-prone as I was. One slipped surreptitiously away in a flying boat from Poole Harbour without any of the usual distractions – being seen off, finding things to say up to the last moment while looking round anxiously for one's luggage, and listening with half an ear to the loud-speaker for the announcement of departure and the gate to make for. Everything silent and clandestine. It was like a premature demobilisation. Now in civilian clothes again; more than that, with every trace of military accoutrements scrupulously removed from my luggage lest prying neutral eyes should detect them and ask awkward questions – though this was probably an imaginary danger; it may be doubted whether the Portuguese authorities cared much either way about camouflaged service men, whatever their nationality or allegiance, passing through Lisbon. On my brand-new passport my profession was given, for the one and only time in all my life, as a government official;

at the earliest possible moment, I had it crossed out and 'journalist' written in. The other passengers were as inscrutable as I tried to look; some of them probably also serving officers, and maybe on Intelligence missions, too. There were one or two whom I took to be genuine diplomats, British and foreign, and a sprinkling of business men in well-preserved suits, and carrying brief-cases, which they opened on their laps as soon as they settled in their seats in the plane, for the purpose of scribbling notes and studying figures and diagrams. We were silent together, fearful of giving ourselves away; heedful of Fougasse's little drawings of Hitler as an eavesdropper. It all added to our sense of self-importance; clandestinity being a form of vanity, as abstemiousness can be a form of self-indulgence.

In any case, the mere fact of being allowed to depart to a neutral country – which seemed so infinitely remote in beleaguered Britain that it was like going to another world rather than just abroad – was in itself a kind of distinction. We were a little group of the elect for whom, for one reason or another, the drawbridge was raised for an instant, and then at once lowered again. It gave me a feeling of being on some high-priority mission, though in point of fact I had only the vaguest notion of where I was going and what was expected of me. Also, of stepping into the unknown; rather alarmingly in our case, since a plane on the Lisbon run had recently been shot down, allegedly because one of the passengers was the film actor, Leslie Howard, and so much fuss was made about him that the Germans thought he might be Churchill travelling incognito. We looked at one another anxiously to see whether there were any among us about whom a similar mistake might be made; relieved to find there weren't. Our silence continued throughout the flight; scarcely a word spoken. All of us, I daresay, were thinking of that other flight, with the false Churchill aboard, which fell into the sea with no survivors; and those of us on Intelligence missions, doubtless going over the planned masquerade that lay ahead, like actors rehearsing their parts. In my case, it involved presenting myself as a member of the Consular Service, and seeking a visa to go to Lourenço Marques and take up my post as vice-consul there. *En poste* – the expression came into my mind; one of the particles of knowingness which accumulate over the years through the practice of journalism, like *matériel*, or collateral, or Bushido; intimations of a bogus expertise.

Lisbon, with all its lights, seemed after two years of blackout like a celestial vision when we landed there by night. For the first day or so I just wandered about the streets, marvelling at the shops, the restaurants with their interminable menus, the smart women and cafés sprawling over the pavements; all the affluence and bustle of a city not at war. Was this how we, too, should one day live again? Or was it all done with mirrors? I couldn't be sure: I'm not sure even now. With escudos in my pocket, I wanted to buy something, and stared in at the goods displayed, tormented by indecision. Likewise, as to which restaurant to go and eat in; irresolutely studying the menus, and in the end munching a sandwich washed down with coffee. There were two almost adjoining shops exhibiting Nazi and British propaganda pictures and publications; oddly resembling one another, like different brands of the same commodity – Coca and Pepsi Cola. Then all those wax figures beauteously arrayed in the shop windows! By night the cabarets, the dancing lights, the bursts of jazz music coming through half-opened doors! Pleasure stalking the streets, with many trailing it, I a forlorn straggler. Magically, the war had disappeared; hey, presto! – gone. The only thing I could find to buy was a coat which I saw in the window of an obscure tailoring establishment, billed as late of Savile Row, and displaying some sort of royal coat-of-arms. It was made of drill, very strong; originally, I should suppose, ordered by some retired British officer resident in Lisbon, and for some reason never collected by him. It gave me good service over many years.

Having spent my statutory period of careless living to put any enemy counter-espionage agents who might have noticed my arrival off the scent, I presented myself at the British Embassy, where I was expected, and directed to the relevant department. These SIS corners of British Embassies, of which I got to know quite a number before the war was over, all had a character of their own. They were different from the other departments, like Chancery, or Trade, or Information; more free-and-easy – men in shirt-sleeves, their feet up on their desks, a lot of coming and going, and strange visitors. The old Secret Service professionals, it is true, tended to look more like diplomats than diplomats did, and were given to spats and monocles long after they passed out of fashion among the regulars. The prevailing fashion among the wartime MI6 intake, on the other hand, was to aim at being as unlike the conventional idea of a diplomat as possible; slouching about in sweaters and grey flannel trousers, drinking in bars and cafés and low dives rather than at diplomatic cocktail parties and receptions, boasting of their underworld acquaintances and liaisons. Philby, in this sense, may be taken as the prototype of them all, and was, indeed, in the eyes of many of them, a model to be copied.

It seemed there was nothing for me to do but wait for the Portuguese Foreign Office to accept my credentials and grant me a visa to Lourenço Marques. This might well, it was explained to me, take time. When the war was going badly for us – as just then – the Portuguese authorities fell over themselves trying to please the Axis Powers; when our prospects looked up, they were ready to do us an occasional favour. I may add that things went on like this throughout the war. For instance, I noticed that the number and standing of Portuguese officials who would show up for a garden party at the British Consulate-General in Lourenço Marques bore an exact relation to the latest communiqués from North Africa and the other fronts; until, finally, when Hitler's body had been consigned to the flames outside his Berlin bunker, Portugal resumed her role as our oldest ally, and the Consul-General might expect the Lourenço Marques élite to turn out in the same strength for the Queen's Birthday as they previously had for Hitler's.

While waiting for my visa, my colleagues told me, I should employ myself in studying the language, and familiarising myself with the Salazar regime, and its colonial policy. It seemed an unexacting assignment, and markedly unlike the role I had imagined for myself when I first thought of participating in the war. Having settled these matters, we all went off to lunch together at the Avish Hotel, notable as being the residence of Mr Calouste Gulbenkian, then reputed to be the richest man in the world.

It was one of those twilit, enormously expensive, old-fashioned, restaurants which have continued to function in places like Lisbon and Monte Carlo and St Moritz, seemingly unperturbed by the many convulsions taking place around them; the ageing waiters in their shabby black suits continuing to carve and pour and serve with sad serenity, refusing to be put out by a changing world, and looking with the same coldly indifferent eye at young girls wearing elegant shorts as at old dusty dowagers mumbling and muttering over their toasted tea-cakes. Other Intelligence Services, my companions told me, were well represented. The Germans were seated at a nearby table entertaining a bronzed film star who had been holidaying in Estoril; there was a solitary Vichy colonel covered with decorations, eyed contemptuously by a noisy party of Gaullists, and three Italians in earnest conversation. Also, a White Russian with a sallow boy friend and a lot of gold teeth, who, it seemed, was on everyone's books. The war was clearly raging in the Avish. While I was hearing these and other piquant details of the various belligerents present, Mr Gulbenkian came into the restaurant. He was preceded by his secretary and followed by a valet; two waiters approached as he took his place at a slightly raised table reserved for him. All eyes were upon him. He lunched alone, the secretary and the valet seating themselves at another table within reach, in case at any time their services might be required; his face sallow and expressionless, the movements of his hands the minimum required to get food and drink to his mouth, the mastication barely perceptible. Was he not, I reflected, a totem figure? Some cherished image which like the king in chess, needed to be protected and sustained, or the game was lost.

Mr Gulbenkian did not linger long over his luncheon, and after his departure we, too, got up to go; my companions back to the Embassy and their counter-espionage, I to stroll in the sunshine. What with the wine and the talk and a general sense of well-being, I found myself not quite touching down on the pavement; borne along on a wave of contentment in which the white jangling trams, the passing faces, the flowers that I seemed to see everywhere, and snatches of music I kept hearing, presumably from some café orchestra, were all comprised. A posting to the Lisbon Front was certainly an agreeable change from other forms of war service I had experienced; it was difficult to believe that only a little way away the war was still in full swing. What was it really about anyway? *Lebensraum?* Defending Mother Russia? Unconditional surrender? Roosevelt's Four Freedoms? Ah, how easily it might have happened that I had to handle them! At the *Guardian* office in Cross Street, asking: What's our line on Freedom from Want?, and being told: The same as from Fear, only more so. At the Ministry of Information, labouring to show that, despite appearances to the contrary, Stalin must be regarded as a doughty champion of Freedom of Worship and of Speech; as one burning to deliver mankind from fear. It would have been heavy going; I was glad to have missed it, and to be strolling about in Lisbon, sans blackout, sans rationing, sans Blitz, sans war, thinking almost affectionately of Mr Gulbenkian; a war aim in himself – five per cent without end, amen?

I managed to arrange to leave my hotel and become a lodger in a modest Portuguese household. It was an agreeable change. The way of life in a hotel is, to me, the most hateful there is. And the more expensive, the more desolating. Those restless, unnecessary trips up and down in the lift; the constant visits to Reception to see if there are any letters when none are expected; the effort to find something on the menu one wants to eat, and then, having ordered it, to eat it! It is not surprising that residents often throw themselves out of upper-floor windows –

I have toyed with the idea myself – or are found dead in their beds of a surfeit of barbiturates. The first meal I sat down to with my Portuguese family, with a plate of their soup before me, I almost wept for thankfulness. Through practising Portuguese with them I managed to learn a little, and acquired a certain facility at reading the language from spelling out the newspapers, which I did seated at café tables, the newspapers conveniently fixed to bamboo frames. I also started reading *Don Quixote* in Portuguese, and a sermon that took my fancy because it was addressed to the fishes; these creatures, the preacher contended, being specially beloved of God, since the flood He sent to punish men, benefited them. Thus, unlike the inhabitants of Lisbon, they might perhaps heed his words.

The head of the household I was staying in was a retired shop-keeper, some eighty years old and diabetic; his wife, also old, a little plump woman who served him with his food, watching him closely while he was eating it, as though to note his reaction to each mouthful. For servant they had a huge Negress from Cap Verde, always smiling and cheerful, who put great splashes of rouge on her black cheeks, where they stood out like British colonies in the old Empire maps, used when I was at school, in which I first saw the shape of the world. She brought me my morning tea, and I used to long for her to come and dissipate – as she invariably did – the sleepless hours' deposit of *angst*. My Portuguese teacher, who also sometimes took meals with us, was an enthusiast for Esperanto; a little man in a black suit, with a wife to match. I occasionally passed an evening with them, and we argued, he in his scanty English, I in my even scantier Portuguese, about the efficacy of Esperanto as a counter-irritant to the Tower of Babel. He turned out to be a reader of *Time and Tide*, who thought *Punch* was funny, and the *Guardian* the greatest newspaper in the world.

From time to time I dropped into the Embassy to collect mail and some money, and also to find out if there was any news of my visa for Mozambique. There never was, and I really believe I might have spent the entire war quietly studying Portuguese. Wars scatter many forgotten men about the world, and I looked like being one of them. A letter from Kitty brought me the news that my father had died. She described the scene in her incomparable way. How his angina had got worse, and he had taken to his bed; then had gone to hospital, where she visited him regularly with my mother. Towards the end he rallied, sitting up suddenly with the old animation in his face – that expression I knew so well, compounded of unquenchable high spirits, a shrewd appraisal of how the world works, and a not so shrewd hope that somehow it might be drastically rearranged in accordance with his heart's desire, topped up with a Cockney cheekiness which advancing years and venerability quite failed to extinguish. He told me once that it was only because his beard got white and his eyes grew dim that he came to behave more sedately; he never *felt* any differently in himself. Sitting up and seeing my mother's tears falling, he turned on her one of his splendid grins, and then with a wink slipped out of bed, and offered her his arm. 'Come on, Annie,' he whispered gaily, 'we're off to the Greyhound!', and swaggered down the passage with her. It was, Kitty wrote, a glorious wink; knowing and joyous and infinitely reassuring. On their last visit he lay in a coma, and my mother, irritated that she could get no sign of recognition from him, tried to turn back his eyelids. 'It's me, Annie,' she said sharply, as though that was bound to bring him back to life. This time it didn't work; there was no response.

Even though I knew my father's life was moving towards its end, I still felt very sad not to have been with him when he died, more particularly because my absence was due to my being in Lisbon, where I had nothing particular to do but wait for a visa. If I had been engaged in some enormously hazardous secret operation requiring my presence abroad, I might have felt differently. As it was, there was really no good reason why I should not have been at his side, which would, I knew, have brought him comfort. His partiality for me, and irrational pride in me, survived all the follies I engaged in and disappointments I caused him. His presence seemed very near, and once more I was waiting at East Croydon station, anxiously scanning the commuters' faces as they came off the trains; catching sight of him at last, well to the fore. An indomitable figure, striding out, bowler hat a shade too large, somewhat low down on his ears; wearing the City's livery, yet so evidently not of it. So evidently a man on his own, a man apart; serving parties and movements and causes loyally and ardently, but without ever being wholly committed to them. Hence, perhaps, his relative isolation at the end of his days. No place reserved for him in the pantheon of the rebels; like the Abbey for the Webbs, or the Miserden churchyard for the Whiteway colonists. Just some family and a few friends at his funeral, which Kitty organised; then forgetfulness. When, after the war, we set up a stone to mark his burial place in the graveyard of the little church at Whatlington, I asked my eldest son, Leonard, what should be written on it, and he suggested, 'A good man, and a just', after Joseph of Arimathea, who was also a councillor. It seemed exactly right. There is an empty space beside him under the same tree where I hope to lie.

As the days got hotter I moved out to a small pension at Estoril in order to be nearer the sea, bathing daily and going for walks along the coast. In the pension I made the acquaintance of a Russian lady, Mme Sazanov, also staying there, with her son Dmitry. She belonged to the family of a well-known Russian diplomat of the same name, and had left Russia at the time of the Revolution. Now she managed to eke out a precarious livelihood for herself and her son by writing travel books. Hence her presence in Portugal, where, in collaboration with the state tourist organisation, she was engaged in preparing some sort of guide-book. In talking to me about it, she grew lyrical on the subject of *le folklore Portugais* (we usually spoke in French, which she knew better than English, having, she explained, been accustomed to speak the language as a young girl in Petrograd), of *la dance folklorique et les chants folkloriques* which so enchanted her. With her thickly coiled nebulous hair, and general impression of having been kept for a long time in a damp cupboard, and so in need of airing, she reminded me very much of the clientele at Sonia Chamberlin's salon in the Borisoglebsky Periulok. It was another example of how revolutions change things much less than might be supposed; if Mme Sazanov had remained in Russia, and managed not to get killed by one side or the other, her life would have been very much what it was as an exile. Only, she would have been staying by the Black Sea instead of in Estoril, and writing, doubtless in an equally *folklorique* vein, about workers' holiday resorts.

Dmitry was what used to be called simple; with a gentle face and disposition. He took the greatest possible delight in all sounds and sights when we went for walks together. In his eyes Mme Sazanov had the genius of a Mme de Staël combined with the mystical insights of a St Teresa of Avila; he listened, enthralled, to her long reminiscences, how-ever many times he had heard them before, and never seemed to tire of her company. She likewise showed no impatience over his sometimes vagrant thoughts and meandering talk and movements. He hoped, he told me, to be an aviator. One evening he arranged chessmen on the table to illustrate the Russian Front; the Queen, Leningrad, the King, Moscow. Another time he came up to my room with *des petites choses qui peuvent vous interesser*, which turned out to be a collection of British and Gaullist propaganda. It was very beautiful to see Dmitry and Mme Sazanov together, and easily compensated for the tedium one sometimes felt as she ground remorselessly on about the glories of Portugal's historical past and enlightened present. A favourite remark of Dmitry's, which he might repeat several times in the course of an evening, was: *'Je suis plein d'enthousiasme, Monsieur'*; on the other hand, small misfortunes were liable to upset him unduly – as when he came to breakfast, having cut himself shaving, and kept muttering: *'C'est affreux! C'est affreux!'*

On one occasion, when the three of us went on an expedition to Cascais along the coast, we saw the fishing fleet being blessed, with the wives of the fishermen going from ship to ship carrying candles and singing ancient songs. The occasion unleashed in Mme Sazanov a great flood of *folklorique* enthusiasm, but Dmitry just fell on his knees, completely captivated by the scene. I hovered uneasily between the two of them; taking the shock of Mme Sazanov's massive bombardment, and enchanted by the light shining in Dmitry's face. It was the same scene, as I learnt subsequently, that led Simone Weil, in a moment of great illumination, to conclude, 'that christianity is pre-eminently the religion of slaves, that slaves cannot help belonging to it, and I among them'. A thought that has often echoed in my heart.

A day or so after our visit to Cascais I got an urgent call to the Embassy, where I was informed that at last my visa had been granted, and I must present myself at the Foreign Office to collect it. I was beholden for this, not to the Ambassador or other senior figures in the Embassy who allegedly made representations on my behalf, but to Rita Winsor, an energetic, kindly and resourceful member of our Section Five Lisbon contingent, who managed to propel the relevant Portuguese official into action. One of the few useful things I learnt in the course of my five years of war service was that one gets little help at the top in any organisation, but only in the lower reaches; the favours of brigadiers are rare and fragile, it is the sergeants, especially in the Quartermaster's branch, who have it in their power to attend to one's practical needs. The same principle applies in civilian life. At the Foreign Office I duly received my visa, written in red ink – *Bon para Lourenço Marques* – and dated 9 May 1942. Now, at last, I could book a passage on a Portuguese boat and be off. I still occasionally, I may add, get a letter from Dmitry in his spidery writing. The last one told me, sadly but not despairingly, that Mme Sazanov had died.

I sailed from Lisbon in the Portugese liner *Colonial*, with, in my charge, some six or seven large sealed diplomatic bags to be handed to the British representative at the various ports-of-call on the way to Lobito, where I was to disembark. My instructions were to keep these bags always in sight to ensure that they were not tampered with, it being the easiest thing in the world to run a hot knife through the seal, thereby opening them up for inspection. Or, for that matter, to X-ray them. Resultant discoveries, as I understood from experienced SIS practitioners, were sometimes curious – as, black market articles like bottles of scotch, lingerie and silk stockings, as well as supplies of contraceptives, porn, and, in the case of one particular ambassador, tennis balls and a set of new uniforms for his flunkeys. A man from the Lisbon Embassy handed over the diplomatic bags to me on the quay, whereupon they were at once whisked off by the porters with my luggage. I thought despairingly that I had lost them before my journey had even begun, especially when I found my luggage safely deposited in my cabin, but no sign of the bags. Later, I discovered them in the hold with the not-wanted-on-voyage luggage, and was able to peep in at them from time to time to make sure that they were still there – the best I could do to ensure their inviolability. This sense of the sanctity of diplomatic bags did not long survive my becoming HM's vice-consul in Lourenço Marques, and consequent familiarity with them. I soon got into the way of travelling about carrying my own private diplomatic bag, in which I kept my liquor and other personal accessories secure against the prying eyes of customs and security men. It was a convenience which I sorely missed when my brief and lowly tenure of diplomatic status came to an end.

The departure of the *Colonial* was noisy and emotional, with many tender farewells and passionate embraces; handkerchiefs continued to be waved till the shore was lost to view. Most of the passengers were military or administrative officers posted to the colonies, and leaving their families or sweethearts behind; though there were some wives and children on the ship. As we drew away from the dock, I waved with the others, pretending to myself that one or other of the dark-haired girls was weeping so profusely at my departure. We sailed down the coast of Africa with all our lights blazing, occasionally catching a glimpse of darkened, furtive belligerent vessels. Once we even thought we saw a submarine, but with our name and neutral status so brightly illuminated, felt no qualms. I soon fell in with two other non-Portuguese passengers, and spent most of my time with them. One was a French naval officer on his way to Tokyo to take up the post of naval attaché there; the other a Swiss diplomat, also on his way to Tokyo to join the Swiss Embassy, whose responsibilities had been greatly expanded through having to act on behalf of all the Allied Powers when they broke off diplomatic relations with the Japanese. They were extraordinarily different; the French naval officer stern, austere, with closely cropped hair and sparing with his words, which, however, when he did speak, were uttered with great intensity, and the Swiss, extrovert, cheerful, verbose and good-natured.

The three of us carried on a marathon discussion, specifically about the war, but generally about the state of the world and future prospects; interrupted when we put in at the Portuguese colonies along our way – Madeira, Guinea, Cap Verde, San Tomé – and then resumed when we found ourselves on the high seas again. Walking up and down the deck, in the bar and the dining-saloon, seated in deck-chairs or leaning over the side of the ship, we talked and talked. At first the naval attaché was sullen and ill-disposed to me, obviously with Mers-el-Kebir in mind, though he never once mentioned it; but gradually he melted, and though he continued to be reticent and taciturn, began to give us occasional glimpses of his real feelings and attitudes. I became completely absorbed in this running conversation, to the point of forgetting that I, unlike the other two, was an actual participant in the war. Anyone listening would have formed the impression that the Swiss was the only one who truly hoped for and believed in an Allied victory, that the Frenchman entertained some expectation that a stalemate of sorts might develop, and that I saw only disaster and confusion ahead whatever the war's outcome might be.

The truth is, I never could shake off the feeling that the war was 'theatre'; like my mother's antics when jealousy afflicted her, or my own tantrums when I succumbed to any of the rages of the will. For that matter, like history itself – a kind of running soap-opera whose actors and script-writers change, but whose essential theme remains the same. I think the Swiss was vaguely shocked by my attitude; between the naval attaché and me, on the other hand, a certain sympathy developed, and when I got to Lourenço Marques I found a long affectionate letter from him, written in his neat hand and couched in his stately French, expressing the pleasure he had taken in our companionship and talk. I sent the letter back to London with the suggestion that perhaps he might be approached as a useful contact when he took up his post in Tokyo. My true motive – rather a shabby one, I fear – was precautionary, in case the Swiss repeated some of the things I had said. In such a case, the letter would have enabled me to claim that I was playing a part with a view to getting on good terms with the naval attaché. In Intelligence stratagems there is always a built-in emergency exit; like those iron staircases in case of fire that one sees outside brownstone houses in New York. I never saw the naval attaché again, but always asked about him when an opportunity offered. In this way I heard that after the war he had joined a religious order with a particularly strict rule; then that he had died. I wish I had kept his letter.

At each port-of-call I was met for the handing over of diplomatic bags, about whose arrival in my charge advance advice had been given. I handed them over as though I had kept them in sight throughout the voyage, but this subterfuge was quite unnecessary. Taking a drink with a local consul, I learnt that the bags contained, for the most part, material from the Ministry of Information, which could scarcely be considered top secret. There might even have been one of my articles, written while I was at the Ministry, on defending our free way of life, though whether this would have gone down particularly well in, say, Säo Tomé, where we saw prisoners chained together and working under an armed guard, may be doubted. My two friends and I regarded the Portuguese Empire as *opéra bouffe*, and noted how run-down the colonies we visited seemed to be. How surprised we should have been to know that the British and French Empires, which still in 1942 seemed quite substantial structures, were shortly going to drop to pieces and disappear, while the Portuguese Empire remained more or less on its feet. In the last century attempts were made to devise a means of giving away the Portuguese colonies – to the Germans, for instance, to keep them quiet – but as it turned out, by a strange quirk of history, they were fated to be the last to survive. It was a sort of *misère* result, with the weakest and most decrepit player scooping the pool – such as it was.

For me, the voyage ended at Lobito, in Angola, where I was to take the train to Elizabethville in the Belgian Congo, and from thence a plane to Nairobi where 'C' 's man in East Africa was stationed. I had farewell drinks with my friends the Swiss diplomat and the French naval attaché, and then stood waving on the quay as the *Colonial* was gently unloosed and moved away in the evening light. It gave me a pang – something familiar disappearing, and I left standing alone as darkness suddenly came down. The British Consul in Lobito arranged my tickets and saw me off on the train which left only once a week – a modest three or four carriages and dining-car, puffing and rattling across the vast spaces of Africa, stirring up the dust, frightening the cattle, and causing a momentary stir of activity and excitement at its various stopping places, where any local Europeans, or near-Europeans, were liable to assemble and stare at the train and its passengers, seeing in them their only link with what they conceived to be their own world, as distinct from this dark Africa where they were fated to live. I liked thus being cut off from everyone and everything; on my own, for ever moving, and through a countryside which never seemed to change – dry and dusty and interminable. Soon I found myself wishing that the journey would never end. It seemed like a way of life, to keep moving; just as, at the Ministry of Information, it had seemed like a way of life to keep still, and at Mytchett to keep drilling. I spent most of my time looking out of the window at the huge dusty vistas as we rattled along; watching the sun rise murkily and set gaudily, and in between ride relentlessly across the glaring, empty sky, with only an occasional herdsman or shepherd to be seen, his black limbs graceful and at ease, as though even then confident of being the ultimate inheritor when the storm raging in the world at last subsided.

After a while, in the restaurant car we started chatting together. There was a little farmer, a doctor, and a veterinary surgeon – a huge man with a large impassive face who illustrated all his remarks with appropriate actions. For instance, when he was arguing that men were unequal because they had different tastes, he showed this individual driving a car, that one drinking, and that other saying his prayers. At one station a priest got in who was carrying a pastoral staff to be delivered to his bishop. He showed it to us, gleaming and jewelled, and we much admired it. As each passenger arrived at his destination, he said good-bye to those of us who were continuing on the train, until, at the Angola frontier I alone remained. The last to get down was the doctor, who bought me a present of a basket of fruit, which he handed to me when he said good-bye.

At the frontier there was a long wait, and I was entertained by some missionaries, who turned out to be Plymouth Brethren – an elderly man, his two daughters and some ladies. We sat round a table drinking tea together and talking about God and the Bible. 'If the Bible is lies,' the elderly man said at one point, 'then we've lived on lies for two thousand years.' I assured him earnestly that I didn't think it was lies – most certainly not. We stayed together till the train left at midnight, walking up and down the platform affectionately, and going on talking. The thought occurred to me then: Suppose I stay with them here, and go no further! But, of course, when the guard's whistle blew, I got back in the train, as I always have. An old steam train, naturally, that slowly picked up speed; so I could lean out of the window and wave to them for quite a time, where I saw them standing with their lanterns in the darkness and waving back. My compartment, when I returned to it, seemed quite desolate. I remember my encounter with the missionaries on the Angola–Congo frontier so very vividly, and even now with a kind of anguish.

Whatever I might wish, the train rolled inexorably on to Elizabethville, and I had to leave the little home my compartment had become and grapple with getting a plane on to Nairobi. For me, the town had a familiar air, being so very like Heliopolis where Kitty and I had lived while I was teaching at Cairo University. Both Elizabethville and Heliopolis were Belgian built; even the tramway bore an uncanny resemblance to the one I used to take to Abbasiah. The European shops were full of all the things like whisky and cigarettes and silk stockings unobtainable in England, the reason being that the Congo's copper production was of great importance, and it was considered essential to keep the local producers in good heart. The Belgians who ran the place looked very large and self-confident and pink in their khaki drill. With ancestral memories of Roger Casement, King Leopold I and E. D. Morel, I looked for signs of brutishness in them, and, as it seemed to me, not in vain.

'C' 's man in Nairobi turned out to be a kindly avuncular figure whose attitude to me was rather like that of a bishop briefing a curate for work in some distant and possibly hazardous mission field. In the pre-war years he had been stationed in Cairo, and told me that, dating back to the time I was resident there, my name appeared in his card-index of subversives and undesirables. He and his Russian wife were very kind to me, and took me to the club, which still retained something of its smart-set character, but was beginning to look a little faded and worn; as, even more so, was Government House, where I was invited to stay because of my friendship with Arthur Dawe, an Under-Secretary at the Colonial Office. It always fascinates me to observe how what is to happen reveals itself in advance; so that though politicians may make speeches proclaiming that we shall never yield here or cede there, their words are belied in peeling paint and fallen tiles and patches of damp. In Government Houses I have visited shortly before the regimes they represented have collapsed, there has always been a musty smell of decay; a premonition that a change of tenancy is imminent.

I felt this very strongly in Nairobi, even though ostensibly Government House was in full swing, with all the usual appurtenances – a car with a flag flying, black soldiers who sprang to attention and presented arms whenever I went in or out, a respectful servant to lay out my clothes and an attentive A.D.C. who led me to His Excellency as and when required, meanwhile ready to engage in polite conversation for an indefinite period. The Governor was a Pickwickian figure; a civil servant translated from his Colonial Office desk to the glories of being an Excellency. These posts, in the last stages of the British Empire, began to be relinquished to civil servants, presumably as a solatium, or maybe just because no one else wanted them. The Governor's wife, on the other hand, had rather a savage look, I thought, as though she might have been more at home among the Kikuyu. Over dinner, served majestically by waiters in gold and red, in Raj style, the Governor remarked that an indication of our present lack of belief in ourselves and our civilisation was that we no longer attempted to make our African and Asian subjects like ourselves, but insisted that they were better as they were. Later in the evening, when we were chatting together, he developed the theme.

There were, he said, three things that had held the Empire together – the military security it offered, the economic advantages it provided, and the institution of the Monarchy. The first could scarcely be expected to survive our military reverses, even though in the end we were technically victorious; the second had been dissipated in the enormous expenditure of two world wars; the third was a matter of sentiment, notoriously fickle and fragile. A young secretary who was with us interjected that, on the contrary, wonderful new prospects were opening up of an Empire based, not on fear, but on genuine collaboration and mutual good will. His words seemed to come from far away; I had written them long before in the columns of the *Guardian*. It was obvious that the Governor thought the game was up, and obviously he was right. What he could not have foreseen was that the preposterous frontiers the colonial powers had drawn when they carved up Africa would come to demarcate independent sovereign states, ruled over by black African demagogue-dictators, each with a flag, an airline, a hydro-electric project and a seat at the United Nations; the conduct of whose affairs would provide a rich, and often cruel, burlesque of the institutions and practices of the governments which had initially brought them into existence.

A flying-boat carried me down the African coast, and at last I arrived at my destination, Lourenço Marques. My first impression was of a rather run-down Mediterranean resort, with bathing beaches, picture postcards, souvenirs, cafés, restaurants, and, at night, cabarets and casinos; except that the sun was hotter and the air more humid. I

stayed at the Polana Hotel, overlooking the sea, and only lately completed. The idea of the Portuguese authorities was to attract clients with
money to spend from Johannesburg and other cities in the neighbouring
Union of South Africa by offering a style of living and of entertainment
more 'continental' in character than was permissible in the Union under
the aegis of the zealots of the Dutch Reformed Church. This worked
even in war-time, and there was a steady influx of South Africans looking for a gamble, and even an occasional clandestine visit to a brothel.

Both my opposite numbers – the Italian Consul-General, Campini,
and the German Consul-General, Leopold Wertz – also lodged at the
Polana Hotel, so I was able to examine them at my leisure in the hotel
restaurant, where, like me, they came for meals. Campini was a large
ebullient man, who obviously tried to look as like his Duce as possible;
wearing a cloak whenever an occasion offered, and given to using
extravagant gestures and rhetorical flourishes. Wertz, on the other hand,
was not at all like Hitler or any of his henchmen; unless it was Ribbentrop, who, as Foreign Minister, was his ostensible boss, and to whom he
might have been said to bear a passing resemblance. He had the youthfulness common among Germans of his type; blond and pink and
spectacled and earnest. I had occasion later on to read some of his letters
home, which a friendly purser on the Portuguese ship carrying the mail
gave me a sight of before sailing. They were addressed to his mother;
very affectionate and filial, if not sentimental, written in a rather formless
hand sprawling across page after page. After the war I also read some
of his official dispatches made available from captured *Abwehr* archives.
They, too, were decidedly verbose, and in them I appeared as a ruthless
intrepid spy-master, with a chain of agents extending over the whole
of Southern Africa, whom he, Wertz, was able nonetheless ultimately to
pulverise. Diplomats and Intelligence agents, in my experience, are
even bigger liars than journalists, and the historians who try to reconstruct the past out of their records are, for the most part, dealing in
fantasy.

If, as sometimes inevitably happened, I bumped into Campini or
Wertz, or passed through a door at the same time, we bowed politely,
but never spoke. Or we might meet in the lavatory, there, too, maintaining a coolly distant manner. Yet, of course, we were conscious of one
another, living, as we were, under the same roof, eating the same meals,
sharing the same servants; not to mention bribing the same local
officials and police officers. Espionage and counter-espionage, as far as
the Portuguese were concerned, made good their war-time losses on

tourism; we secret agents represented an invisible import, if not a capital gain. It was altogether a curious relationship I had with Campini and Wertz; a kind of wordless intimacy. Even now I feel as though, if I ever ran into one of them, it would be as an old acquaintance – 'My dear fellow, how are you?'

Ledger, the British Consul-General, a kindly low-keyed man, treated me handsomely, though it was obvious that he had considerable scepticism about my supposed duties, and disliked handing out money to me even though it did not affect his own careful accounting. The other members of the staff likewise regarded me as a kind of pampered interloper whose activities were not to be taken seriously. I had a room to myself in the Consulate-General, and there I sat, with my typewriter, and a safe, in which I kept my code-book, my invisible inks and my cash, my general assignment being to try and stop the enemy from getting information about our convoys sailing to North Africa up the Mozambique Channel, where they were being torpedoed by German submarines. This was happening on a large scale, greatly assisted by the ease with which a message could be sent from Durban to Lourenço Marques giving details of Allied shipping passing through the port. The task was daunting, and I scarcely knew where to begin, seeing I had no local contacts, and my knowledge of Portuguese was sketchy to say the least. To while away the time I deciphered a long telegram which had come for me via Ledger. It was a laborious business, and the kind of thing I have always been bad at. First, one had to subtract from the groups of numbers in the telegram corresponding groups from a so-called one-time pad; then to look up what the resultant groups signified in the code book. Any mistake in the subtraction, or, even worse, in the groups subtracted, threw the whole thing out. I toiled away at it, getting into terrible muddles and having to begin again, but finally managed to disentangle the message in an approximately legible form.

It came from Philby, as I knew from the style, and provided a résumé of the espionage scene in Lourenço Marques in the light of Wertz's and Campini's latest telegrams. All their traffic was being intercepted and cracked at Bletchley; so I had the inestimable advantage of knowing just what they were up to – like having access to the answers at the end of the book in an arithmetic test. This benefit was available to Montgomery fighting the Battle of North Africa just as much as to me fighting the Battle of Lourenço Marques. It also meant, of course, that my activities showed in the Wertz–Campini traffic, so that any bluff, or any pretence practised on my own account without reference to London was bound to become known there at once. Nonetheless, to show at all in the Bletchley material was considered in MI6 circles to be an enviable distinction; exactly like having a leader quoted in the foreign press in my *Guardian* days. The Philby directive suggested that it might be a good idea to concentrate on infiltrating the Campini *apparat* rather than the Wertz one, since the personality of Campini, to judge from his boastful, high-flown style, seemed the more vulnerable of the two.

That evening at dinner at the Polana Hotel I looked across at Campini's table – where they seemed to be in a particularly festive mood – wondering how I could hope to plant an informer among them, or otherwise get at their secrets. Signora Campini, for instance – what about her? Might she be approachable? A short, compact lady, not particularly beautiful, but quite vivacious looking, and about a third of Campini's bulk. I began to think of her almost amorously, and after dinner, when the Italian party went for a stroll in the cool moonlight, followed at a distance, only, however, catching vague echoes of their voices and their laughter. I sent a longish message to London, ciphering with anguish late into the night. It announced my arrival and establishment at the Consulate-General, and gave an account of how things were at the Polana Hotel; as it were, setting up the board and beginning to arrange my pieces.

Like Brighton rock, a war spells out the same word wherever you bite into it; on the various fronts, from Stalingrad to the Polana Hotel, the same essential line-up. Only the scale varies; not the dramatis personae. Wertz and Campini, Führer and Duce – what's the difference? Lipski, a Polish diplomat, told me once that when he saw the accused at Nuremberg he could not believe they were the same men he had treated with so deferentially in Berlin. That shambling figure, surely not Ribbentrop; that woebegone clown couldn't be Goering. But they were; it was just that they had changed their positions on the board, moving from an attacking position, to a defensive one, and then to surrender.

So, the drama of the war was played out on the Polana Front as on any other, though it has to be admitted that actual hostilities occurred but rarely. On one occasion, a South African lurched as though by accident into Campini, and a fracas of sorts followed; on another, after a drunken party, someone went round muddling up all the Axis boots and shoes put out in the corridor for cleaning. There was also an ugly scene about which particular radio station should be turned on for the news, to the point that the management decreed that the public transmission of broadcast news bulletins, from whatever source, was forbidden. Naturally, we all believed that our rooms were bugged and our bags searched; and I occasionally prowled about the hotel corridors and peered in through windows, though the only discovery I made was that Dr Wertz wore a hair-net in the privacy of his room – an interesting, but scarcely significant, item of intelligence. It piqued me slightly to observe that when visitors from South Africa arrived in the hotel it was always Wertz and Campini they wanted pointed out to them, never me. However, I comforted myself with the thought that, in war, the enemy enjoys the advantage of being glamorous; like other men's wives.

It was through the good offices of Ledger that I recruited my first sub-agent; Camille, a Polish Jew who had managed to escape from the Gestapo and make his way to Lourenço Marques, where he subsisted largely on bridge, which he played extremely well. He came to see me often. Through his bridge-playing he had a large circle of acquaintances among Portuguese officials, including the police; and in his long conversations with me – in French, which he spoke with rather a thick accent – he always presented himself as a sort of *chevalier* or dashing cavalry officer, who, through the fortunes of war, found himself in strange, if not disreputable, company, towards whom his attitude was one of tolerant condescension, as I, a fellow *chevalier*, would readily understand. It is the measure of his essential decency, and of my fondness for him, that we maintained this fiction intact to the end of our relationship, despite the fact that money passed hands, and sometimes led to wrangling which could easily have become acrimonious, and that sometimes the information he passed to me likewise partook of the fantasy which governed so much of his life in Lourenço Marques. I can see him now – the close-cropped hair, the jaunty appearance, the carefully pressed linen suit that had seen better days and white shoes always meticulously pipe-clayed, the cane, the ravaged face liable to carry an afternooon shadow even in the morning, and, above all, the eyes peering out from this ensemble anxiously, courageously, and with a touch of sheer consternation.

Quite early on in our acquaintanceship he brought to see me one of the more senior police officers in Lourenço Marques – Inspector Y. From his colour and bearing the inspector seemed to be decidedly a local product; as, indeed, were a good proportion of the officials in Mozambique. The Portuguese, I found, had no colour prejudice as such. Any resident in their colonies who acquired money and was generous in handing it out to his betters; who adopted a name like Costa da Silva, went to Mass regularly, and generally conducted himself in a responsible, respectable way, became automatically socially accept-able. The pawn got through to the back row more easily than in other African colonies. I used to think because of this, that, had I been a black African, I should have preferred to live under Portuguese rule, despite its brutality, incompetence and corruption, than under that of any of the other colonial Powers; certainly than under the rule of Afrikaners in the Union of South Africa across the border.

Camille had given his police inspector friend a great build-up before bringing him to see me – '*Vous savez, un homme très intelligent, très cultivé, très fin. Franchement, je m'étonne; même en comparaison avec les cercles intellectuelles les plus estimées de Varsovie. Un homme exceptionnel.*' He lingered over the syllables of this last word – *ex-cep-tion-nel.* Inspector Y did not, at first glance, live up to this panegyric. He had one of those bashed-in faces which look as though lumps have fallen off them here and there; like a plaster bust which has been left exposed to the weather. As he spoke only a few words of French and English, I had no means of appreciating his wit and learning, so highly praised by Camille. Despite linguistic difficulties, I managed to convey to him the suggestion that if, in the course of his duties, he came across anything that might be of interest to the British Consulate-General, I should be most grateful if he would communicate it to me via our mutual and esteemed friend Camille. The suggestion was well received; something in the nature of a smile broke across the waste-land of the inspector's face, followed by a pause in which we all three looked at one another, aware that we had reached the heart of the matter.

Diffidently – it was my first bribe; later, I became brazen enough – I produced from the drawer of my desk an envelope in which I had put some hundred escudo notes, and mentioned that, no doubt, certain expenses would arise in connection with the assignment the inspector had so graciously undertaken which I hoped he would allow me to defray. Thereupon, I passed the envelope to Camille to pass on to his friend. Camille opened it, took out the notes and counted them, with the other's eyes closely upon him. I noticed in the Inspector's face, as he watched Camille counting the notes, a faint but unmistakable look of dissatisfaction; a barely discernible shake of the head, a touch of cold-ness breaking in on the amiability he had previously displayed. It would not do. Camille, as ever, master of the situation, very courteously asked permission to enter into a private colloquy with me. Drawing me aside, he said in an undertone that his friend was too polite (*trop gentleman*) to say so, but the amount I had handed over was quite inadequate. Wertz, in such a case, paid at least three times as much; Campini even more, *et même les Japonais, bien plus.* As I well knew, he went on, he never cared to discuss money with me; the subject was highly distasteful to him. Where money was concerned he was *un enfant nouveau né.* Even so, in this particular case, his honour was involved, and he must ask me to increase the amount paid to his friend, even if it had to be deducted from his own paltry honorarium. I suggested another three hundred escudos; his lips soundlessly formed the word *cinq*, and *cinq* it was. I should add that Camille's notion that he disliked discussing money was scarcely in accord with the facts; we discussed little else, invariably to the disadvantage of HM's Government and the British taxpayer. Having settled the matter of the escudos, Camille and his friend departed, with many courtesies, leaving me to work out a telegram to London announcing the new recruit to my *apparat*, and seeking approval for the rate we had settled on for the job. I anticipated no difficulties.

I found that bribing, which inevitably played a large part in my Lourenço Marques activities, had as many subtleties and diversities as seduction. Thus, in certain circumstances the passing of money had to be engineered in such a way that it seemed to happen of itself, which, in seduction terms, was the equivalent of lolling or reaching out an arm as though by accident. Alternatively, there were occasions in which one yelled or banged the desk, insisting that not a cent more would be forthcoming. This might be compared with violent assault. It is interesting, incidentally, as bearing on the close relation between the two activities, that the same word is used for both – to pass money or to make a pass. I became quite an adept as time went on, knowing just when to show the colour of my (or rather HMG's) money, and how much was needed to provide the necessary incentive in this or that case. In Intelligence operations, money is an essential ingredient; even where other motives arise – as patriotism or ideological affiliations – money, however little, or its equivalent, must be dropped in, like a touch of bitter in a mint julep, to validate the deal. Only when money has passed is the mystical union fully established; it's money that makes Intelligence go round. And money, as it were, on trust. For obvious reasons, I couldn't ask Inspector Y for a receipt. In bribery there are no accounts; only good, or, more often, bad, faith.

As it turned out, Inspector Y proved to be well worth his pay. In numerous operations his help was invaluable. Thus, when we arranged for some South African troops interned in Mozambique to be taken into Swaziland, then British territory, the good man was able to ensure that there were no traffic hold-ups or other misadventures along the way. The troops in question had been torpedoed off the Mozambique coast, the troop-ship transporting them to North Africa sunk without trace in a sea infested with sharks. At the Consulate-General we heard of the catastrophe, and I went along with the rest of the staff to receive the survivors when they came ashore, wet and shivering and bewildered; some of them, especially the lascars, babbling incomprehensibly, and letting out strange anguished howls which merged with the cries of the scavenger birds the scene had attracted. It was an eerie spectacle; a moonless night, pitch-black, the sea stormy, and, apart from our flickering lights, only the white of the breakers to be seen as they came roaring in. The survivors, as belligerents landing in a neutral country, had to be interned by the Mozambique authorities, and were put in the *Assistencia Publica*, a place of such squalid horror that even rebellious seamen planning to desert in Lourenço Marques, after a sight of it, returned meekly to their ships and the boatswain's whistle.

I managed to get a message to the interned South Africans that, if they would arrange to take a stroll along the road to the Swaziland frontier on a particular Sunday afternoon, I'd hope to have some cars going in the same direction that would stop and give them a lift. First, I tried the South African business community resident in Lourenço Marques to see if any of their cars would be available, but none were. They feared trouble with the authorities which might damage their business. In the end, it was the taxi-drivers of Lourenço Marques who saved the day; especially one of them who brought in the others – a little man with a big mouth strikingly like Lord Beaverbrook, and known thenceforth by the name. Happily, he knew nothing of the original; otherwise, as I told him, he might well have been tempted to sue me in the courts for defamation. Some ten of them happened to drive their taxis in the direction of Swaziland on the afternoon in question, and loaded up with the interned troops, depositing them at the frontier some fifty miles away where I had arranged for them to be admitted. In no time they were in Mbabane, the capital of Swaziland, and thence whisked away to Johannesburg and home. The taxi-drivers would accept no more money than the normal fare, though the risk they ran was far greater than the South African business men would have had to face. It is true, of course, that, thanks to Inspector Y, the risk was far less than they supposed, but I doubt if they knew this. I really believe they would have done the job for nothing, so delighted were they to have a chance of serving the Allied cause. Thenceforth, they were all my firm friends. Years later, when I was banned from entering the Union of South Africa, the story of the escape of the interned soldiers was resurrected in the South African press. I was happy to learn that some of those who took the Swaziland road had survived the war, and remembered their deliverance from the *Assistencia Publica.*

Another episode in which Inspector Y's part was even more useful concerned a local resident known to be an organiser and collector of shipping intelligence for Campini. He, too, we decided, should be given a trip to Swaziland. The problem was to ensure that he took a drive in that direction on a specific evening and at a specific time. As it turned out, we were able to arrange a stratagem on the best Hollywood lines. Our man, it appeared, was enamoured of a white South African girl dancer, who, however, had so far repelled his advances. At the same time, she very much wanted a return visa to Johannesburg, this having hitherto been withheld on the ground that her way of life in Lourenço Marques was immoral. As so often happens, Afrikaners tend to combine tolerance of collective wickedness, as embodied in the vile doctrine of *apartheid*, with particular squeamishness in matters of personal behaviour. Similarly, the privately immoral are often the loudest in protestations of public virtue. Hence the insistence in the New Testament that a balance must be struck and maintained between our duty to God and to our neighbour.

The girl came to see me, and I encouraged her to tell me about her life in Lourenço Marques and wish to go home. She was rather pretty in a dusky way; like so many ostensibly white South Africans, probably by no means of pure European stock. Financially, I remarked, she had presumably not been doing too badly. She nodded; there was plenty of money about; but the Portuguese! She pulled a face; the bars and cabarets of Johannesburg, she said in effect, were scarcely Cheltenham Ladies' College, but by comparison with their Mozambique equivalents, delectable. Anyway, she was sick of being passed around from hand to hand, with everyone wanting the same thing and wanting it at once. Like so-and-so, I said, mentioning the man we proposed to kidnap. Yes, like him, she agreed readily. Then we got down to business. We wanted this man, for reasons she could easily guess, somewhere on British territory where he could be questioned. Would she help to get him there? All she had to do was to induce him to go for a drive along a particular road at a particular time. In return I'd guarantee to do everything possible to overcome the difficulty about her visa. It was a very dishonest proposition on my part. I had no reason to suppose that

I could persuade the South African Consul-General in Lourenço Marques – who certainly had no great liking for me – to change his attitude towards allowing her to return to Johannesburg, and I deliberately let her form the impression that I could pull strings on her behalf in high quarters, which was, of course, quite nonsensical. I hadn't even referred the project to London for approval, as I was bound to do before embarking on anything of the kind. It was extremely unlikely that approval would be given, at least without a whole lot of questions being asked, and consequent delays. I found very early on in Lourenço Marques that it was better to act first and ask afterwards. If the action was successful, everyone was delighted; if not, there was bound to be trouble anyway, irrespective of whether or not prior approval had been sought.

Rather to my surprise, the girl readily agreed, and we went ahead. She duly induced her aspiring paramour to take her for a drive; Inspector Y stopped the car at the agreed place, where another car was waiting, and our man was expeditiously transferred into it, and then driven to Mbabane, where I lost sight of him. Later, I vaguely heard that he had been taken to England for interrogation, and spent the rest of the war there. Fortunately, when he arrived in Mbabane he had notes of Allied shipping movements in his pocket. His disappearance from Lourenço Marques created a minor sensation, and was widely attributed to financial difficulties. It was said that the accounts of his business were in disarray. I was tempted to claim this as a piece of deliberate deception on our part, but in fact it came about naturally, which is always the best kind of deception. The girl behaved impeccably, and said nothing to anyone about what had happened, which made me more than ever ashamed about my shabby bargain with her. Intelligence work necessarily involves such cheating, lying and betraying, which is why it has so deleterious an effect on the character. I never met anyone professionally engaged in it whom I should care to trust in any capacity.

In due course I nerved myself to approach the South African Consul-General about the girl, trying to make him believe that my interest was due to a personal infatuation. I overdid it, of course, dwelling on the girl's desire to make a fresh start, and on the essential purity and goodness of her nature. The Consul-General had one of those lean, dry antipodean faces – he was Australian by origin – and seemed unimpressed by my apologia. After I had finished, he brought up the subject of the kidnapped man, and asked me if I had any views on it. I said I hadn't, apart from vaguely hearing that he was in financial difficulties. 'I think you did it,' the Consul-General said quietly. I let that pass, and got up to go. A few days later, to my great relief, I had a scribbled note from the girl saying that she now had permission to return to Johannesburg, and thanking me. I sent her some flowers. By a happy chance, Inspector Y was put in charge of the police investigation of the missing man, and he looked in to tell me how his enquiries were going. It was the only occasion during our acquaintanceship that I knew him to laugh heartily. He laughed and laughed, and I handed him an extra envelope.

It was curious how quickly I became used to this weird business in which I engaged. Going each morning to the Consulate-General, opening my mail, telegrams deciphered now, happily, not by me but by an expert elderly Scottish lady, Miss Stewart, sent from London for the purpose; in- and out-trays, telephone calls, visitors, appointments, all the usual procedures of office work. Back to the Polana Hotel for lunch, and a glimpse of Campini and Wertz, or, if they were absent, speculation as to where they were. In the afternoon, a stroll by the sea, and then back to the office till the evening when there were liable to be social occasions. The various consulates celebrated their national days, like embassies; receptions were held, uniforms worn, gossip exchanged, just as though Lourenço Marques were an important capital, and no war raging throughout the world. For news I was dependent on the local newspaper, which I spelled out each morning, and on a cyclo-styled sheet issued by the Consulate-General. It was thus that I learnt of the Battle of Stalingrad, and of the continuing triumph of Japanese arms. Far, far away these momentous events were taking place, but we on our African coast, in tropical heat and humidity, dozy and amorous and scandal-mongering, went our way; for us, the struggle symbolised by Campini in his cloak, Wertz in his shorts, and me, contending together. Occasionally I relieved my feelings by despatching a message to Graham Greene in Freetown; it, too, scrupulously coded with one-time pads, as though most secret, and replied to in similar style.

Occasionally, too, I would find some reason for visiting South Africa; driving there, dusty mile after dusty mile, or, when it rained, churning and floundering through mud. After green Swaziland, the parched Veldt, where I came upon little Boer townships and villages; strangely silent and deserted, almost as though unoccupied, until I suc-ceeded in knocking up some large, somnolent inn-keeper who, with slow sulky movements, produced beer and a hunk of bread and cheese, gazing suspiciously the while. A weird survival, as it seemed to me; some brontosaurus from another age, lumbering, barely articulate, brutal in a slow kind of way, but also lost, dazed, as though involved in a bewildering situation beyond his understanding, yet stubbornly resolved to stay as he was because there was no alternative. Brobdingnagian, towering, brooding, but with some valid relationship to this country where fate had put him; blindly resolved to live out his destiny there to the end, whatever it might be. The black Africans serving him, working his land, digging out his gold and his diamonds, seemed utterly subservient; yet beneath their oppression, strangely enough, I thought I detected a sort of patient confidence and satisfaction; almost a quite joy, that the future was theirs. All they had to do was to wait – which they were well accustomed to, and good at.

It is one of those situations in the world which everyone, consciously or unconsciously, recognises as being somehow crucial; more so than others seemingly more momentous. In South Africa itself this sense of momentousness is made more poignant by the very fascination of the countryside itself – something Alan Paton has conveyed beautifully and vividly in his writings. What is happening there, I realised, is not just a political squabble, a matter of ins and outs; but rather a great drama, in whose working out the Afrikaners, the ostensible villains, have their own peculiar nobility, as the black Africans, the present victims, their own special exaltation. It may even be, I sometimes speculated, that this land is earmarked to be the scene of the last battle between our expiring civilisation and the up-and-coming barbarism threatening it. By an accident of history and geography, the Afrikaners have been cut off from the demoralising currents of the twentieth century, and in their isolation have been able to go on believing in themselves as a people chosen by God to maintain and defend the beliefs and ways of their forebears; to see themselves as the guardians of Christendom in a dark continent. Despite the, in contemporary terms, lunacy, and even criminality, that such an attitude has led to, it has a great fascination; even those who find it most abhorrent and scandalous are still held by it. In the American Deep South there is plenty of anger and fear, but in South Africa there is something else – this weird, distorted, grotesque, in its own way, heroic attitude of the Afrikaner, defying, not just contemporary anti-racialist principles, not just the propositions and hypocrisies of the conventional liberal attitudes and the World Council of Churches, but history itself. Dull, sullen, paunchy men, obstinately, stupidly, standing up to the currents which have swept aside in our time ancient dynasties and social orders, and reduced to rubble and despair so many proud cities and citadels which, only a few short years ago, seemed strong and rich and enduring.

I usually arrived at Johannesburg after nightfall; the city ablaze with lights, headlights bearing down on this rough Babylon prospering so mightily, gold being no less needed to fight wars than men and machines. So, every effort made; backs straining and bending, sweat pouring over dusky faces, furnaces glowing, winches turning, to extract the last yellow ounce to forge into ingots to stock bank vaults and Treasuries. I had seen some of the requisite labour being recruited in Mozambique. Good biceps, a fine chest expansion, straight legs and solid thighs; all this surveyed and felt by the recruiters, like a cattleman at a market. He'll do! Now, in Johannesburg, the recruited to be seen, wild looking, separated from tribe, home and family, and in their own way likewise engaged in the feverish quest for gold. On Saturday nights when they received their pay, rolling about drunk in the streets, with notices warning white motorists – Beware, Natives! lest they should run them down like straying dogs or cats. A wild feverish city, awash with new red wine and raw brandy; a place of violence, with more to come – smelling already of the blood that must flow. A city of gold and blood; yellow and red.

On one such occasion, I went on to Cape Town, where there was an MI5 man to liaise with; MI6 not being permitted to operate in a British Dominion, as South Africa then, of course, still was. Through this MI5 man I made the acquaintance of Brigadier P, a South African who was a strong and avowed Anglophil; a genial host and interesting talker. At the time he was dealing with the case of Robey Leibrandt, which had made a considerable stir in South Africa, and even caused some ripples in Lourenço Marques; Leibrandt being a German agent who had been despatched from a U-boat in a rubber dinghy to land on the South African coast. This he succeeded in doing, and in setting up some sort of radio transmission, but he was fairly soon caught. The man primarily responsible for turning him in, and whose evidence was essential in the forthcoming court proceedings, was, Brigadier P told me, lurking in the top storey of the Post Office building. Would I like to come and see him? I said I would, and the Brigadier took me along. Never have I seen a man so scared. He had an armed guard watching over him night and day, and nothing would induce him to venture out-of-doors, where he considered, Brigadier P believed with reason, that he was bound to be murdered. By way of camouflage, he was in the process of growing an enormous moustache, and so eager was he for the protection he hoped this foliage would afford him that he seemed to be fostering its growth, strand by strand, like an assiduous gardener. Was it not, I remarked to Brigadier P, a strange case for a man to be in who had apprehended an enemy agent in time of war? He shrugged significantly, and agreed that, to anyone who did not know South Africa, it doubtless did seem strange. I should have paid more heed to the object lesson he had kindly arranged for me. Afterwards, I heard that the man, by this time his moustache having reached stupendous proportions, was taken under the most stringent security conditions to give evidence for the prosecution at Leibrandt's trial, and then whisked off to some distant place where the fury of the Afrikaner nationalists at what he had done could not reach him. Leibrandt was sentenced to a term of imprisonment, of which he served some five years, and then was predictably released when Dr Malan became Prime Minister. I vaguely heard that he set up as a butcher, and now is dead.

In Lourenço Marques I acquired another informant, Serge; a small, eager Jew from somewhere in Eastern Europe. One of those veterans of persecution who had somehow made his way across half the world, hiding, scurrying to and fro, changing his name and documentation from time to time; an expert on identity papers, in and out of prison, settling for a while – in Constantinople, in Beirut, in Alexandria, then on the run again. Any hat he wore a shade too large, clothes with some remote stylishness of their own, a cut about them, shoes pointed and perforated. It was his face I loved; so full of knowingness and woe and wistfulness. What battered endurance and heroism traced in it! He would come in to see me two or three times a week; sitting in front of my desk, occasionally gesticulating or getting up to illustrate a point – this person and that who'd turned up, gossip he'd heard, conversations he'd listened to. India-rubber features screwing up, the suspicion of a wink – '*J'ai joué la comédie avec lui*'; his favourite saying, perhaps because life had so often played the tragedy with him. He'd done everything, but had no trade or profession; with the traditional Jewish veneration for learning still in him, he occasionally picked up a book, but was only vaguely literate. A polyglot if ever there was one, with snatches of every language under the sun, including German, which he knew quite well, but would not speak if he could possibly avoid it. We spoke in French, with occasional English words breaking in. With me, he never once played the comedy; I treasure his memory.

It was thanks to Serge that I became involved in what proved to be, in MI6 terms, the most successful of my Lourenço Marques operations.

In one of his *tours d'horison* he mentioned that he had made the acquaintance of a Greek sailor who told him that the captain of his ship was working for the Axis, and had a rendezvous with a German U-boat operating in the Mozambique Channel, for the purpose of handing over stores and equipment. It fitted exactly with a rather obscure reference in my latest dollop of Bletchley material to a Greek boat Wertz was to keep a special look-out for. There was only one place, Serge told me, where we could be sure of running into his man, and that was the oldest established and best-known Lourenço Marques brothel, invariably referred to as Marie's Place after the proprietress, herself a veteran in the business. He mentioned this establishment with a certain diffidence, having, as I well knew, a wholly undeserved respect for me as someone removed from the sordid necessities to which such as he were subject. Sometimes, in our conversations, I sought to disabuse him of this notion, trying to explain that I considered his life to be heroic compared with mine, and his instincts purer and more disinterested, but it was no use; he continued to see me as a creature living on a different plane. As far as visiting Marie's Place was concerned, I was able to convince him that, in the course of duty, I was ready to present myself there or anywhere else, however unsavoury, at any time. He said he would alert me, and there we left the matter for the time being. I may add that of course I gave Serge money from time to time, and of course he took it, but he never once raised the question of the amount or counted it in my presence, or came to me – as every other agent I ever had, did – with some hard luck story requiring an additional sum urgently.

The very next day I got a message from Serge to meet him that evening at a café near the waterfront. He was looking more dapper than usual; wearing an old-fashioned boater with a coloured ribbon of a kind still worn when I was an undergraduate, which he had acquired somewhere or other in the course of his wanderings. We went together to Marie's Place, where, in the old style, a red light was shining over the heavy front door, corresponding, I decided, to 'C' 's blue one. We rang, and a grating opened, and a face peered out. On recognising Serge, we were at once admitted – something that embarrassed him a little, and led him subsequently to explain at some length how it was only since working on my behalf that he had become a frequenter of Marie's Place, which was so very useful for making contacts and picking up gossip. The old-fashioned appearance of the exterior was matched within – heavy plush curtains, deep dusty divans similarly covered, with brocaded cushions; little mother-of-pearl tables, a large leopard-skin rug with a snarling head, and the whole bathed in heavy, all-pervasive perfume. There are two interiors which scarcely seem to have changed through the centuries – brothels and the anterooms of ecclesiastical dignitaries, both expressing, in their heavy hangings and upholstery, a certain continuity, a relationship with what is changeless in us and our lives; in the one case, sensual, in the other, spiritual. Serge and I sat down side by side on one of the divans, and presently Mme Marie herself swept in; an ageless lady, with a curled blonde wig, pendulous ear-rings, and much jewellery gleaming and jingling about her person; a large bosom amply displayed, a voluminous dress of red satin, and at the heart of all this infra-structure, a gaunt, bony, lavishly rouged face. It was said that she had arrived at Lourenço Marques some sixty years before from Marseilles to join the present establishment, becoming in due course the patron and enormously rich. There was always a reigning gigolo, the current incumbent being a young Tunisian named Mustapha.

Yes, Mme Marie told us, the young man we were interested in was expected that evening, and it was Monique who would entertain him. Monique, it seemed, had got to know him quite well, and could tell us more about him. At the moment she was working (somehow it went even better in French – *pour l'instant, elle travaille*), but – looking at her little jewelled wristwatch – she should be free soon. Meanwhile, could she offer us a glass of champagne. This was brought in on a tray by a negro boy in a red coat and turban, While we waited, sipping it, clients came in and were attended to – mostly South Africans, fairly tipsy and on a spree, one or two obvious sailors very drunk, and a local Portuguese, immensely respectable-looking, who took off his glasses and carefully wiped the lenses before going upstairs. At one point Camille's friend, Inspector Y, put his head in through the door, saw me, and, with an expression half leering and half astonishment, at once withdrew. When, later, I referred jocosely to our encounter, thinking this the course of prudence, he went to great pains to explain that inspecting the *maisons de tolérance* was one of his more disagreeable duties.

In due course Monique appeared, unruffled by her recent labours. Incidentally, we saw the clients come in, but not go out – there was another exit. So I never knew on whose behalf Monique had been working. She turned out to be an exceptionally amiable woman, well, even heavily, built, rough featured, with a pleasant smile and smooth, cheerful voice; my idea, to the life, of Oblomov's wife. Yes, she knew our Greek quite well; a nice boy, but young, naïve, inexperienced – the last slightly accentuated. He had told her about the goings-on on his ship, and she had considered them important enough to pass on to Serge. If there was any way she could help further we had only to mention it; she would do anything – but anything – against the Nazis. No idle boast, as I had occasion to learn later. Now she must go; the Greek might arrive at any minute, and she would not wish him to find her with us. It was not so much a matter of security as of etiquette, of delicacy. I could quite see why. If we talked all four together, she and the Greek, at a certain point, would have to leave us, or be left by us, and we should know why, and they would know that we knew, which would be inelegant, and, in any case, possibly add to the difficulties of his lack of experience.

As it happened, the Greek arrived immediately after she left us. He was extraordinarily beautiful; one of those faces you still find among modern Greeks whose features exactly recall the broken statues in Ephesus or Corinth. Yes, they could easily take over the ship; the first officer was wholly on our side. All that was required was that I should arrange for them to be able to sail the ship into Durban after they had disposed of the captain and the one or two members of the crew on whom he could count. 'Dispose?' I asked. He smiled. That was optional; they could be thrown to the sharks, or, alternatively, secured and handed over to the Durban authorities. It was obvious where his own preference lay, but I opted for the latter course. He promised to bring the first officer to see me at the Consulate-General the following morning, there being a certain amount of urgency as they were due to sail in forty-eight hours' time. On this note we parted, leaving him with Monique.

I found myself greatly excited by this venture. Everything about it seemed wonderful – cast, plot, *mise-en-scène*. Serge was equally delighted; for the first time I saw him truly excited. His only disappointment was that the sharks were not to be fed, but I argued that what could be got out of the captured men would be more useful than killing them, and anyway I could guarantee that they would be immobilised for the rest of the war. This had to satisfy him, but I could see he was thinking of the extermination camps, and of all it had cost him to have to dodge and run across half the world. My argument, anyway, was specious; it was extremely improbable that anything of importance could be got out of the captain. He and his associates could be thrown to the sharks with impunity; no one would ever know or care. I chose to have them kept alive, even though they had been engaged in fuelling and provisioning the U-boats that were sinking our convoys in the Mozambique Channel. This, not out of humanitarian or pacifist

sentiments – I read without undue perturbation of the saturation bombing of German cities – but because I could see in my mind's eye their
bodies being thrown overboard, hear their cries, observe the shadows
of the sharks as they gathered, and the blood staining the water after
they pounced.

It was rather absurd, I admit, when one of the great holocausts of
history was taking place, to fret like this, one way or the other, about the
fate of a Greek captain and a sailor or two. Yet I did fret. Why rob
Serge of a taste of legitimate vengeance? I asked myself. This tiny
drama – what was it by comparison with the global one being enacted?
Well, the difference was that in the tiny drama I had a part to play,
lines to speak, whereas in the other I was only an extra; part of a crowd
scene, shouting obediently Hosanna! or Crucify him! according to the
exigencies of a script I had no hand in writing. So the Greek lived, and
I knew that I was a fraudulent belligerent, with no passion like Serge for
victory and vengeance – the same thing, really; no sense of being engaged in a life and death struggle against the powers of darkness. If I
had been truly honest, in the light of this realisation I should have
turned in my Mozambique assignment and returned home to grow
potatoes in Whatlington. Instead, I threw myself with renewed zest into
our plot, spending half the night ciphering a long message to London
about what we proposed to do, and meeting the first officer the next
morning, as arranged, to work out the final details with him. To my
great satisfaction I was able to get from him the precise bearings of
where the projected rendezvous with the German U-boat was to take
place, and telegraphed this information, along with the ship's probable
time of arrival at Durban, to Cape Town for transmission to Naval
Intelligence.

In the event, everything happened according to plan; the ship duly
arrived at Durban with the captain locked up in his cabin and his
associates likewise secured, and I had every reason to hope that the
rendezvous would be effectively kept. A long message from London
indicated that at last they had realised there that the ship I had been
telegraphing about and the one Wertz was being urged to keep an eye
on, were one and the same. There was also some criticism of the procedures I had employed, especially my communicating direct with
Naval Intelligence rather than through them. I could afford to take a
light-hearted view of these strictures because, shortly after receiving
them, I had a congratulatory telegram from 'C'; considered in the
Service a rare and precious accolade. I never knew for sure whether I

could claim to have contributed towards reducing by one the submarines operating in the Mozambique Channel, or heard what happened to the Greeks, pro or contra, but the operation enhanced my
standing in MI6.

Thenceforth Monique and Marie's Place became part of the Lourenço
Marques scene for me. Oddly enough, in retrospect, they seem the only
homely – if I dare use the word – aspect of the whole adventure. There
was a down-to-earth quality about the establishment which was very
appealing. As for Monique herself – she, as I came to see, had some
truly admirable qualities, partly due, perhaps, to her very profession,
which served to canalise into workaday channels emotions and desires
which otherwise can become unduly pretentious, overstrained and
ultimately even destructive and demented. The only point on which we
differed, was over whether or not she should knife one or other of the
visiting Germans to whom, when they visited Marie's place, she was
liable to be allotted. It would be so easy, she insisted, and showed me
just how it could be done when the German, however husky, might be
expected to be quiescent. She did not accept my arguments against such
an action, but she bowed to them.

I am happy to think now that my last word of her related to an episode
in which she was at her most sublime. A small black box she left at the
Consulate-General was found to contain charts, a log-book and a code-
book belonging to a British ship's captain who had recently put in to
Lourenço Marques. It appeared that the captain had brought the box
ashore with him for security, got drunk and gone along to Marie's Place,
where he had been handed over to Monique. In view of his condition,
she thought it more prudent to take the box off him for safe-keeping, and
the following day, not knowing where or how she could find the captain,
thought it best to bring it to the Consulate-General to be returned to
him. Without any question, she could have got for it from Wertz or
Campini a sum that, to her, would have been a fortune. Equally certainly,
she knew that this was so, but never, I am sure, for a moment even
considered such a possibility.

One late afternoon, sitting in the Polana lounge, I noticed a young
woman, obviously Portuguese, come into the hotel and speak to the
clerk at the reception desk. Something about the way she moved, some
special ease or grace in her, at once held my attention, and without
thinking what I was doing, I went up to her and said, 'Hullo!' It was
a risky thing to do; she might easily have responded in a way that

would have been highly embarrassing for me – by being angry, or complaining to the clerk, or just ignoring me. There were all kinds of possibilities. As it was, she smiled, and returned my greeting. Her beauty was even more striking near to than I had supposed; with her large dark eyes and hair, and the sallow complexion that went with them. Also – though this was more apparent later, when I got to know her – some quality permeating her whole being that I can only describe as the innocence which comes of accepting life in its totality, all it has to offer, to the mind, the body and the soul. When she had gone I risked asking the clerk who she was. The wife of a local German business man, he told me, who might be described as the Gauleiter of the German community resident in Lourenço Marques; adding that she and her husband were moving into the hotel in a day or so. This information added a professional dimension to a personal inclination.

Thenceforth, I was, of course, on the look-out for her; saw her arrive with her luggage, and managed to make a rendezvous for that evening, at the end of the hotel terrace overlooking the sea, where it was dark and unfrequented. I stationed myself at the end of the terrace – much too early, it goes without saying. In the dining-room I had noticed she was seated at Wertz's table, so that, in addition to the excitement of meeting her, was the thought, that she would be coming, as it were, hot-foot from the company of my chief antagonist. I dreaded that someone else might choose that particular evening to be on the terrace, and resented every footstep I heard that was not hers. At last she came, with a characteristic swinging gait she had that I got to know well and recognise at once. It is always easy to talk to someone with whom one is going to become intimate; the future casts its shadow backwards, and there is no explaining to be done, even though there is everything to explain. A stumbling, awkward first encounter rarely ripens into intimacy. The first thing I learnt was her name – Anna. We talked about the war; she was much more sanguine than I about the Eastern Front, and absolutely certain that the *Wehrmacht* would be routed. She easily guessed that I was wondering how she could feel so when she was married to a Gauleiter. Their marriage, anyway, she said, was breaking up; hence the move to the hotel, where, in fact, they occupied separate rooms and rarely saw each other. As for Wertz – she detested him because he was a Nazi.

All this came out, not perhaps in the course of our first talk, but certainly in the early days of our acquaintanceship. She told me, too, of another German, Johann von X, a refugee, whom she loved and hoped to marry, and would like me to get to know. He had come to Africa as a fugitive from the Nazis; had been interned in Rhodesia, then escaped and made his way to Lourenço Marques, where they had met. I had to consider, of course, whether the attitude she took might not be a plant on her part to lull me into confiding in her, to the point when I might perhaps be pulled into the German network, or at any rate exposed. The delight of her company, the charm of her full, rich voice and occasional misuse of English (which she had learnt at a school in South Africa), especially slang; the sheer pleasure of being with her on those warm Lourenço Marques evenings, on the terrace, or, as sometimes happened, I in my car, driving slowly along until I saw her, a vigorous, striding shadow – how, in such circumstances, could I possibly suspect her of engaging in deliberate deception. As it turned out, my instinct was correct; in all her dealings with me she was never other than straightforward and truthful. All the same, I had to cover myself by reporting the contact to London, giving her a code name, and seeking authorisation for going on seeing her. It was as well I did this; an Englishman staying in the hotel who had spotted us together on the terrace sent the Consul-General a letter complaining of my behaviour. Ledger showed the letter to me before sending it on to the Consular Department of the Foreign Office. So I was able to forestall it.

The gap between my relationship with Anna as presented in my Intelligence reports, and as it actually existed when we were together, was so wide that it amounted to a sort of schizophrenia; being two people in one, and at times getting confused between them. Double agents quite often go off their heads, and I can easily see why. They begin to doubt both their identities, or imagine a whole multiplicity; one fitting into another, like those dolls which get smaller and smaller, until, right at the centre – nothing. In this particular case, the situation was greatly eased by the inclusion of Anna's friend Johann in our relationship. He was a highly intelligent and perceptive person of whom I also got very fond, and so somehow, as it were, completed the circuit; whereas before there had been open wires sparking and spluttering, with the risk of a fuse at any moment, now the current flowed smoothly.

The first time we picked him up in the car we went for a picnic by a rock pool some miles away. I had brought provisions and a bottle of drambuie, which for some reason, though I did not particularly like it, became our regular drink. It was a perfect moonlit evening, warm and still. I realised when I saw Johann that I had noticed him about in Lourenço Marques; a tall striking figure one could scarcely miss, with fair hair, blue eyes and the standard sabre cut down his face. At one point I saw him on the beach directing a fat German dentist named Dr Schwab in some reducing exercises. We often laughed about this. He spoke English well, but with a characteristic lilting German intonation. In his own style he was decidedly handsome, so that he and Anna made an impressive pair; he so blond, she so dark. Their intimacy was strong and deep; they were wrapped up in one another, two castaways who had found a sanctuary together. Though, alas, I am very prone to jealousy, even in the most ridiculous circumstances, so that I can find myself feeling jealous of two total strangers who, maybe in a railway carriage or some other public place, seem totally preoccupied with one another, to the exclusion of anyone else who may be present, including myself – nonetheless, being with Johann and Anna on our outing together, I had not a single twinge, save once, and then only momentarily. This was when Anna turned to Johann to shelter her while she got into her bathing suit, I having meanwhile tactfully jumped into the pool and started splashing about in it. After our swim we ate our provisions, drank our drambuie, and talked and talked, covered with a blanket because the night air began to get fresh. Finally, we dozed off, for how long I can't be sure, but I know that when I awoke I had a curious sensation of not knowing which of us was which; of our being inextricably mixed up together. The sensation lasted, I suppose, for no more than a few seconds; then it passed, and we got back into the car and returned to Lourenço Marques.

Soon, by the operation of Parkinson's Law, the staff in Lourenço Marques began to grow. First to arrive on the scene, as I have mentioned, was Miss Stewart, to take over the ciphering and re-ciphering. Her arrival was a great relief; though I improved a little with practice, the one-time pads continued to baffle me, and I would sweat and groan over them far into the night. Now I just had to type out a message and hand it over to Miss Stewart, and await her ciphered version of any that arrived. One ill consequence, I fear, was that, lacking the restraining influence of having to encipher messages myself, I became ever more verbose. Happily, all this paper has now, as I understand, been destroyed, though, ironically enough, not its counterpart, the *Abwehr* records, which were captured by the Americans, and have been carefully microfilmed and stored in Washington. If, by some infinitely remote chance, anyone in the future wants to know what went on in the way of counter-espionage in Lourenço Marques during the 1939–45 war, it will be Wertz's version, not mine, that will be available. Indeed, this may be said already to have happened in Ladislas Farago's *The Game of the Foxes*, which leans heavily, if not exclusively, on the *Abwehr* records in purportedly recounting the story of German espionage in the 1939–45 war.

Soon after Miss Stewart's arrival there took place in Lourenço Marques a diplomatic exchange which led to a further accretion of staff. Two ships sailed in, one bearing Allied diplomats from South-East Asia, and the other Japanese diplomats from Europe and America. They then exchanged passengers for the return voyages. Journalists arrived to cover the event, among them some old acquaintances amazed at my vice-consular impersonation, and I had the task of organising a press-conference at the Consulate-General at which the British Ambassador from Tokyo delivered a kind of diplomatic incantation; like a monsignor splashing holy water over a missile site. My chief interest in the occasion was meeting the various Secret Service and related personnel who had managed to get in on the exchange. They all came clandestinely and severally to see me in my office (were Wertz and Campini similarly invaded? I never found out) to collect money, send messages to London, and generally establish themselves as being again in circulation. I tried, before they came, to guess which of the passengers might turn out to be in SIS, but failed in every case save one – that of Steptoe. He, I decided, when I first set eyes upon him, was every inch a Secret Serviceman, and so, sure enough, he was. I took an instant liking to him, and persuaded him to stay behind in Lourenço Marques with me.

He was a little cock-sparrow of a man, with a bristling moustache, a high voice, a monocle and a lot of suits, ties, hats and shoes despite the fact that he had been in internment since Japan came into the war. A real pro, I felt, to whom every encounter, however innocent, was clandestine, every letter – even bills – needed to be tested for invisible ink, and everyone near him, in a café or restaurant, in a railway carriage, or just happening to pause in his vicinity to light a cigarette or do up a shoelace, was keeping him under surveillance. He carefully burnt every communication he received that could possibly be regarded as in any way compromising; not just content to set fire to them and leave them to be consumed by the flames, but watching the ash to make sure it mouldered into undecipherable dust. I never actually saw him eat any paper, but he told me – and I entirely believed him – that before the Japanese came to take him into custody, he swallowed his code book, page by page, from A to Z, and was just settling down to consume his one-time pad when he was arrested. He was never, drunk or sober, forgetful for an instant of the burden of secrets that he carried; a treasure trove that he felt the enemy were longing to take off him. By some miracle, he told me, the Japanese failed to avail themselves of the opportunity which his being in their custody provided, but he was ready with all manner of ingenious false confessions if they had pulled off his toenails, roasted the soles of his feet, or otherwise exerted themselves to wrest his secrets from him. Ironically enough, one of his fellow-passengers on the exchange, a blameless British Council representative, a brilliant Japanese scholar with a Japanese wife, who subsequently became *The Times* correspondent in Tokyo, did get the full treatment, the Japanese doubtless calculating that no government would finance and support the activities the British Council engaged in without some ulterior motive. Steptoe, on the other hand, would have struck them as a purely Wodehousean figure of no security interest – the Japanese being, as Wodehouse himself told me, among his most avid readers.

Steptoe's feeling that he represented a prize any enemy Intelligence service would give their eyes to have at their disposition, was not abated by the failure of the Japanese to try to extort his secrets from him. The Germans, he felt sure, would know better, and when at one point it was suggested that he might return to London via Lisbon, travelling there on a Portuguese boat, he indignantly rejected the suggestion. Without a doubt, he said, the boat would be intercepted by a German submarine, and he would be taken aboard to be delivered into the hands of the Gestapo. One imagined the signal going out from Berlin: 'Calling all U-boats, get Steptoe at all costs.'

Apart from these harmless eccentricities, which, I found, he shared with most old SIS hands, Steptoe was a cheerful companion, and in many ways a sagacious counsellor. For one thing, he knew the Secret Service through and through; how it worked and the people who ran it. Every trade has its own particular style and gibberish, and he was a master-hand at letting fall the technical terms of espionage (letter-box, chicken-feed, cover, etc., etc.) thereby giving an impression of effortless expertise. He would come and sit with me in my office at the Consulate-General and read all my telegrams, offering occasional suggestions, which I invariably accepted, for making them seem more authoritative. I soon introduced him to Anna whom he treated with great gallantry, and later to Johann. To both of them he conformed much more closely to their idea of a typical Englishman than I did. Occasionally, we gathered clandestinely in his room, when he would make a great point of turning on his radio as loudly as possible to counteract any hidden microphones or eavesdroppers. Once, when we were shouting to one another against this noise, we suddenly realised that God Save The King was being played on the radio to mark the end of that day's Overseas Service of the BBC. As it resounded through the room at full blast, Steptoe out of habit half rose from his seat to stand to attention, I just shifted uneasily in mine, and the other two looked on the ground. If there had been an enemy agent peeping in at us through the keyhole, I wondered what he would have made of the scene.

During the period of the diplomatic exchange Campini gave a great dinner in the Polana Hotel to the Japanese diplomats, at which I was able to take a peep. The Italian Consul himself was holding forth, with many Mussolini-like gestures, his words being translated into English as he went along by a member of his staff, there being, presumably, no one available who could translate them into Japanese. The interpreter knew English only imperfectly, so that he stumbled along behind Campini's flowery eloquence, with occasional words and phrases – 'Victory... Pluto-democracies... Eastern Front... Bolshevisms finally trampled in the dust...' emerging comprehensibly. It was, however, the faces of the Japanese that held my attention; they seemed frozen in their wonderment, like a moving picture that has suddenly stopped. When at the end they came to applaud, they clapped their hands together mechanically, as though they were little toys which had been wound up to perform this gesture. I was reminded irresistibly of their faces when, after the war, I attended a few sessions of the Japanese War Guilt Trials in Tokyo. General Tojo and his fellow war-criminals wore precisely similar expressions as they listened to numerous translations of the pleas of the various Allied prosecuting counsel, turgidly expatiating upon the evils of tyranny and its guilty instruments in true Lockean style – something between an Eisenhower Inaugural and Laurence Olivier delivering Lincoln's Gettysburg Address. Remembering that the trials had been going on already for two years, that counsel were paid by the day, and no end was in sight, I could not but feel a pang of sympathy with General Tojo and the others, submitted, as it seemed to me, to a protracted refinement of torture. The returning Japanese diplomats got off more lightly in Lourenço Marques, but, as I could see, they, too, suffered.

I, also, had my troubles; a telegram from London required me urgently to screen the Polish citizens from the Far East involved in the diplomatic exchange. The Poles in question turned out to be a party of orthodox Polish Jews who, for some unexplained reason, the Japanese had seen fit to send along with the diplomats. No one knew their names, they had no papers, and during the voyage, it seemed, had kept to themselves, preparing their own food in accordance with their particular dietary requirements, and scrupulously performing the various requisite ceremonies. 'Screening' was a term which had come into great vogue; if someone had been screened, his loyalty and reliability were considered to be impeccable. It was the security equivalent of a medical smear. Actually, as it turned out, Philby and most of the other defectors had all been repeatedly screened, which did not seem to have incommoded them in any way. To have screened my Polish Jews with any degree of exactitude would have taken a whole array of screeners several years, even assuming it was possible at all. I telegraphed back that such investigations as I was able to make gave them a clean bill, and they were shipped to Tanganyika. How they fared there, I never heard.

Another arrival at Lourenço Marques was Hunt, or to give him his full name, Huntington Harris, an enormously tall American who belonged to the Office of Strategic Services (OSS), the first essay of the United States Government in the field of espionage, later to burgeon into the ever-proliferating CIA. They came among us, these aspiring American spy-masters, like innocent girls from a finishing-school anxious to learn the seasoned demi-mondaine ways of old practitioners – in this case, the legendary British Secret Service. Most of the early arrivals were Yale or Harvard dons, who imagined themselves writing Ashenden-type stories when the war was over; in the case of the chestier ones, Hemingway-esque ones. Or they might be the offspring of Senators or Congressmen, adept at looking after their own. Or unsoldierly sons of generals, or the un-nautical offspring of admirals Or advantageously connected in some way with the State Department or the *New York Times*. Or just, like Hunt, unmilitary by temperament, while belonging to rich patrician families. In any case, indubitably an élite corps, presided over by 'Wild Bill' Donovan, a corporation lawyer and friend of Roosevelt. Alas, the period of tutelage lasted all too short a time. The first feeling of awe and respect soon evaporated; and it turned out that the finishing school products had learnt all the tricks and devices of the old practitioners in no time at all, and were operating on their own, sustained by lavish supplies of money whose reckless dispensing sent up the accepted tariff of bribes to astronomical proportions everywhere, making even the cost of trivial services like getting charladies to go through wastepaper baskets quite exorbitant. As for the police – once the OSS appeared on the scene, it cost as much to suborn an assistant inspector, or even a mere sergeant, as would once have sufficed to buy up the whole force.

I got over this difficulty in Lourenço Marques by simply co-operating with Hunt. He was, in any case, a pleasant companion, with a dry drawling wit, and his extra supplies of cash made it possible to gladden the hearts of Camille and Serge, not to mention Inspector Y. We found a convenient residence that we could share, rather on the outskirts of Lourenço Marques, with a garage that had a door into the house through which visitors could pass without being noticed. Johann often visited us in this way; he had a cat-like facility for suddenly appearing out of nowhere. On the whole we lived amicably enough together, though at times Hunt's good nature was severely strained. For instance, once when Johann was driving my car and got into some sort of trouble with the police, it was necessary for Hunt, as the only available person as tall as Johann, to insist that the police were mistaken, and that it was he, not Johann, who had been at the wheel. For some reason which now escapes me, to support this dissimulation, it was necessary for Hunt to grow a beard, which he heroically did.

Then there was Nero, a huge man with a shaved head who was working for SOE, a sabotage organisation set up by Dr Dalton at the Ministry of Economic Warfare. Though SOE and MI6 were nominally on the same side in the war, they were, generally speaking, more abhorrent to one another than the *Abwehr* was to either of them. Fortunately, however, I was soon on the best of terms with Nero and his family, consisting of Andrée, his French wife, and Susie and Anne, their two daughters, of all of whom I became very fond. Susie had long yellow hair, and Andrée herself was one of those well-educated French women who manage to be intelligent without becoming like Simone de Beauvoir. She and Nero had met in Alexandria, where Andrée was a teacher and Nero a business man, some twenty years older than she. I really had – and, for that matter, have – no clear idea of what, if anything, Nero was up to; but his household was, for me, one of the bright spots in Lourenço Marques, and I spent many happy hours there, talking, laughing and planning impossible operations – such as taking over a German ship immobilised in Lourenço Marques harbour. Life did not smile on Nero after the war; he got a job as starter on the race-track at Heliopolis – the one that Kitty and I looked out over from our flat when we lived there. Then, when all the English had to leave

Egypt, he came to see me at *Punch*, and a little later I heard he had died. I wish now that I had tried harder to help him.

Johann continued to interest me, as a person and as a phenomenon of our time. He was ten years my junior; an artistocrat, born into the war of 1914–18, and growing up in the period of famine, inflation, unemployment and corruption which followed. When he was still quite young he joined the Nazis, and rose rapidly in the party hierarchy, though from early on he began to have doubts. Perhaps because of his mood of uneasiness, he took on a crazy mission in Austria which involved organising an attempt on the life of a minister in the Austrian Government with a view to creating a condition of political confusion. This, it was hoped, would seem to justify German intervention, leading, of course, to the Anschluss. An alternative plan was to assassinate Von Papen, then the German Ambassador in Vienna, but this laudable project was abandoned. Anyway, Johann's mission failed, and he was arrested, being later exchanged for an Austrian – von Strachwitz, an ultra-conservative Catholic who abominated the Nazis, and who had fallen foul of the authorities in Munich and been arrested there. On his release, Johann found himself quite disenchanted with the Nazis; indeed, in actual danger from them. So he made off to Africa, to Dar-es-Salaam, and what was then Tanganyika, where there was still a quite large German community. When the 1939–45 war broke out he was interned in Rhodesia as an enemy alien, but escaped, and made his way to Mozambique, the nearest neutral territory.

It was a strange experience, in the middle of a ferocious war, thus becoming intimate with someone like Johann, who, for instance, when we talked about Himmler, could draw on personal experience of working with and knowing him. It would be easy for me to claim that I cultivated his acquaintance solely for Intelligence purposes, and had to choke back my moral indignation at his past association with the Nazis' evil deeds and purposes. This, however, would be quite untrue. I greatly enjoyed his company, and grew to like him very much. It would be equally untrue for me now to say that Philby's double-cross fills me with abhorrence. If I were to run into him, I should, I am sure, pass as agreeable an evening with him as ever I did in the days when we were both in Section Five. I have never been able to relate my feelings about people as individuals to my reactions to their public attitudes and behaviour, whether approving or disapproving – something that has often got me into trouble.

Johann and I played chess together, went for expeditions with Anna, talked incessantly about our plans and hopes and fears for the future. He had a great love of wild animals and places, and was quite at his best in this setting. I think he had come to care little for human beings, having seen them at their degraded worst, and been cheated or captivated into participating in their degradation. With wild animals he was more at ease, holding in his hands a lion cub or baby alligator with great tenderness. Shakespearean tags easily come into my mind, and of him I found myself saying under my breath: 'Timon will to the woods, and there shall find / The unkindest beast more kinder than mankind.' Ironically enough, in our discussions it was Johann who took the liberal, hopeful view of the war's outcome, I who insisted that whoever won or lost – and we assumed, of course, that the American–Russian–British alliance would win – our civilisation had seen its best days, and that we must expect another Dark Age. We even exchanged some letters on the subject, which I still possess; their faded typescript – jejune thoughts are all that remain of many hours of ardent disputation.

By various means, we got to know that Wertz was sending a man into South Africa with funds at his disposal, to make contact with pro-Axis elements there. I knew the man in question by sight; a rather lost-looking soul, often to be seen mooning about, who never seemed to have anything much to do, and was regarded as something of a joke by his fellow-Germans in Lourenço Marques. We even were able to trace in advertisements in a South African newspaper oblique announcements of his coming, and Bletchley provided confirmation. So I decided the best thing to do was to go myself to alert the police in Johannesburg, who should be able to pick him up fairly easily, and find out who his contacts were. It might, I calculated excitedly, put them in the way of infiltrating, and ultimately exposing, the whole enemy set-up in South Africa. Passing through Swaziland, I looked in on Captain T, the head of the police there, who was very co-operative and sympathetic. For instance, he had been most helpful over speeding the shipwrecked South African troops on their way home. Somehow I had the feeling that he wasn't quite as enthusiastic about the project as I was, but still he responded sufficiently to confirm my opinion that my mission was well worth undertaking.

There had been heavy rain, and the mud roads were a morass, with no proper surface at all. My car slithered about in a most alarming manner, and several times I thought I had got hopelessly bogged down. However, at last I reached Johannesburg, where I registered at my hotel, had a bath and a meal, and then went round to police headquarters, taking with me under my arm a file we had compiled in Lourenço Marques, containing all the relevant information. As it happened, the Commissioner was away, but an assistant received me most affably. I remember him as a large dark man, rather handsome, in a smart uniform; not at all like an Afrikaner in appearance. He might even have been Jewish. After compliments and pleasantries, he put on a serious air and asked me just what I wanted of him. As clearly and succinctly as I could, using my documents where necessary, I told him how this emissary of Wertz's, whom I could identify, was crossing into the Union illegally, probably on his way now, with contacts to make and money to hand over. I know pretty well the route he'd take; so couldn't we go after him and get him? The other listened to me attentively; he was sitting on the side of his desk, one leg, very smart and shapely in its tight blue trousers, swinging to and fro, the boot brightly polished, gleaming. Suddenly he began to laugh, positively to shake with laughter. Naturally I looked surprised. The leg stopped swinging; then, glancing at me quizzically, but by no means unsympathetically, he asked me if I realised that there was scarcely a homestead between the Swaziland frontier and Johannesburg that wouldn't be proud to hide Wertz's man, feed him and see him on his way. Did I see the point? I did, of course. He went on to tell me how, an evening or so before, they had been tipped off that a meeting of the Ossewa Brandwag, an extreme nationalist organisation, was taking place at such a house at such a time. So a man had been sent along to see what was afoot. Sure enough, a lot of people had turned up at the house in question, and the man had taken the numbers of their cars. When, back at police headquarters, these were checked, they were found to include the registration number of the then Minister of Justice's car. Again he asked me if I saw the point, and again I said I had. Very well, then, would I come and join them for a drink? This I did; indeed, for several drinks.

When I left the police headquarters, I was feeling very sore and depressed, but worse was to come. The following morning, strolling about the town, I actually *saw* Wertz's man. He was quite unmistakable, looking very lost and forlorn; in blue shorts, too large for him, and unseasonable in the chilly weather. The heavy, German climbing boots that he was wearing over thin socks were likewise inappropriate. From the look of him, I should say he had just arrived at Johannesburg, and had not yet had time to get his bearings. Obviously, I should have done something about him in spite of my discouragement at police headquarters. But what? I just stared at him. Whether or not he spotted me, I have no means of knowing, but while I was staring he disappeared. Afterwards, miserably going over the incident in my mind, I decided I should have grabbed him myself; or at any rate shouted and pointed at him so that people gathered round. But just to do nothing! It was inexcusable.

That afternoon I drove to Pretoria, and on the way saw a car skid and crash. As it turned over, legs were waving in the air; like an insect on its back. For a minute I was the only person present, and got out of my car to approach the overturned one, again with no clear notion of what I should do. The waving legs were subsiding; now with only an occasional faint twitch, and soon they were entirely motionless. Fortunately, others arrived on the scene, more capable than I; a doctor and an ambulance were procured, and I drove on to Pretoria more subdued than ever. There I called at Army Headquarters to see an officer I knew in the Intelligence Branch. He was in a Nissen hut, the set-up so like 5 Corps that I almost forgot myself and gave a noisy salute on entering. I told him the whole story of what had happened, only omitting my abortive encounter with Wertz's man that morning. I cannot say that he seemed particularly surprised. When, after the war, Dr Malan became Prime Minister, I was interested to read in *The Times* that one of the first acts of the new Government was to raid this particular office and remove some documents. I think I know what they were, and may even have made a tiny contribution to them myself.

When I got back to Lourenço Marques, feeling very dispirited, I was disconcerted to find that my house was in a state of great confusion, as though it had been burgled. Then I remembered that the burglary had been arranged with Johann to offset any suspicion that he might be responsible for tipping us off about Wertz's emissary to South Africa. As now Wertz would never know that we had been tipped off, I reflected bitterly, the burglary was unnecessary. The only pleasing feature of it was that, among documents left around for Johann to find and pass on to Wertz, was a bogus memorandum, purportedly addressed to me, to the effect that very little information of late seemed to have been coming from Campini, and asking whether it was worth while going on making substantial payments to him. This malign suggestion seems to have registered in Wertz's mind.

From South Africa I was summoned to Cairo to discuss the possibility of using our contacts in Lourenço Marques for the purpose of disseminating deception material. The officer I had to see was Peter

Fleming, whom I had vaguely known for a number of years. We were both staying in Shepherds Hotel, and met in his room, where he was still unpacking, looking, even more than usually, like a beautifully polished piece of furniture – a tallboy, say, or grandfather clock. While he was talking, he absent-mindedly picked up one of his bush-shirts, and touched the crown on its shoulder-strap very gently; like a jeweller picking up and handling some rare stone. He told me that his boss, Colonel Dudley-Clark, would shortly be arriving in Cairo, having, as he put it, God-high priority. He repeated this expression 'God-high priority' several times, as though it established Dudley-Clark's eminence, and the importance attached to his deception activities, which were, as a matter of fact, extremely successful, especially at the time of the Normandy landings. When he finally appeared – by no means as soon as his God-high priority might have led one to expect – he turned out to be a sharp little man with bright, quick eyes, who easily explained to me what he wanted put about in Lourenço Marques – rumours of imaginary Allied plans for invading the continent to put the enemy off the scent of the actual intention to land in Normandy. In this field, too, the results of one's labours, if any, could be monitored at Bletchley, where the injection of the deception virus showed, and then the degree to which it had taken in the enemy's blood stream and nervous system. All Intelligence roads seemed to end in this rather drab little town, hitherto only known as a railway junction; that ritual game of rounders turned out to be a masque of victory.

I spent my time in Cairo wandering about, and trying, without much success, to find old haunts and old acquaintances. The town was full of troops; and GHQ Middle East itself – within whose perimeter an MI6 contingent was installed – covered a large area. There were still a few British civilians to be seen. I overheard one of them at the Gazira Club complaining about the influx of war-time officers as honorary members. The next time I went to Cairo, shortly after the disastrous Suez venture, British nationals were being treated like displaced persons, and Shepherds Hotel, where Peter Fleming and I waited for Dudley-Clark to descend on his God-high priority, had been razed to the ground.

For the moment, however, our position seemed solid enough. The threat of an Axis occupation – which at one point led shopkeepers to lay in stocks of German and Italian bunting – had receded, and over my morning tea I read in the *Egyptian Gazette* the exhilarating headline: AFRIKA KORPS IN FULL RETREAT. An additional satisfaction for me personally was that it meant my job in Lourenço Marques, such as it was, must now be considered over, since troopships would once more be able to use the Mediterranean instead of going round the Cape and up the Mozambique Channel. This knowledge made me more than ever bored and restless when I got back to Lourenço Marques. In every job I have ever had the same thing has always happened – after an energetic start, I have lost interest in it, and spent my time coasting along and waiting to make off. This, I may add, excludes writing, which, as far as I am concerned, is not a job at all, but a necessity; like breathing, or circulating one's blood.

It was in this lack-lustre mood at the end of my time in Lourenço Marques that I became involved in an adventure, at once foolish, squalid and heart-rending. It concerned Hélène, a dancer at a night-club in Lourenço Marques called the Café Penguin. Serge brought her to lunch with the idea that she might be useful, speaking, as she did, French, Spanish, and Portuguese, and having, by the nature of her profession, many contacts among local officials and visiting shady characters. She was, as I learnt afterwards, partly Greek, but had lived and worked in Portugal and Spain; her face, with its large nose and small chin, reminded me vaguely of one of those Egyptian heads in the Cairo Museum. Her voice was rather hoarse, her clothes cheap-looking and flashy; but there was something bright and brave about her that I found appealing.

We spoke over lunch, I remember, sententiously about how people's attitudes towards one changed with one's material situation, and how rare was affection which was wholly disinterested. She obviously enjoyed herself, and promised to come again and prepare a Spanish meal for us. This proved difficult to arrange, and in the end I took her to lunch at Costa da Sol, a restaurant by the sea. Again, our conversation was inclined to be sententious; and without much conviction, since I was thinking of getting away from Lourenço Marques at the earliest possible moment. I broached the question of her keeping her eyes and ears open on my behalf at the Café Penguin. To this, she eagerly agreed. Out in the sunshine, she looked very made up, with black glistening hair; and her coquetry seemed excessive, if not professional. I felt ill-at-ease, and even a little ashamed, to be seen in her company. Then one evening by chance I went with Hunt to the Café Penguin. It was quite a small place; some tables, mostly occupied, a tired orchestra, upstairs a gambling casino, a few faded taxi-girls, lights turned down for the dancing. At about midnight the cabaret began. First a young Spanish girl singing, strutting about, exposing her youthfulness; then Hélène, vigorous with her castanets, and much applauded. Afterwards she came and sat at our table, and at 2 a.m., when the orchestra stopped, I took her home, Hunt having already left. In the car, inevitably, being rather drunk, I made a lurch in her direction. She was astonished, truly astonished: *'J'avais beaucoup de considération pour vous,'* she said in a flat, sad voice. It was not exactly a reproach; much worse than that. No words ever spoken to me, I think, have echoed more wretchedly in my ears, and made me feel more sick with myself.

After this, I went to the Penguin quite often, though I hated the place. Alcohol helped me through the evening till 2 a.m. Hélène, I found, was really two people. She was by nature rather sad and melancholic, liable to say that her life was a *futilité*, or: *'Je ne suis pas une femme pour un quart d'heure,'* or, when I asked her why she was crying: *'Je n'ai pas le droit de pleurer.'* Then, when other people were around, she would assume her professionally gay manner, with the exaggerated coquetry, the too elaborate smile and the too studied gesture. I liked her best when she talked about her own life; about her difficulties with the proprietor of the Penguin, in arranging a new dance, or in insisting on her position as an *artiste* as distinct from a *papillon* or taxi-girl. Once we went into the country on a Sunday, when she wore blue trousers, a red blouse and an enormous straw hat with ribbons. The effect was somehow indescribably poignant. On the way back she sang little Spanish songs, all sad; then when we got to my house and she heard voices upstairs, she at once put on her other manner, becoming a shepherdess in a bawdy French farce.

On one occasion she showed that she had strong nerves. We were driving along a straight road with trees planted on each side, and suddenly the car got totally out of control, lurched across the road, just missed running straight into one of the trees; then came to a standstill. Hélène was perfectly calm, more so than I was. It turned out that a vital part in the steering apparatus had been removed, and as I, very foolishly, had been going to a garage run by an Italian, it was reasonable to assume that Campini was responsible. When, after Italy's collapse, he was interrogated at length, he described how he used to see me going for my morning swim, and had a strong compulsion then to run me over himself. Another time, on an impulse, I took Hélène upstairs to the gambling – something I have always intensely disliked, as the pornography of cupidity – and won three centos straight off, to the great annoyance of the proprietor. I gave them to her, and she stowed them away on her person with great satisfaction.

It was now that the absurdity, the futility, the degradation of how I had been living seized me with irresistible force. The fact that my activities were nominally related to the conduct of war, and might even be interpreted as having been, within their own preposterous terms of reference, effective, even successful and deserving of commendation, only made them the more distasteful to me. One particular night, after returning from the Penguin, I lay on my bed full of stale liquor and despair; alone in the house, and, as it seemed, utterly alone, not just in Lourenço Marques, in Africa, in the world. Alone in the universe, in eternity, with no glimmer of light in the prevailing blackness; no human voice I could hope to hear, or human heart I could hope to reach; no God to whom I could turn, or Saviour to take my hand. Elsewhere, on battlefields men were killing and dying. I envied them; it was a solution and a solace of sorts. After all, the only bearable thing about war is the killing and the dying. That is its point. In the Blitz, with, as I thought, London falling about my ears, I had felt a kind of contentment; here in this remote forgotten corner of the world, I fell into the final abyss of despair. Deprived of war's only solace – death, given and received, it came into my mind that there was, after all, one death I could still procure. My own. I decided to kill myself.

It was before the days of barbiturates; otherwise, I should have certainly swallowed a bottle of them then and there, and not be writing these words. The notion of blowing my brains out – apart from the fact that the only weapon I had was the little pistol acquired at Sheerness when the fugitive French troops arrived there; a shaky and unreliable instrument for this or any other purpose – had the disadvantage, that, so dying, my children could not but know that their father had taken his own life in this particularly squalid way. I decided that the best thing to do was to drown myself. Somewhere I had read that drowning was like falling asleep in the sea. So, I would make of my death one last morning bathe; these bathes being, I reflected, with unctuous misery, the only part of my life in Lourenço Marques that had remained uncontaminated. It was all ridiculously easy. I put on my clothes, got into my car and drove to the sea shore, leaving no notes because I wanted my death to seem like an accident. It was known that I often bathed at unseasonable hours, so there would be nothing out-of-the-way in my having decided to take a dip in the middle of the night, swum out too far, and been unable to get back, with no possibility of being heard when I cried out for help. A telegram to Kitty from Ledger; deeply regret, etc., etc.; grief in Whatlington, but not shame; the end of a relationship, which had been full of separations and betrayals, but also of joy and intimacy. Basically, however, constructed out of the rubble of a broken-down way of life. A shanty structure built on a bomb site, with no foundations, and, at best, no more than a corrugated iron roof.

All the same, at this moment of anguish that I believed to be my last, it was of Kitty, and Kitty alone, that I thought; wondering about her, caring about her, and about no one and nothing else. (The children, also; but only as part of her.) 'Only death will part us,' she had said to me on the night before I left for Lisbon; and now the death I proposed to find would fulfil her words. She was not so much someone I loved as part of me; we had been grafted together to become one. Nothing could alter this; not even my cowardly decision to end a life I could no longer endure. Our union was more, infinitely more, than the means sought to unite us. The clumsy gropings after unity of the flesh – licking the earth, as Pascal calls it; the even more ridiculous gropings after unity of mind, a Sidney and a Beatrice Webb laboriously assembling their facts, jointly stating their conclusions. Perhaps most preposterous of all, the gropings after unity of the spirit; two upturned faces marvelling in unison at the Sistine Chapel, tapping their feet in unison and wagging their heads to Beethoven's Ninth, Brecht, their amour, wit and wisdom of Shaw their edification, Karl Marx and the Brothers their loadstar and their mirth. Such was not the union I had defaced, but something infinitely more profound and enduring. From the depths of the trough into which I had fallen, my soul cried to depart.

I drove to the furthest point along the coast road, some six miles from Lourenço Marques, and there got out of the car and undressed. The lights were still on in Peter's Café and Costa da Sol. As the tide was far out, I had to wade on and on before there was enough water to swim in. So this was the end of my life, my last little while on earth. I kept on trying to think of the French word for 'drown'. Everything seemed to me unreal – had there been a single moment in my life when I had truly lived? Everything false – love, hate, happiness, despair, all equally false. Even this dying seemed false. Was it me, wading on to the open sea? Was it really happening? The bottom I trod on was muddy now, the water creeping up and cold, the air damp. At last there was enough water to swim in. I started swimming, the dark water churning white as my arms beat through it. Soon I was out of my depth, and still swam on. Now I felt easy, now it was settled. Looking back I could scarcely see the shore; only the lights of Peter's Café and Costa da Sol, far, far, away. I began to tremble, all my body trembled; I went under the water, trembling, came up again and reposed myself as though on a bed. I could sleep on this watery mattress, sleep. Then, suddenly, without thinking or deciding, I started swimming back to shore. I was very tired, and kept feeling if I was in my depth again, and wasn't; I shouted foolishly for help, and kept my eyes fixed on the lights of Peter's Café and the Costa da Sol.

They were the lights of the world; they were the lights of my home, my habitat, where I belonged. I must reach them. There followed an overwhelming joy such as I had never experienced before; an ecstasy. In some mysterious way it became clear to me that there was no darkness, only the possibility of losing sight of a light which shone eternally; that our clumsy appetites are no more than the blind reaching of a newly born child after the teat through which to suck the milk of life; that our sufferings, our affliction, are part of a drama – an essential, even an ecstatic, part – endlessly revolving round the two great propositions of good and evil, of light and darkness. A brief interlude, an incarnation, reaching back into the beginning of time, and forward into an ultimate fulfilment in the universal spirit of love which informs, animates, illuminates all creation, from the tiniest particle of insentient matter to the radiance of God's very throne.

Now I felt the bottom, and began to wade laboriously back to the shore, reaching it by the estuary of a river, a long way away from where I had first gone into the sea. All round me was deep black mud, through which, shaking with cold, I floundered, until, by luck more than any sense of direction, I saw my car where I had left it. Even at the time I realised, and realise now ever more clearly, that this floundering was a sort of parable. Plodding and floundering on through the black deep mud, but never again without hope; thenceforth always knowing, deep in my heart, remembering even when I forgot, that it was not by chance or for nothing that the lights of Peter's Café and Costa da Sol had called me back. That I, too, had something I must try to say and be, until the time came for God to put me to sleep, as I had tried, in my own fatuous and sinful wilfulness, to put myself to sleep in the sea off Lourenço Marques. When, finally, I reached my car and my clothes, the morning was just breaking; the black African sky just beginning to be tinged with grey. I breathed in the dawn air, greedily; after all, I was still alive.

Though I scarcely realised it at the time and subsequently only very slowly and dimly, this episode represented for me one of those deep changes which take place in our lives; as, for instance, in adolescence, only more drastic and fundamental. A kind of spiritual adolescence, whereby, thenceforth, all my values and pursuits and hopes were going to undergo a total transformation – from the carnal towards the spiritual; from the immediate, the now, towards the everlasting, the eternal. In a tiny dark dungeon of the ego, chained and manacled, I had glimpsed a glimmer of light coming in through a barred window high above me. It was the light of Peter's Café and Costa da Sol calling me back to earth, my mortal home; it was the grey light of morning heralding another day as I floundered and struggled through the black mud; it was the light of the world. The bars of the window, as I looked more closely, took on the form of a Cross.

The next day I took the precaution of reporting to London, giving the impression that I had gone through the motions of trying to drown myself as a deliberate ruse to delude Wertz into thinking I had completely lost heart. In the end I began to wonder whether, after all, it *had* been a ruse. In all deception, whether of governments, or demagogues, or press lords, or media pundits, or advertisers, down to little con-men and columnists and street-corner *exaltés* – the ultimate doom is that the deceiver comes to believe his own deceits. Wertz heard from Johann what had happened, and duly sent a long message on my suicide attempt, which he attributed to despair at my inability to measure up to him in Intelligence work. It was in this message that he so exaggerated the importance of my position in the Allied Intelligence network in East Africa in order to enhance his own achievement in laying me low. Graham Greene, who was back in London now, and dealing with my telegrams, as well as seeing the Wertz intercepts, minuted that he was sceptical about my explanation of the suicide attempt, and considered it to have been genuine. With his novelist's eye, he understood.

When I left Lourenço Marques for good, Nero's daughter, Susie, was allowed to come with me in the launch that took passengers out to the flying-boat. So the last thing I saw as we climbed into the sky was her long yellow hair. When we got to Kampala, in Uganda, I was afflicted with acute abdominal pains, and rushed to hospital for an emergency appendix operation. I rather doubt if this was really necessary. Indeed, when I was under the anaesthetic, before it had fully taken effect, I overheard two doctors talking in Scottish accents, and one of them was saying to the other that the operation seemed rather precipitate, but they might as well go ahead now. Illness, in my experience, is often a device for opting out for a while. Even so, according to the doctor who cut me open, my appendix was in poor shape. I only stayed in the hospital five days, and then managed to get on a Belgian plane to Lagos. What I remember most about Kampala hospital is how gentle the African nurses were, with their smiling faces and clumsy, kindly hands.

At Lagos I was met and taken to an SOE establishment there, being still rather weak and inactive. A seat had been booked for me on a plane to England the next day, but a colonel with a wooden leg claimed priority, and took my place. This priority game was played in all the transit camps; junior officers whose places were constantly being pre-empted by majors and colonels and brigadiers, were liable to be stuck in one of them for weeks at a time. One saw them, unshaved, wild-eyed, rushing out in packs whenever a plane landed or took off, in case some last-minute cancellation left a seat vacant. I felt pretty annoyed myself with the one-legged colonel, until I learnt that the plane in which he had taken my place ran into the mountains round Shannon Airport and crashed with no survivors. As Kitty had been alerted that I was on this plane, when I did turn up it was as one risen from the dead. My welcome would, I am sure, have been warm in any case, but in the circumstances it was positively ecstatic, and added to my own wonderful sense of homecoming; of being in contact with something real and lasting after my fantasy life in Lourenço Marques. It was tempting to regard my ejection from the crashed plane as a kind of miracle (as, when he was serving in the army in the Civil War, Bunyan did his replacement by another soldier, who was subsequently killed in a siege; this being, incidentally, his only reference to the Civil War in all his writings), but on reflection such a view seemed disrespectful to the memory of the one-legged colonel, who would certainly see the incident in a different light.

4 *The Victor's Camp*

... Justice, that fugitive from the Victor's camp.

> – Simone Weil

When truth conquers with the help of 10,000 yelling men – even supposing that that which is victorious is truth; with the forms and manner of the victory a far greater untruth is victorious.

> – Kierkegaard

AFTER SOME SICK-LEAVE, I reported back to Section Five, now installed in Ryder Street in premises that were subsequently to house the *Economist*; an appropriate succession. Everything seemed very much the same as it had been at St Albans, with Philby more than ever the dominant personage. He still, when working at his desk, wore his father's old 1914–18 war officer's tunic, and still had his same little circle of ardent admirers. My performance in Lourenço Marques – which looked so much better in the telegrams than when actually happening – was considered to have been impressive, and earned me a certain prestige, but I never felt other than an outsider when I was with Philby and his friends. They were altogether more serious than I was about our plans and stratagems, and found my derisory attitude towards SIS, and refusal to accept the USSR as the one just Power engaged in the war, particularly distasteful.

Occasionally quite sharp arguments developed. I cannot recall that Philby ever joined in these, save once – and that might have been significant. It arose out of someone complaining very bitterly that invaluable intelligence from Bletchley relating to the enemy order of battle and operations on the Eastern Front was being withheld from the Russians for fear that they might compromise the source. I argued that such caution was legitimate, especially in view of the way the Russians had passed on to the Germans everything they knew about us and our intentions during the period of the Nazi-Soviet Pact. Another similar occasion for treachery might arise, and we were right to guard against it. In any case, Stalin was bound to disbelieve anything coming officially from the Allies, and assume it to be provocation; as he had when Stafford Cripps, as British Ambassador in Moscow, informed him – correctly, as it turned out – of the date and place he must expect a German attack on the USSR. This line of talk for once infuriated Philby, who spluttered and shouted that we were in duty bound to do everything within our power, whatever it might be, to support the Red Army, including risking – if there was a risk – the security of the Bletchley material.

It occurred to me afterwards, when Philby's double-cross was officially admitted, that it might have been this particular issue, on which he felt so strongly, that first involved him in illicitly handing over documents to the Russians. Giving them intercepts relating to the Eastern Front was something he would certainly have considered it to be perfectly proper and honourable to do, and from this start he could easily have got fully enmeshed. We shall probably never know for sure, but I find the possibility more plausible than that he was specifically a Soviet agent – on the books, as it were – from his undergraduate days. In any case, if he had been a fully fledged Soviet agent at the time, it is reasonable to assume that he would have been supplying the Russians with Bletchley material anyway, and so would have kept out of any dispute about the rights and wrongs of so doing. Incidentally, I learnt from Alexander Foote, who had been the radio operator in the famous Lucy Ring in Switzerland, that, in fact, Stalin *was* getting the requisite Bletchley material. It was being sent to him via the Lucy Ring; acquired, purportedly, from sources in the German High Command. This, given its detail and invariable accuracy, was quite inconceivable. It could, in fact, only have come from Bletchley. I found it highly appropriate that Stalin could only be persuaded to believe in the reliability of Allied Intelligence if it reached him from an undercover network on a dubious channel.

I got to know Foote after the war, when he was working as a clerk at the Ministry of Agriculture and Fisheries, then located in Regent's Park near where I was living. He used to drop in for a chat on his way home; a large stolid-looking Yorkshireman, who could be very funny about his time in the USSR and the training in espionage methods that he was given – no less fatuous, I was relieved to learn, than our own essays in the same field. He went there in the first place as a drop-out of the depression years and a Communist sympathiser, and then managed to get himself trained for a foreign espionage mission with a view to being sent abroad. By this means, in due course he got to Berlin, where he re-defected. When the 1939–45 war began he made his way to Switzerland, to be taken on there by the Lucy Ring. No one could have been less like the popular idea of a secret agent – he was much more like an insurance agent, or possibly a professional cricketer – but he had developed a taste for clandestinity, and found his overt life with Ag. and Fish. very tedious.

Philby had lately moved into a new smart house in Chelsea, which was still being decorated when I visited him there. Given wartime conditions, it struck me as surprisingly luxurious, and knowing that his pay would scarcely extend to such a style of living, I assumed – wrongly as it turned out – that his wife Eileen must have private means. I should perhaps point out that all SIS salaries were supposed to be a closely guarded secret, kept even from the Inland Revenue men by making them tax-free. Actually, of course, we all knew what everyone else got. Looking back, it seems clear that at some point Philby's income must have been substantially augmented from Soviet sources – something that would certainly have played a part in his suborning. He was by nature generous, extravagant and hospitable, and so liable to be impecunious and in dire need of money. The Russians were adept at taking advantage of such personal situations.

In his new home, with his wife and children round him, he seemed particularly cheerful and well content, but I thought I detected a shadow over Eileen's face from time to time. I heard afterwards that she had some sort of mental collapse, which may well have been due to getting an inkling of what her husband was up to. I always found her especially sympathetic; if only because, in the rather exotic company in which Philby habitually moved, she seemed as alien and vaguely uneasy as I felt. When I said how nice the house was, and how pleasant for them all to be settled there together, Philby told me that Eileen and the children, like other MI6 families in London, were shortly moving into the country. It seemed that the Bletchley material clearly indicated some new devastating development in the German air offensive – as it turned out, the use of V weapons. It strikes me as curious now that I cannot recall making any use of this information myself; either to alert Kitty and our friends, or just to show off by dropping dark hints about what lay ahead.

Trevor Wilson was already in Algiers, having gone there when the

Allied landings took place in November 1942. It was decided that I should join him and take over liaison duties with the *Securité Militaire*, whose head was Commandant Paiolle. While waiting to leave for Algiers, I spent my time fraternising with the French, and getting to know the various warring factions, ranging between straight Vichyist and straight Gaullist, all with supporters and patrons in SIS, SOE, and OSS, to whom they could look for money, supplies and patronage. One of the most ardent Vichyist supporters in SIS was Claude Dansey, a veteran of many intrigues, and by this time at odds with most of his fellow-Broadway *apparatchiks*. He summoned me to come and see him, for no reason that I could discover except that he wanted to have a look at me. We sat for a half an hour or so, staring at one another across his desk, and exchanging banalities. I carried away an impression of a grey, tired, angry face; an adroit player in a game whose rules had been changed beyond recognition.

Personally, I felt drawn to the Gaullists from the beginning; I found Jacques Soustelle, de Gaulle's Intelligence chief – a brilliant anthropologist who had been Assistant Director of the *Musée de l'Homme* in Paris in his twenties – more interesting and easier to talk to than his rivals, most of whom were professionals, and very military in their bearing and attitudes. Also, I felt sure the Gaullists would win in the long run anyway. The other factions had no leader who could compare with de Gaulle; the alternatives produced by Churchill and Roosevelt – Weygand, Giraud – being derisory. The first glimpse I had of de Gaulle in the flesh was in the lift in the Connaught Hotel where he was staying. I was struck at once by the woebegoneness of his expression; but more like a clown's than a martyr's. The face of a man born to lead a lost cause, with the additional sorrow that it would ostensibly triumph.

The London Gaullists proved, on closer acquaintance, to be a curious collection of zealots and adventurers, some, like Passy (de Wavrin), belonging to the extreme Right, others, like Soustelle, to the Left, with all sorts of variants – devout Catholics and anti-clericals, civil servants, admirals and professors (whose numbers noticeably augmented as the Gaullist cause prospered), and other miscellaneous hangers-on – united only in their devotion and allegiance to their aloof, ungainly leader, with whom most of them had barely exchanged a word, and whose very names he was liable to confuse. I went in and out of their various offices, dotted about in the region of St James's Street, lunched with them at the Écu de France, where most days a row of *képis* was to be seen in the

cloak-room; had talks with them at Ryder Street, and briefed myself
by reading Section Five's own collection of their communications at
home and abroad – a field which Bletchley in no wise neglected. It is
sad now to reflect that the person of them all I should most like to have
known – Simone Weil – was at that very time sitting in one of their
offices preparing the document, subsequently published as *The Need
for Roots (Enracinement)*, which made so profound an impression on
me.

When, through my friend Richard Rees – now alas dead – I first
became acquainted with Simone Weil's life, it was this part, in London
with the Gaullists, that I found most poignant, doubtless because I
was so familiar with the scene, and thus could the more readily imagine
her reactions. She managed to get to London under the auspices of
André Philippe and Maurice Schumann, and hoped to be dropped in
occupied France to join the Resistance. This, of course was quite
impossible, if only because of her noticeably Jewish appearance. Her
temperament, also, unfitted her; as Soustelle (who was with her at the
famous *École Normale Supérieure*) remarked to me once, her kingdom
was not of this world, whereas the Resistance was. I think she must have
suffered, too, through what would have struck her as the essentially
worldly, if not frivolous, attitude most of the Gaullists had towards
what she thought of as their sacred mission to liberate France. De
Gaulle himself said of her: *'Elle est folle'*, as in a sense she was, but with
the madness that St Paul commended to the first Christians. In the
end, she was bitterly disillusioned with the Gaullists and Gaullism, and
actually wrote a letter resigning her post. Her passionate sense of
identification with the French in their suffering led her to insist that she
must eat no more than would have been available to her in France,
where by this time, in theory at any rate, rationing was very strict. The
result was that she in effect starved herself to death. I cannot help
feeling that, in taking this decision, the row of *képis* in the Écu de
France, may well have been in her mind.

The Gaullists had not known what to do with her, and so had given
her the task of considering the various moral and social problems that
would arise when France's Liberation was achieved. Few of them read,
and none heeded, her brilliantly perceptive analysis of the dilemmas the
post-Liberation situation would present, but it may well prove to be
the case, when the final accounting is made, that *The Need for Roots*
will be seen to represent the only lasting achievement attributable to
the Gaullist presence in London. Simone Weil's death took place at a

sanatorium in Ashford, the coroner's verdict being that it was suicide. Thinking about this long afterwards by the stone that marks her burial place, it occurred to me that it was perhaps a special mercy, to spare her the agony she would undoubtedly have suffered at the spectacle of what actually happened when France was, *soi disant*, liberated. She was quite on her own when she died, so was buried in a pauper's grave, thus achieving in death what she had so ardently sought in life – identification with the poorest and lowliest of her fellow-humans.

Algiers, when I got there, was teeming; like a boom town when oil has been struck or gold discovered. Everyone moving about eagerly and energetically, talking, gesticulating; many varied uniforms, male and female, to be seen. In the hot summer nights, with the stars bright in the sky, no one wanted to go to bed. I joined the throng myself, drifting along with the others; an officer again, in khaki drill, a crown on my shoulder, having been advanced one notch on resuming military status. From HM's Vice-Consul to major. There I stayed, a major to the end; it sounded better in French – *mon commandant*. What particularly excited us all was that Algiers seemed so unmistakably French, with policemen in blue carrying white truncheons, blowing whistles and directing traffic, just as if they were in the Place de la Concorde; with cafés sprawling onto the pavements, and waiters in white coats sweating profusely as they miraculously steered trays of drinks to those who had ordered them, and, above all, that composite smell of *gaulloise* tobacco smoke, cheap scent and *pissoirs* which still, across half a century now, carries me back to the first time I stepped off a Channel steamer and found myself on French soil. Algiers was a half-way house to France.

The SIS contingent had established themselves in a large Arab house high up above Algiers, presided over by a handsome naval captain in a white uniform with a row of interesting looking ribbons. There, the spy-masters lived together, operating into Italy, Jugoslavia, Greece and adjacent territories. Our Section Five office was downtown, in the Rue Charras; a busy street, more in keeping with Trevor Wilson's temperament, to which noise and confusion were congenial. He was a short, unaccountable man with a toothbrush moustache, who had been a bank-manager in France; knew the language perfectly, but spoke it in a strange muttering whisper, with his head bent down, and usually a cigarette in his mouth which got affixed to his upper or lower lip, wagging with his words. In this manner he would carry on a running monologue, only partially comprehensible, and whether in English or

French barely discernible; in any case, broken up by sudden furious exclamations, as: 'Where's that fool Brent?' – Brent being our long-suffering driver. Nonetheless, he managed to get inside the skin of our French associates in a unique way; something for which having to decide, in his capacity as bank manager, whether or not to grant an overdraft to some peasant farmer or small tradesman or industrialist, doubtless provided an inestimable training. Take him for all in all, he was about the ablest Intelligence officer I met in the war, with an instinctive flair for the work, including all the deceits and double-crosses involved.

His own opinions were fanatically held and frenetically expounded. He leant, if anywhere, in the direction of Maurras and the *Action Française*, which did not, incidentally, prevent him from being on the best of terms with Philby, whom he enormously admired and endlessly praised; one fanaticism, in my experience, finding another congenial, irrespective of its ideology. At this time, he was violently anti-Gaullist, to the point that if, driving about in Algiers, he happened to see the General, solitary and sedate, in the back of his car, he would actually shake his fist and shout abusively: 'Look at him! Look at him!' He correspondingly admired de Gaulle's rival, General Giraud, who enjoyed the support of the Allies; the Americans in particular. Algiers was plastered with posters displaying a message from Giraud: UN SEUL BUT: LA VICTOIRE! I myself felt instinctively, but did not say, that Giraud hadn't a chance; especially after I saw a photograph of the two generals shaking hands in the presence of Roosevelt and Churchill – like a seal and a hippopotamus nibbling the same bun under the eyes of their keepers at the Zoo. It was, indeed, soon after this fraternisation that Giraud just seemed to fade away.

Even Trevor Wilson's laughter was extreme; something would amuse him, and he would return to it again and again, laughing more hysterically each time. Once, for instance, someone remarked that Chinese sages were in the habit of cultivating a single strand of hair on their chins, till it grew to an inordinate length. This so took Trevor Wilson's fancy, that he almost exploded with mirth; I quite expected him to have a go at the fashion himself. His loves were as strong as his hates, and he handed over Paiolle – whom he revered – to me, as though dealing with him must be regarded as a sacred trust. We went along together to the *Sécurité Militaire*, then housed in some army hutments on the outskirts of Algiers; rather like Mytchett. The form in seeing Paiolle was invariable; on being admitted to his office by his adjutant, one saluted, with a '*mes respects, mon commandant*', and then shook hands. Commandant to commandant. First, causal observations were exchanged, followed by the business in hand – usually relating to a communication from London based on Bletchley material (which Paiolle was supposed to know nothing about, but did), pointing to a suspect, or requiring an investigation to be undertaken. This dealt with, more casual talk followed, and perhaps a drink, or lunch in the mess. One way and another, I saw a lot of Paiolle, and got to like him very much, but never to know him well, or to find talking to him easy, as I did with Soustelle. He was through and through a professional soldier, a St Cyr product; of a type I imagine to be now virtually obsolete in France. A dignified, handsome man; in all ways honourable and correct. The Gaullists were very hostile to him, and but for his close relations with us might easily have got him out: '*Le Général a voulu le saquer,*' Passy said to me once, *à propos* Paiolle. As it was, he managed to hold on; ultimately accepting the inevitable and serving under Soustelle.

Thenceforth I spent much time at the *Securité Militaire*, getting to know the other officers, and sometimes passing an evening with them in their *popotte*; which I was able to manage, but with nothing like Trevor Wilson's ease and panache. For one thing I lacked his capacity to drink vast quantities of what Paiolle called fire-water – very new brandy, the only liquor in good supply in Algiers just then. The aching boredom of some of these evenings weighed heavily upon me; especially the French dirty stories, which I found even longer and less funny than their English equivalents, and the marching songs which they had sung as cadets, and managed still to bellow out despite swelling stomachs and thinning hair.

Paiolle took me on a tour of North Africa, visiting units of the French army whose morale, reportedly shaky, he wanted to check. I was strongly reminded of the situation in India, though, as it turned out, the French had before them an even longer weariness to endure than had the upholders of the Raj, while their rule was being defended in order to be liquidated. The young officers were very touching; wondering what had gone wrong, and why their dedication and enthusiasm, and the – as they thought – loyalty of their Zouaves, seemed to count for nothing. The only really cheerful unit we visited was the Foreign Legion, consisting mostly of Germans, who, it appeared, were perfectly content to be ranged against their fellow-countrymen, though, had they wished to, by the terms of their enlistment, they could have contracted out when France declared war on Germany. I heard one of the legionaries singing a song as he polished his equipment, whose words continued to echo in my mind.'

> *Il y a des pierres dans toutes les routes*
> *Il y a des femmes dans tous les chemins.*

We drove along the coast road; pine trees and blue sky on one side of us, and the blue Mediterranean on the other. In Fez we stayed in the Citadel, in the middle of the town, guests of the then commander, a general with one arm. After dinner he and Paiolle went into the garden, walking up and down in earnest conversation. I watched them from my bedroom window, the distorted shadow cast by the one-armed general in the bright moonlight exaggerating his infirmity. While watching them, I heard a trumpet sounding the Last Post, announcing to the troops in the Citadel that the day was over.

Other people's empires tend to seem more tolerable than one's own, and in this last view I had of French North Africa I was reminded of stories and films which had excited me as a child rather than of the tirades of my father and his friends against the villainies of colonialism. The immediate impact and the colourfulness was stronger than the sense of outrage at the exploitation involved. Driving along, Paiolle and I talked about the assassination of Admiral Darlan in December 1942, which fell so conveniently for all concerned (perhaps even including Darlan himself, who may well have felt himself at the end of the road), that many assumed it must have been planned, with the assassin, a young royalist named Bonnier de la Chapelle, a conscious or unconscious instrument. More probably, he was just, as I gathered from Paiolle, allowed to go about his business; like Van der Lubbe when he set fire to the Reichstag, or like Lee Oswald when he fired at President Kennedy in Dallas. History, like wood, has a grain in it which determines how it splits; and those in authority, besides trying to shape and direct events, sometimes find it more convenient just to let them happen.

A bearded British Council man kindly took me to tea with André Gide, who was staying in Algiers as the guest of a professor in the Rue Michelet. He had been wandering about in North Africa – a milieu that he found very much to his taste – and after the Allied landings, came to Algiers to, as it were, adjust himself to the new phase of Liberation that was obviously on the way. The adjustment was necessary because, from a Gaullist point of view, his comportment during the occupation had been somewhat equivocal. For me, it was an exciting visit even though I had not read much Gide – only *Si le Grain ne*

Meurt, and his two books on the USSR, the one highly adulatory and the other as highly critical. The fact that he was a famous writer was quite enough to make me feel more uplifted, as I climbed the steps to the apartment he was staying in, than if I had been about to make the acquaintance, at one and the same time, of General Eisenhower, President Roosevelt and King Farouk of Egypt. We found Gide sitting by an open window, and looking down at the Rue Michelet, up and down which GI's were endlessly passing, rolling their buttocks inside their tight uniform trousers in a way which is very characteristic of North Americans – so much so that even strangers settled briefly among them soon acquire it. For Gide, the spectacle, for obvious reasons, held a special attraction. I was aware at once of his grey, coldly luminous face; almost priestly in style – an impression enhanced by a skull-cap that he wore. But priestly on the Devil's side; the sanctity somehow foetid, the luminosity unearthly without being heavenly – studio lighting rather than light, an effect. Nonetheless, there was something enchanting about his words, as he chose them and used them, the timbre of his voice; so clear and so true, like the bells of those little Swiss churches sounding out on a Sunday morning in the chill mountain air.

At this time Gide was preparing his translation of *Hamlet*, and we discussed it briefly – translating being, for writers in ideological distress, a ready recourse; for instance, Pasternak, who also turned to Shakespeare. Gide was puzzling over some of the more obscure phrases – 'a bare bodkin', I seem to remember – but I was unable to offer any help. Then he described how he had been trying to meet John Steinbeck, whose work he greatly admired, and who was in Algiers as a war correspondent. Whenever he managed to get hold of him, Gide said, he was drunk. He had tried at different times – in the evening, at lunch-time, and finally at breakfast; but always with the same result – *Il etait soûl.* There was something very funny in this picture of the great Gide making sudden forays by day and by night to find Steinbeck sober; always without success.

I had a strong sense of something evil in Gide; not just in the way everyone has evil in them, but in a particular concentration that can be eerily attractive as well as repellent. This prevented me from truly appreciating his company. It was like being in some very beautiful place – say, the Duomo in Florence, or in Chartres Cathedral – when the drains have gone wrong. An exhalation from him hit me in a similar way. To believe in evil today is not considered permissible, or, if evil is allowed to exist, it tends to be elevated, as having some inherent creativity, beauty, joyousness, of its own. Yet what I saw in Gide was the terrible desolation of evil, the total alienation from the principle of goodness in all creation; he seemed to be imprisoned in darkness, like someone waking in a strange room, and looking in vain for a switch or a door or a window.

Inevitably, the subject of the USSR cropped up between us. Gide said that not being allowed to visit Russia any more was like a physical deprivation to him, he so longed to be there. I could understand this; quite irrespective of the Soviet regime, there is something about the people and the countryside, something in the very air one breathes, that exerts a tremendous pull. The impression I had was that Gide now regretted the break with the Soviet authorities that the publication of his second book about the USSR had caused, and looked back nostalgically on his first visit, when he was treated as an honoured guest, like any Bernard Shaw or Henri Barbusse. His disillusionment, in any case, seems to have resulted rather from the changed attitude to pederasty in the USSR, making its practice a penal offence, as it had been before the Revolution, than from any outraged sense of the injustice, inequality and cruelty Soviet rule involved for its ostensible beneficiaries. I was tempted to pass on to him something the British Consul-General in Algiers had told me. He had been instructed to present to Bogomolov, head of the Russian Mission, a list of Soviet nationals who had found their way to Algeria, and ask him what he wanted done about them. Bogomolov took a pencil and ticked the names of those who were forty and under. When the Consul-General asked what should be done about the others, he just shrugged expressively. So Alaric, King of the Visigoths, might have shrugged if someone had asked what should be done about the old and the sick when Rome was sacked.

The only person I had ever met who knew Gide was Alfred Douglas, and it was on the tip of my tongue to mention him to see how Gide would react; but I desisted, vaguely remembering all the rows and charges and counter-charges that had accompanied the notorious visit Wilde, Douglas and Gide paid to Algiers in 1895. Hugh Kingsmill and Hesketh Pearson took me to see Douglas towards the end of his life, when he was living in a small villa in Hove, and in the habit of taking his evening stroll along the promenade. Other local residents might well have been surprised if they had known who was in their midst. By this time he was a small shrivelled-up man with a large bulbous nose. As though to accentuate the disappearance of the beauty Wilde had so extravagantly praised, the walls of his little sitting-room were covered with portraits of himself as a young man; blazered, straw-hatted, exquisite. It was a narcissus room; the Dorian Gray story come to life. Douglas was still very indignant about Gide's scabrous account of their Algiers adventures. He told us how Robert Harborough Sherrard, Wilde's romantic champion, was in the habit of insisting, to refute Gide, that anyway Arab boys were not available in Algiers; but Douglas added softly: 'They are, you know; they are!' I didn't feel capable of conveying this scene to Gide, and, in any case, it would scarcely have been appreciated. We left him back at his window, watching the GI liberators rolling their buttocks up and down the Rue Michelet, and maybe meditating another foray to find Steinbeck sober. When I thought of his grey, cold face, and his exquisite words rising out of it, like a clear spring out of stony ground, it seemed more than ever fitting that the Devil should be a fallen angel.

This same bearded British Council man persuaded me to give a public lecture in French. The moment I had agreed to do it, actuated, no doubt, more by vanity than good-nature, the prospect of actually standing up and holding forth in French became a nightmare, which, every time I contemplated it, filled me with panic fear. However, thanks to the kindly assiduous help of Bobby Barclay, who, fortunately for me, was in Algiers, I managed to produce a text, and to stumble through it without breaking down. The audience carried me back to my Cairo days; even in war-time Algiers there were nooks and crevices where devotees of culture lurked, ready to sally forth when a suitable occasion offered; as well as a certain number of Anglo-French and American *littérateurs* who had begun to gather in the wake of the advancing Allied forces, like white penguins behind a plough. The theme of my address (the text has, I am thankful to think, long since disappeared) was my joy as an Englishman at being in Algiers, where I felt nearer to France than ever I had since the war began, and how I had been going over in my mind all the different reasons, seldom expressed but deeply felt, that France meant so much to us on our side of what Churchill had called our moat. It might have been Charles Morgan or André Maurois speaking. I must have laid it on pretty thick because there was positive acclaim at the end, and I found myself for a day or so in some social demand. I am always surprised when anything I do is well received. Also disconcerted, since, I can never manage, ultimately, to persuade myself that what is applauded is ever any good. In this particular case, my predilection received abundant verification.

At our MI6 establishment up on the hill I was particularly taken with one of the faces. It was older and more mature than the others, more, properly speaking, a face; like some ancient manuscript, creased and smudged, rather than mint-fresh off the rotary presses, and done in tens, if not hundreds, of thousands of exemplars. The name he went by – Adrian Hunter – was obviously a *nom de guerre*; and I learnt later, when we had become intimate, that he was none other than the von Strachwitz who had been exchanged for Johann following his abortive assassination attempt in Austria. After being thus exchanged, Adrian just managed to get away from Vienna before the *Anschluss*, and made for London, where he allowed himself to be recruited by SIS, being convinced that the Nazis meant war, and nothing but war. We spent many of our evenings talking together, and laughing – in my case, jeering – at the young spy-masters, who, with a seemingly infallible instinct, supported, supplied and financed the Communist guerrillas who were already preparing their own offensive to follow the final overthrow of the Nazis. When our war was won, theirs would begin. At one end of the scale, Adrian insisted, Roosevelt and Churchill did everything in their power to ensure that, when Germany finally collapsed, Stalin easily occupied and dominated the countries adjoining his frontiers, and, at the other, our young spy-masters showed a like determination so to arrange matters that, in countries further away, he was presented with a well-armed, well-financed and well-organised underground army.

To someone like Adrian, with his deep-seated Catholicism and sense of history, it all seemed crystal clear. He himself worked in the MI6 Jugoslav Section, where the others, much younger than he was, and Philby-like in their ways and attitude of mind, automatically assumed, for instance, that Mihailovitch must be dropped and Tito adopted as our man in Yugoslavia. Why? Adrian asked. Only because Mihailovitch was on our side, whereas Tito hated and despised every-thing we purported to stand for and believe in. We sat talking in this strain, looking down on the lights of Algiers, and on the Mediterranean beyond – the same coast from which Augustine in Hippo had watched the collapse of Rome as we were now watching the collapse of Christen-dom. Adrian's face, with its ironical creases and wrinkles, its tired eyes, which yet, behind their tiredness, held an impregnable serenity, was like a veritable map of what we were talking about.

Another favourite theme of Adrian's was of how the Allied strategists had unaccountably failed to push against the door Mussolini's fall left open. Here, of course, he was thinking of his Austria, and of how, as we both knew from Bletchley, the *Abwehr* actually withdrew from Italy when Mussolini was deposed, assuming that all was up; then, when nothing happened, drifted back, dumbfounded. The long, slow campaign up the peninsula was delayed still further when the Americans insisted on transferring all available troops from the Italian front to reinforce an operation into Southern France; surely one of the most bizarre in history, being against no one and serving no purpose – unless it was Stalin's. I went with Paiolle to Bastia in Corsica to watch the convoy leave – a majestic sight, if we hadn't known, from the empty order of battle, that there were no troops to oppose a landing and no military or strategic gain in effecting one. Not even Adrian in his darkest mood of prophesy foresaw the final *dénouement*, when the Anglo-American forces checked their advance, standing by while the Red Army occupied the countries of Eastern and Central Europe, never to be dislodged thence in our time. It is a curious and little noticed fact of history that it is the strong, not the weak, who are most prone to surrender, and that usually before they are even called upon so to do.

Adrian remained a friend till his death. After the war, he returned to live in Vienna, where he edited a magazine which provided a platform for his own conservative view, in matters ecclesiastical as well as political. On his visits to London we always met. On one of these occasions, he described to me how, late one evening in Vienna, he had happened to take a tram going in his direction. At one of its stops a drunk Red Army soldier had got on, and when he found that the tram would not be passing what was then the Soviet Zone, he pulled out a pistol and forced the driver to alter his route. Adrian just sat where he was, smiling drily to himself at being thus confronted with the brave new world that lay ahead, until, the Russian having been put down, the tram resumed its regular route. It was another parable to which I should have paid more heed.

Such considerations scarcely arose in AFHQ (Allied Forces Head-quarters), packed tight in the Hotel St Georges, where General Eisenhower reigned supreme. It was laid down that every staff post might be filled by a matching Anglo-American pair, so that instead of one colonel, two majors and four captains, there would be two colonels, four majors and eight captains, with the requisite in- and out-trays and other impediments. It seemed a cumbersome and expensive way of promoting Anglo-American understanding. To my great delight, I found Colonel Ross-Atkinson still at his old post in charge of what was now called Counter-Intelligence. His matching American had, I thought, a somewhat puzzled air, but they seemed to be on cordial terms. I dined with him one evening in his mess, and found that he was more prone than ever to fall asleep; but he still had the same rough, shrewd way of judging everyone and everything which I liked so much, and determination to stay with the Headquarters caravanserai till the end – as he succeeded in doing.

My only business with him now was to bring him occasionally a Bletchley intercept of special Security interest. This I had to do by hand, showing it to him, and then taking it away. Once, having shown him one of these intercepts – about enemy intimations of a forth-coming meeting between Roosevelt and Churchill – we got talking, and I forgot all about it. Back in the Rue Charras, I hunted through my brief-case and pockets, and there was no sign of it. Had I dropped the piece of paper somewhere? Or left it on Colonel Ross-Atkinson's desk? This was a hope, and I rushed back to the Hotel St Georges to find that his desk was bare and that he had gone to lunch. So I sat in his office waiting for his return, and woefully speculating on what was likely to happen to me. Should I be shot? Or just sent to the Glass-house? Or court-martialled and disgraced? To have lost a Bletchley intercept, thereby jeopardising the whole invaluable cipher-cracking operation, was the most serious offence I could possibly have com-mitted. When Colonel Ross-Atkinson returned, I explained my plight, and he was extremely sympathetic. We considered all the different possibilities, and when and to whom the loss should be reported. While we were thus talking, his clerk came in with a pile of papers, on the top of them being the lost intercept. It seemed that I had absent-mindedly put it in the out-tray while the Colonel and I were talking, and that it had been automatically circulated to various Headquarters branches, in none of which had it made any particular impression. This was vaguely disconcerting, considering the importance we attached to such material; but anyway the intercept was back, to my intense relief.

A regular duty I had was to attend a weekly conference on security matters presided over by Duff Cooper, who had arrived in Algiers as special emissary to de Gaulle's Provisional Government – which is what his CFLN (*Comité Français de Libération Nationale*) had now become. I used to look forward to this, as I liked Duff Cooper and admired his book on Talleyrand. The matters which came up for discussion at our meetings cannot have been very weighty, because I am unable now to remember one single item. I also grew fond of the Foreign Office official in attendance, Patrick Reilly, who has one of those wonderfully steady, clear minds I so admire, doubtless because my own is so unsteady and prone to obfuscation. These two favourites of mine – Duff Cooper and Reilly – both had, relatively speaking, disappointing careers; whereas the other governmental personage in Algiers – Harold Macmillan – who always struck me as a parody of a Conservative politician in a novel by Trollope, became Prime Minister.

It was at a picnic party given by the Duff Coopers (Lady Diana had joined him in Algiers) that I caught my only war-time glimpse of Evelyn Waugh. He had recently been involved, along with Randolph Churchill, in an air accident on their way to Jugoslavia, and looked a little shaken. I had the feeling that his uniform was not as smart as it was meant to be; likewise his moustache, which readers of his brilliant war trilogy will remember. Altogether, he seemed dispirited. We sat for a while side by side on a bench, and I recalled gratefully the very generous notice he had written in the *Spectator* of my book *In A Valley of This Restless Mind*. I knew that what I wrote and said afterwards disappointed him; in another notice, he spoke of the promise of 'serious interests' which had not been fulfilled.

Thereafter, on the few occasions that we met, it was always a matter, as Serge would have put it, of *Jouant la comédie*. For instance, at a literary luncheon for the publication of *The Ordeal of Gilbert Pinfold*, over which I presided, words I intended as homage to a writer and a book I greatly admired, turned into a meandering, facetious discourse, while Waugh himself engaged in a pantomime act with an ear-trumpet he then affected. Similarly, without any conscious intention on my part, a note of acrimony always seemed to come into anything I wrote about him – even his obituary. When I became editor of *Punch* he wrote me a gratifying letter saying that my appointment could be revolutionary in its consequences; but here, too, the results that followed were distasteful to him, and I declined to publish an article of his which I considered to be libellous.

Now that Waugh is dead, I greatly regret that I made no serious attempt to overcome our mutual antagonism. Probably I should have failed, but I wish I had tried. Most of his friends and admirers regarded him as a superb clown, or as a brilliant trafficker in nostalgia; but I saw him as like Bernanos, 'between the Angel of light and the Angel of darkness, looking at each in turn with the same enraged hunger for the absolute.' His true charity comes out in some letters he wrote to George Orwell in his last illness which I have read; perfectly phrased in their consideration for someone in affliction, despite the fact that, ostensibly at any rate, he and Orwell were, temperamentally, and in many of their opinions and aspirations, as opposed as any two writers could possibly be. I was given a last chance when he was staying in a rather dismal hotel in Menton, near Roquebrune, where Kitty and I had rented a villa. We used to see him sitting, as it seemed, disconsolately, in the lounge with a book in his hand. I had then an almost overpowering longing to go up and speak to him, and twice drafted a letter proposing a meeting, but in each case resisted the impulse through a cowardly fear of being repulsed or made to look foolish. When I heard the following Easter that he had died, I felt quite stricken; not just because he was so talented a writer and satirist, but because there would now never be another opportunity in this world to gather strength and courage from him for the lost battles that lie ahead.

I came into contact with his ghost in curious circumstances some years later. The Soviet writer, Anatole Kuznetsov, had sought asylum in England, and was staying with Waugh's mother-in-law, Mary Herbert, and her son Auberon Herbert, a long-standing and dear friend of mine. I was asked to interview Kuznetsov for BBC Television, and it was necessary to find a more or less clandestine location for fear that the KGB might seek a chance of organising his murder, as had happened in the case of other distinguished fugitives from the USSR. Evelyn Waugh's widow, Laura, kindly offered their house, and there we all duly assembled – cameraman, sound-recordist, David Floyd to be interpreter, Tony Smith and Peter Chafer as joint producers, and, of course, Kuznetsov himself.

It was a scene that the late owner of the house would scarcely have relished, but its piquancy on his premises would surely not have escaped him; and from the beginning I was conscious of his presence. Kuznetsov, as it turned out, was all too typically a Soviet product, with granite features, broad trousers, gold teeth and a fathomless conceit of himself. However hard we tried, it proved impossible to get him to assume the role of a literary Nureyev – which was greatly to his credit. Every time we took our eyes off him he raced over to a hired car that we had, got behind the wheel, and, never having driven before, began pulling the levers and releasing the brake, until the vehicle started moving, and he disappeared round a bend in the drive, to the great concern, particularly, of the MI5 men who were keeping an eye on the proceedings. In the house itself – a huge Victorian mansion with furniture to match – there was in the dining-room a bust of Waugh on whose head his war-time army cap had been placed; I thought I caught an ironical smile flitting about the mouth from time to time. We spent our evenings in Mary Herbert's house, with Auberon and Kuznetsov, who there seemed like an intruder into Brideshead; or, alternatively, to have been given an extra part written into a Soviet version of the *Forsyte Saga.*

Far the most interesting aspect, to me, of Intelligence operations was providing appropriate material (known as chicken feed) for transmission by enemy agents who had been turned round – that is, induced to go on functioning under control. This needed to be very carefully and subtly concocted; on the one hand, sufficiently high grade to impress their *Abwehr* masters, thereby building up their reputation; on the other, not so high grade that it gave away anything of major importance to us. Then, at the required moment, they could be used for deception purposes, at the risk, if necessary, of being blown. Fortunately for us all, Sir John Masterman, a dab hand at the business, has been allowed to publish his official record of just how this double-cross system functioned in the 1939–45 war. Here again, as he points out, the Bletchley material was invaluable, if not essential, since it enabled the credibility in the enemy's estimation of agents under our control to be continually checked, and any tricks they might try to engage in to be at once detected. It was astonishing how, on both sides in the war, agents continued to be believed in even when they had been under control for years, and regularly sending grossly misleading information. The reason was, I think, that the officers controlling double-cross agents became in time very fond and proud of them. After all, they gave them their words, and built up their fictitious characters, so that they were as much the creation of their officer-controllers as the characters in a novel are the novelist's. If one of them was awarded an enemy decoration – as sometimes happened, again on both sides – it added lustre to the whole operation; and when the time came to blow a double-cross agent for some ulterior purpose, the controlling officers were as grieved as Dickens was when he felt bound to kill off Little Nell. In time, as Sir John shows, all the enemy agents in the United Kingdom were brought under control and turned round, so that, in effect, he and his colleagues were running the *Abwehr's* British service for them. My impression is that they ran it better, and transmitted higher-grade material, than ever the *Abwehr* would have been able to manage on its own account. Which side in the war gained thereby is a difficult equation to work out.

In North Africa we had a number of turned-round enemy agents under control. There was, for instance, a well-born English beach-comber in Tangier who was so well in with the Germans that they continued to believe his reports even after he had persuaded them that the Allies' North African expedition was making for Dakar. Also, a French colonel stationed near Algiers who continued to function successfully right up to the end of the war, and who could today, if he cared to, wear an Iron Cross in one lapel and a *Croix de Guerre* in the other. An aspect of this use of turned-round agents which greatly appealed to our French colleagues was that it could be made to pay for itself, if not yield a handsome profit. There was nothing they liked better than getting our double-cross colonel to apply to his *Abwehr* masters for money, to be dropped by parachute in specie rather than notes, which, they made him say, were dangerously detectable. They also, at one point, being short of motor tyres, induced him to apply for some on the ground that if he were to try and buy them locally at the then prohibitive price, it would draw attention to him undesirably. A set duly arrived in an air-drop, which proved, incidentally, to be Dunlops. I made the suggestion that the colonel should send a message complaining of being troubled by his sexual appetites, to the point that it was impossible for him to concentrate on his work, and that he hesitated to avail himself of local facilities for fear of giving himself away. I had a picture in my mind of Rhine maidens floating down from the sky, but our French colleagues were more sceptical. The most that could be expected by way of response, they insisted, would be a supply of bromide.

War, Napoleon is alleged to have remarked, is a matter of mobility. This, I discovered, applies especially to Intelligence officers, who are always on the move; liaising, getting into and out of the picture, bustling about, here, there and everywhere, with their maps, their talcum, their coloured chalks. A stationary Intelligence officer is a contradiction in terms, like a sedentary eagle; he moves, therefore he is. As the Allied forces pressed forward in Italy, the area for roaming steadily enlarged. Thus, I visited Brindisi, where Marshal Badoglio set up his brief Government in the Hotel Imperiale, which likewise had to accommodate civil servants, service chiefs, advisers, envoys ordinary and extraordinary; all the miscellaneous camp-followers who

go racing after authority in all its guises, and however transitory its
tenure. Just as an alcoholic will, in the last resort, drink anything,
down to and including methylated spirits or surgical spirit, so the
power-addict will procure his fix on any terms. Governments on the
run, governments in exile, shadows of shadow-cabinets, all have their
jackals whose hands reach up for coloured ribbons, honorific titles,
imaginary portfolios and other such offerings of the great. At his trial,
Laval was able to point to one of the presiding judges, and recall that
the last time he had seen him was outside his office at Vichy, where
he was waiting to solicit a favour.

So, the Imperiale was teeming; under-secretaries sleeping in bath-
rooms, monsignoris dossing down on a couple of arm-chairs in the
hotel lounge, ambassadors-to-be with nowhere to lay their heads, and
carrying their sashes and their orders and their letters of credence
about with them for lack of anywhere to stow them safely away. Italian
officers in prodigiously wide breeches and jack-boots gleaming like a
seal's back, wandered hither and thither looking for someone to
interrogate them; war correspondents – including the inseparable trio,
Alan Moorehead, Christopher Buckley and Alex Clifford – likewise
questing; in their case, for communiqués, hand-outs, interviews, anything to tap out and dispatch, datelined Marshal Badoglio's Headquarters. I spent some pleasant hours with them. An amiable Air
Force officer, who was acting as Badoglio's interpreter-in-chief, took
me to pay my respects to the Marshal. He was accommodated in what
must have been one of the Imperiale's best rooms, with a view of the
sea and a bathroom of its own, and seemed, I thought, rather dazed
as he sat there, as though wondering what had happened, and who he
was supposed to be. There were others waiting to see him, and after a
brief exchange of courtesies I withdrew, to listen to the ecomiums of
the Air Force officer. A truly outstanding man! What a remarkable
intelligence! How understanding! Ciano in his *Diary* describes how,
when Goering and his retinue waited upon Marshal Pétain, they were
all vying with one another to get a word with Laval. Sycophancy, like
other frailties, in the last resort has no standards.

That evening, a radio link with Rome – still under German military
occupation – was being tried out, to see whether our man there was
operating freely or being controlled. It was rather exciting, waiting to
pick up his signal. What would he send? Details of German troop
movements and installations? Something about Italian morale? What
was happening in the entourage of King Victor Emmanuel? When he

finally came through, it was to tell us that we must not suppose that all the good democrats and patriots were in Marshal Badoglio's Government; there were others, as good, and better, in Rome. I voted that the link was evidently not under control; no *Abwehr* officer, I argued, would have had the wit to invent so authentic a message. So it was agreed.

In Brindisi I acquired a car and a driver. It was an ancient vehicle, but with one inestimable advantage – above its number-plate a notice bearing the legend: INTERNATIONAL CONTROL COMMISSION. When and how this notice had been acquired, who the International Control Commission were, and what, if anything, they were controlling, I never found out; but the effect of ostensibly travelling under their auspices was magical. We were never held up, or asked for papers, or in any way interfered with. The roads were crowded with military vehicles of one sort or another, and in an appalling state; the bridges had nearly all been blown up and replaced by temporary structures; the villages were largely deserted. The war seemed to have laid a particularly heavy hand on this landscape and its people. In the cities bombardment brought great misery and destruction, certainly, and the wasteland left behind was desolating; but still it was somehow inherent in them. They contained so much violence and conflict anyway, that their destruction was more like a volcano erupting from within than an attack coming unaccountably and savagely from without; whereas there seemed no place for marching men and rolling vehicles and prowling aircraft in the countryside of Southern Italy, so poor and so everlasting, cultivated over the centuries with such loving care, enshrined for me in the descriptions of Silone, dug out of his heart in love and fury.

In Naples one bright afternoon the whole population were evacuated in order that booby traps and other devices left behind by the Germans when they withdrew might be dismantled without risk to the inhabitants. A vast concourse gathered on the hills around the city; like a vision of the Last Day, when all the dead arise. In Naples, too, I was taken to a house lately occupied by the Gestapo. It was a scene of squalor and disorder; the lavatory bunged up, everything broken and torn, the grate piled high with burnt paper, books on the floor, a desk, once elegant, with inlaid wood and brass fittings, dragged halfway to the door as though to take it away, and then abandoned; in one of its pigeon-holes a family group – all in Bavarian costume – plump mother, father smoking a curved pipe, two sons wearing student caps, three daughters in dirndl dresses, and written at the bottom some illegible inscription in old Gothic characters, and in one of the drawers, an illustrated erotic book, with pictures of elephantine women and bestial men. Violence, sentimentality and porn, and finally, to round things off, sheer imbecility, in the form of a propaganda record lying about which played a Lili-Marlene-type song into which a soft, persuasive voice broke from time to time, saying, in English: 'You know you're losing the war . . . You'd far better give in. . . .' So short a while before the others had been there, living presences; and now, surveying the debris they had left behind, came the realisation that these ashes were still warm. Capri abandoned; Pompeii, too, with fresh bullet marks on its crumbling masonry. After the great eruption of two thousand years ago, this supererogatory, man-made one scarcely showed – ruins to ruins. At Caserta another huge headquarters was in course of preparation, where the enemy's final surrender in the Italian campaign would take place.

My last visit to Italy ended in Rome, which had lately fallen to the Allies. I was lodged in the Banco di Roma; a vast marble structure for the accommodation and celebration of money, not men. Now, it seemed, the god had failed; its temple was empty and chill, like a tomb full of battle-dressed intruders. Elsewhere, the presses were rolling off Occupation money at top speed, with, on the back of the notes, Roosevelt's Four Freedoms printed, including Freedom from Want, which, it must be admitted, this particular currency did little to sustain. Peeping into the Banco di Roma some years later, at the time of the Second Vatican Council, the rites seemed to be in full swing again; the god was back, and the battle-dressed ghosts had long since departed.

At dawn on the morning of 12 August 1944, we took off for France in a small plane piloted by a Canadian. Besides the pilot and myself, there were Paiolle and Pelabon, whom I had met from time to time with Soustelle; both in uniform, the latter as a naval officer. I had not known he was in this service; in his new, unfamiliar uniform, he looked younger than his years. We flew low enough to follow our course – over the Downs, then Dover and the white cliffs, the Channel, and, finally, France. It surprised me that, seen from above, the countryside looked exactly as it had four years before. Yet, after all, why not? What did we expect? I scarcely knew, but not assuredly, those familiar little towns and villages grouped so serenely around their churches; those tidy fields and massive horses, that I remembered so well from times past. There ought, surely, to have been a haze of smoke, gutted houses, refugees on the roads, troops and military aircraft. Our troops, I heard, when they landed suffered a similar disappointment at finding only a surly, well-fed prosperous-looking peasantry when they had been led to expect a starving, desperate population overjoyed to see them. The worst feature of propaganda, advertising, or any form of organised lying, is that, try as one will, one comes to believe it; as press lords come to believe what they read in their own newspapers, and television producers what they see on the screen.

None of the four of us said anything, or looked particularly uplifted or moved. I as, in a sense, the host, belonging, anyway, to the country which had provided the aircraft and facilities, felt I ought to utter, and tried desperately to think of suitable words. About how, at this historic moment . . . privilege of sharing together . . . resolved never again to allow . . . sectarian or selfish interests. . . . It was another of those fraudulent sentences which will never end, carrying me back to leader-writing days. Put into French it seemed even worse. I decided to stay silent. Only Paiolle, who had kept his fore-and-aft cap on, saluted, murmuring what sounded like: '*Je salue mon pays.*' Pelabon, who had taken off his peaked naval hat, which seemed to bear rather heavily upon his head, looked uncomfortable at this gesture, as though he felt he, too, should have responded in some way; but by then it was too late, and whatever he did would have looked like following Paiolle's lead. Apart from my abortive effort to bring out an appropriate sentence, I had no particular sense of drama. It is the words that make the drama, rather than the other way round; 'Now he belongs to history,' establishing, rather than defining, Lincoln's part.

Our pilot, his headphones on, indicated that we shouldn't be able to land as planned at Le Bourget, where there was still fighting going on, and he landed finally on an air-strip some seventy miles from Paris. There was a good deal of confusion there, too, and no one took much interest in us. We gathered our luggage together, and managed to get a lift in a military truck loaded with miscellaneous regular and irregular French troops, some of them with FFI (*Forces Françaises de l'Intérieur*) arm-bands. As we had an air of being senior officers, we were put up in front, with the result that, as we went along, whenever we passed through cheering crowds – which happened all the way to Paris, getting thicker and noisier the nearer we got – we responded officially, saluting and waving like royalty, on behalf of the others, many of whom were already fairly drunk, and very wild and excited; shouting, dancing about, and even occasionally letting off a gun. In time, we, too, became infected with the prevailing excitement; the more so because, every time we were brought to a halt, swigs of cognac and glasses of champagne were pressed upon us.

As a British officer I had a certain rarity value. The Americans had insisted that, because of El Kebir, not to mention the Battle of Trafalgar and Crécy, the British were unpopular among the French, and should as far as possible be kept out of sight; whereas, because of Lafayette, the Americans were correspondingly beloved. I never myself came across anyone among the French, military or civilian, with whom such considerations weighed. They belonged only to the calculations of public relations experts, whose divorcement from the world around them is vastly greater than anything of the kind achieved by the most resolute hermits; a St Simon Stylites lives in close contact with his fellows compared with the Madison Avenue men. In this particular case, the moment it became known that there was *un officier Anglais* aboard our lorry, the offerings of champagne and cognac became ever more pressing; as did my readiness to accept them, and to exchange embraces with any agreeable females in the vicinity. In this exalted frame of mind, I gradually, as it were, got integrated into the show; until I really became convinced that I was a liberator being received with love and gratitude by the liberated.

By the time we arrived in the centre of Paris, and our truck put me down at the Petit Palais, where Allied Forces had their headquarters, I was in a very exalted state indeed, and parted from my fellow-travellers with many protestations of affection and esteem. Paiolle went off to find his wife, whom he had not seen since he left France; Pelabon made his way somewhere or other – anyway disappeared. The Petit Palais was a scene of great confusion; there was no electric light or water, Paris being then without any municipal services. Occasional electric torches or hurricane lamps showed up shadowy figures among the statuary, sleeping GI's stretched out under some Perseus or Venus, or, seated, sending up Lucky Strike oblations to a Pallas Athene. A cultural bivouac which might have been compèred by Kenneth Clark. With some difficulty I managed to find Trevor Wilson; he was in his element, having acquired a long *poilu* greatcoat which swept the ground, making him seem even smaller than he naturally was. A cigarette was, as usual, more or less permanently attached to his lower lip, and occasionally smouldering, making his always indistinct speech more so than ever. He was the perfect companion for a Liberation; I greeted him warmly and affectionately, and he responded in the same spirit. He would, I knew, combine his seemingly surrealist manner with a magical cunning in procuring food and shelter, and in finding his way to exactly the right places at the right time.

First he took me to an American mess, where we ate baked beans washed down with coffee; then on to a haunt of his on the Left Bank – already, in some miraculous way, he had procured a vehicle and a driver – packed out, mostly with civilians, and thick with tobacco smoke. Trevor, of course, knew the *Patron*, and a place was found and a bottle put before us. There were only flickering candles to light the tiny stage, where a man, completely bald, with a large, sad clown's face, was intoning a soliloquy, in which he recalled all the terrible things that had happened to him since the Germans came to Paris. *Et maintenant*, he concluded, with an expression of infinite woe, through which he struggled, to break into a wry smile – *Et maintenant, nous sommes libérés!* The audience roared their approval, and looked quizzically at Trevor and me. Somehow it seemed the most perfect comment on the situation, and ever after, when I have thought of the Liberation, I have seen again the solemnity of his vast expanse of face, and heard his woeful declaration. Only clowns and mystics ever speak the truth.

The next morning we went to a Requiem Mass for six heroes of the Resistance, their coffins side by side, and covered with flowers, each one bearing the Cross of Lorraine. Mourners processed by, shaking Holy Water over them as they passed. Trevor Wilson, still wearing his *poilu* greatcoat, did this with particular zest, to the point that I feared he might have emptied the receptacle used, leaving nothing for the next-in-line who took it off him. I had not previously known that he was a Roman Catholic, as he now appeared to be from his familiarity with the order of service and ceremonial usages. At Nôtre Dame, there was a special thanksgiving service attended by de Gaulle. The cathedral was packed tight, with a great array of cardinals and archbishops at the altar. The choir sang melodiously, and up in front the heads of the General and his associates could just be seen. It was at this point that someone fired a pistol; as was subsequently discovered, by mistake. The effect was fantastic; the huge congregation who had all been standing suddenly fell flat on their faces, supposing that some plot – Communist, Pétainist, Nazi, maybe even Gaullist – was about to be put into operation. There was a single exception; one solitary figure still standing, like a lonely giant. It was, of course, de Gaulle. Thenceforth, that was how I always saw him – towering and alone; the rest, prostrate.

As things turned out no posture could have been more appropriate. In those first days after the German withdrawal, without a doubt, de Gaulle's presence alone prevented a total breakdown, probably followed by a Communist takeover. As soon as he appeared on the scene, Allied plans, so painstakingly worked out, for setting up a military government, prior to the holding of elections, all ran into the sand; the brigadiers who had assembled at embarkation ports, putative gauleiters, lawyers, men from the city and of a certain age, briefed in the *Code Napoléon* and other lore for taking over their allotted districts, stole silently away, unwanted. Wherever de Gaulle appeared, he was the government, and recognised as such. Witnessing this performance I realised that it was not just his political acumen, and the undoubted charisma of his weird angular disposition, which made him the unquestioned master of the situation. Rather, he had some second sense arising out of his complete confidence in himself and in his destiny, which guided his steps, fed out those rumbling and so telling words of his, and showed him exactly where he should be and what he should say. He was like, I decided, one of those circus clowns who ride a bicycle clumsily into the ring, seeming always about to fall off, until you realise that they are in fact consummate riders, who will always recover their balance and end up standing majestically on the saddle and saluting a wildly applauding audience.

From this time on I always assumed that he must win, however strange and self-defeating his tactics at a particular moment might seem to be. When, for instance, in 1946 – Soustelle, then one of his Ministers, vividly described the scene to me – he brusquely ended his first brief spell of being head of the government by coming into a cabinet meeting and, without any prior warning, banging the table and exclaiming: '*J'en ai marre!*' I felt quite sure that the move, though inexplicable at the time, would prove to have been correct from the point of view of his larger purposes. As, indeed, it did, since it left the ghosts of the Third Republic, still extant when the Pétain Government expired, to give a public demonstration of their inability to rule France, thereby providing him with an opportunity, in due course, to take over on his own terms, and to shape a regime in accordance with his own notions of durability.

This conviction served me well when, after the war, I became a journalist again. Thanks to Soustelle, I was able to interview de Gaulle at the lowest point in his political fortunes – the only circumstances in which men of action are at all informative. At the time, he had only some six members of the *Assemblée Nationale*, one of them being Soustelle; in the Crillon Bar the foreign correspondents were unanimous that de

Gaulle was finished, and the French press was either against him, or dubious about his prospects. I, remembering my circus trick-cyclist image, thought otherwise. He received me in his office in the Rue Solférino; seated at a desk that was much too small for him, so that he seemed, at the same time, to bulge out of it and to tower above it. His stomach already protruded noticeably, his complexion was muddy and his breath bad; yet, as always, I found in him a nobility, a true disinterestedness, even a sort of sublime absurdity, which overcame his physical and mental gaucherie. We spoke in French, of course; to the best of my knowledge, during the years he spent in London he failed to acquire one single word of English. On the occasions that he uttered a few words in a foreign language, he always had to learn them phonetically beforehand. The encounter remains memorable; more so, I think, than any other of the kind I ever experienced, not so much because of what was said – predominantly by him; I scarcely spoke, a somewhat unusual experience for me – as because of the sense that I had of being in the presence of someone of enormous significance, who was, at once, as such men are, the hero and the victim of the times we were living through.

Our conversation began with one of his tirades about the *pourriture* of French politics, and ended with my asking him what he proposed to do now, to which he replied with a majestic: '*J'attends!*' At the time I wrote an account of what he said, as exactly as I could remember it, in the *Daily Telegraph*, whose deputy-editor I then was. At one point I summoned up my courage to ask him why, if the present regime was so abhorrent, he had not tried to fashion a better one himself when, just after the war, he dominated France as no one else had since Napoleon, or even *le Roi Soleil*. He glowered at me for this, indicating, as I thought, by the very intensity of his reaction that it was something he had asked himself from time to time; then rumbled out his answer: '*Ce n'était pas l'heure.*' I had to leave it at that; the timing would have been wrong – as, indeed, one can see now, it would have been.

The only other contact I had with him was to write to him after his retirement suggesting that, as his astonishing career as a world figure had, in effect, begun with a broadcast on BBC Radio in 1940, he might consider it fitting to conclude it with a last word on the same channel. I quoted the case of Tolstoy who, in the very last sentences he wrote, concluded: 'That, my dear brothers, is what I have been trying to say.' How wonderful to have a similar last word from de Gaulle! He replied very charmingly that he appreciated the suggestion, but had resolved not to venture upon the air (*utiliser les ondes*) again. There was one other tiny connection; when I became a waxwork in Madame Tussaud's I was put in a room between Twiggy and the Burtons, with a massive de Gaulle staring down upon the four of us. Not a sparrow can fall to the ground, we are told, without concern in Heaven; so, likewise, the *placement* of waxworks.

Soon after arriving in Paris I looked in at the Hotel Scribe where the war correspondents were accommodated, and found one or two old acquaintances among them. How familiar a scene! The fingers questing over a typewriter keyboard, the faces momentarily pulled together to concentrate wavering attention, the cigarette pulled at for inspiration, the glass to hand to fuel the motor when it faltered. TONIGHT TRICOLORE BRAVELY OVERFLYING PARISES FAMOUS ARCDETRIOMPHE FIRST TIME SINCE GERMANS UNDERGOOSE-STEPPED . . . 'Hey! can anyone tell me, is there a flag over the Arc de Triomphe? Not! Well, what about the Eiffel Tower?' A centre of attention was Hemingway, fairly drunk, surrounded by admirers, and hung round with hand-grenades like monstrous beads – which everyone hoped had been immobilised, since, as he lurched about, one might so easily have gone off. Occasionally, he doubled up as for a fight, fists clenched and beating the air; the beard surrounding the face like an artist's shading, making it nebulous, indefinite. Looking at him, there was some comparison I was reaching after; someone he closely resembled. Then I remembered; it was the beard which gave me the clue – of course, Walt Whitman. A similar ribald figure, boozy, preoccupied with the image rather than the reality. Music in *muzak*, speed in a speedometer, beauty in cosmetics; virility in the pederastic posturings of a Whitman and strength in a Hemingway's fists beating the air – these two, pre-eminently, the dreamers and the dream.

I spent the next few days wandering about in liberated Paris in varying states of intoxication, having, in the confusion which reigned, nothing particular to do and nowhere particular to be. My French colleagues had not yet surfaced, and the *Services Spéciaux* not yet taken down the shutters and opened for business. A British uniform continued to procure friendly smiles, embraces, bed-fellows even, as and when required, as well as limitless hospitality; food, in so far as supplies were available (which they only were, for the most part, in rather dubious company), and, more plentifully, drink. For what must have been the one and only time in French history, the more expensive paris restaurants like Maxim's refused to present a bill to Allied officers, doubtless hoping thereby to *épurer* themselves from having been, during the occupation, similarly attentive to German officers. It was after benefiting from this unusual dispensation that Trevor Wilson, Victor Rothschild (who had now turned up in Paris), and I, a substantial luncheon under our belts, decided to make contact for the first time with a British Forces Headquarters which we heard had been set up in the Roger et Gallet building in the Rue St Honoré. Thither we repaired, in high good humour, to be told that the brigadier who was then in charge had not yet returned, but that we might wait for him in his office, which we did, our high spirits noticeably diminishing as the minutes passed. A project entertained at a festive meal, needs, like Brutus's plot, to be taken at the flood if it is to lead on to victory.

By the time the brigadier turned up we were decidedly deflated; he, clearly, found us an astonishing, if not distasteful, spectacle. It was not difficult to see why. He looked particularly smart in his service dress, his buttons shining, his red-tabs glowing; whereas we presented, from his point of view, a lamentable appearance. Trevor had on his *poilu* greatcoat, which had not improved with the wearing; the stub of a Gaulois cigarette still clung tenaciously to his lower-lip. Rothschild was a massive, but scarcely a soldierly figure; and I doubtless bore marks of my Liberation celebrations. The situation was not made easier when it came out the lieutenant-colonel among us (Trevor and I were majors) was none other than Lord Rothschild; a name that clearly represented, in the brigadier's eyes, all that was most alluring and splendid on earth. Could this be he? And in such company? Clearly not; they must be impostors. His hand, I thought, began to move towards the bell on his desk, no doubt to summon an orderly and have us removed, when Trevor once again made himself master of a difficult situation.

We were, he explained to the brigadier, cloak-and-dagger men, leaving him to assume that what he had taken to be uniforms were, in fact, an ingenious and carefully devised disguise for some purpose of our own. He was further mollified when Trevor went on to say that we had merely come to report to him as our, pro-tem, commanding officer, with no requirements in the way of billets or rations or pay. Trevor, I should add, by this time, had moved into an elegant apartment in the Rue de la Paix, formerly occupied by an *Abwehr* officer, and I was shortly going to move into the Rothschild mansion in the Avenue Marigny, prudently requisitioned on Victor Rothschild's behalf, in which he had kindly offered me accommodation. When we got up to go, our relations with the brigadier had become positively cordial, which led me to remark that if at any time there was anything we could do for him, he had but to mention it. At this, he looked suddenly thoughtful. Yes, he said, there was one thing over which we might be able to help. He had been asked to procure a white Rolls-Royce for an air marshal's wife. Could we possibly lay hands on one? Trevor had the air of a man with a whole fleet of Rolls-Royces in all colours at his disposal; it was just a matter of picking the right one. I murmured weakly that we would keep our eyes open. Rothschild, I thought, looked a little surly; he, after all, might well have had a white Rolls-Royce.

In these first days after the Liberation, France (apart from the war-zone itself), and more particularly Paris, was in a virtual state of break-down, without organs of authority or law. The police, heavily tainted with Pétainism, if not collaboration, were lying low for the time being, until it became clear who was going to emerge to give orders and command obedience. By day, it was not so noticeable, though even then in places like the Palais de Justice and the prisons, which I had occasion to visit, there was total confusion; the judges having mostly disappeared or been arrested themselves, and the prisons being glutted with alleged *collaborateurs*, brought along by no one knew who, and charged with no one knew what. It was when darkness began to fall that one became aware of the breakdown; with no street-lighting, and the tall houses all silent and locked and boarded up, like sightless eyes. Inside them I imagined cowering figures, hopeful of surviving if they remained per-fectly still and hidden. Then, as night came on, sounds of scurrying feet, sudden cries, shots, shrieks, but no one available, or caring, to investi-gate. It is unknown to this day how many were shot down, had their heads shaved, piteously disgorged their possessions in return for being released, but certainly many, many thousands. Outside Paris – for instance, in Orleans, where I spent a week-end in a country house – the situation was even more drastic. Our host had to make his terms for us to come and go with the local FFI, who terrorised the district. There, too, many were shot down or summarily executed and never accounted for. We dined by candle-light; the meal dished up and served by one or two old servants. Afterwards, we played parlour games and danced, talking a little too eagerly, and laughing a little too shrilly, to be convincing; most of us full of thoughts of 1789.

In Paris I spent several evenings with an FFI band, accompanying them on some of their nocturnal expeditions. We first met at a parade at the Arc de Triomphe, when Churchill and de Gaulle laid wreaths on the Unknown Warrior's Tomb, and then marched side by side down the

Champs Elysées. A curious pair, the one so rotund and merry, the other so tall and grave; like Mr Pickwick and Don Quixote. I struck up a friendship with the FFI band then and there, and they invited me along to an apartment they had taken over in the Avenue Foch, formerly occupied by the Gestapo; large and elegantly furnished, well stocked with champagne, and, like the *Abwehr* house in Naples, with erotica. They were a mixed lot who had come together by chance; the leader, I was told, an actor of sorts, and certainly given to striking attitudes – for instance, one arm in a sling, and flourishing a revolver with the other. His second-in-command was, I should say, an Algerian; rather vicious-looking, and probably a figure from the underworld. I never knew any of their names, except that the actor-leader was called Alain and the Algerian, Marc. There was also a girl named Chantal; pretty, but ravaged looking, in a khaki drill skirt and tunic, and wearing a cartridge belt. The others – some seven or eight – I scarcely distinguished from one another. They were mostly very young, with that curious hunted animal look that street life gives. One of them spoke in a more cultivated way, and might well have been at a Lycée. Today, one would take them to be students; or *Bezprizoray* who had stepped straight out of *The Clockwork Orange*.

I was never able to decide whether they were just a marauding gang, or whether patriotism or ideological fervour played some part in their activities and antics. They certainly took things from people – cigarette cases, jewels, money; anything like that – but for my benefit made a great point of handing them over to Alain, who kept them in a box, which he locked up, and whose contents he carefully listed, to be handed over, so he said, to his superiors. Equally certainly, they were given assignments; to go to such a house, conduct a search, interrogate such a person, make an arrest, and even – as they boasted, but I never saw them do it – carry out an execution. If a door was not opened to them, they would batter it down; everyone cowered before them, and did what they were told. Considering their youth, they behaved with horrifying callousness, arrogance and brutality, recalling a saying of Tolstoy to the effect that revolutionaries in authority always behave worse than those they replace because they come fresh to it. In the years ahead, I was often to be reminded of this. After I stopped seeing them, I vaguely heard that Alain had been arrested, and found to have a collaborationist record.

I got another glimpse of the dark face of Liberation, though this time from the other side of the fence, in connection with a notorious

Paris gangster named Laffont, who during the occupation, in his sinister establishment in the Rue Lauriston, worked closely with the Germans. In return for his services, they tolerated his nefarious activities, and provided him with many amenities and privileges. It was by making use of such criminal elements that the Germans were able, despite the Resistance, to maintain their position in France with very few troops, and those often elderly reservists. Laffont, I should say, was about the most hated and wanted man in Paris when his German protectors disappeared, and it is not surprising that quite soon he was caught and taken into custody. The police hoped to get a lot of information out of him about other underworld operators, and used the usual methods, with the result that he was soon in very poor shape, to the point that he threatened suicide. They particularly did not want this to happen, not, it goes without saying, out of any consideration for Laffont, but because his public trial and execution might help in restoring their morale and prestige. Laffont himself knew quite well that his situation was desperate, but had got it into his head that somehow, if he tried hard enough, the French might be induced to hand his case over to the Allied military authorities for them to deal with it. The police encouraged him in this totally impractical, not to say nonsensical, notion in order to counteract his suicidal tendencies, and wanted a British officer – as Serge would have put it – to *jouer la comédie* with him, and go through the motions of listening sympathetically to his plea. Through the *Sécurité Militaire*, the unappetising task fell to me.

My rendezvous with him was a room at the Sûreté; one of those impersonal, stale rooms in walnut and black leather, that you find in police stations all over the world. Two officers brought him up from the cells, handcuffed, and looking very pale and battered; a dark, sallow man, his black hair brushed, reasonably well shaved, and wearing his own clothes, but with no collar or tie. I could imagine him as something of a dandy in his time; fond of a manicure, silk shirts, well-cut suits. His dossier indicated that he had been a great womaniser. He struck me as being rather slight in stature; but others who had seen him before the police got to work on him said he was burly. Obviously, the purpose of our talk could not be achieved if the two officers remained in the room. Their withdrawal had been arranged beforehand; also the removal of his handcuffs. I hadn't liked to ask if they had facilities for keeping us under close observation, but assumed they must have. All the same, it was an eerie moment when I found myself alone with him. I felt more embarrassed than afraid of anything he might do, to me or to himself;

he seemed so listless and broken and dumb. To start the conversation I tried to put on an impersonation of a brisk staff-officer, and for the purpose had a briefcase with me from which I took out a paper or two. I gathered, I said, that he considered his case should be an Allied, rather than a French, responsibility. Why precisely? His voice, when he spoke, was flat. I thought I could detect a Midi accent. Because, he said, the offences that he was charged with took place during the German occupation. How, then, could his guilt be investigated by French police who had themselves continued to function under the occupation authorities? Or, for that matter – and here his flat voice acquired a touch of animation – how could he be tried by some upstart Gaullist military court whose members had been in exile when his alleged crimes were committed?

It was not very convincing, especially in the light of his dossier, which I had, of course, read, outlining his criminal record, going back to long before 1940. Continuing my role as a brisk staff-officer, I said that I assumed he wanted me to put this to the Allied Command, which of course I would do, though with what result I naturally could not foretell. Yes, he said, he wanted it put to General Eisenhower personally. Suddenly the overweening vanity of the criminal mind showed; he had seriously persuaded himself, it was clear, that once Eisenhower heard of his predicament, he would bang the table, and insist on the French handing him over – 'Bring me Laffont!' Now, perhaps calculating that as a British officer I might resent this undue preoccupation with an American Commander-in-Chief, he went on to tell me how he had hidden RAF pilots who had baled out over France, and helped them to escape to Spain. This had become almost a routine reaction by now; I scarcely ever met a Frenchman who had not, at some point or other in the war, had at least one RAF pilot hidden in his attic. If there had been as many RAF pilots as these revelations would seem to suggest, I often reflected, our Air Force would have been so huge that we should have won the war almost before it had begun.

Laffont's anglophilia was not exhausted by his efforts on behalf of RAF pilots; he went on to tell me that the only woman he had ever loved – this, with a dim smile, as though to say that he had known a woman or two in his time – lived in Hull, and he had sent her food parcels all through the war. However had he managed that? I asked him. Again, that atrocious vanity of his manifested itself. Oh, he said, he could do anything he liked in that line through the Swiss Red Cross. It was true, as a matter of fact, that even before the war he was on amicable terms with senior police officers, and during the occupation with leading political figures as well, including Pierre Laval, who actually visited him in the Rue Lauriston. The only comparable egomaniac I have encountered was Hitler's banker, Hjalmar Schacht, who told me, when I interviewed him in Düsseldorf, where he opened a bank after his Nuremburg ordeal, that during the war he had received food parcels from Montague Norman, also via the Swiss Red Cross, sent on the theory, presumably, that bankers, whoever they might be, should in no circumstances be allowed to go hungry. With his rimless pince-nez gleaming, his hair *en brosse*, his tall stiff collar and air of impeccable rectitude, he seemed astonished that I should find anything bizarre in this. It would be interesting to have a look at the Swiss Red Cross records for 1939–45 – if any such exist – to see just who sent parcels to whom.

Laffont seemed reasonably content with our talk, from which I deduced that it had served its purpose, and got up to go; whereupon the two officers came back into the room, and handcuffed him again. In their presence he visibly wilted; the bounce that had been stirred up in him by his talk of his lady friend in Hull, and of what a master-hand he had been at dealing with the Swiss Red Cross, dissolved under their iron gaze. Perhaps, after all, he didn't really have much hope of escaping from their clutches. It was a relief to get away, and out into the street, but the memory of my macabre encounter with him continued to haunt me; not because I had any particular pity for his plight, or sense of horror at what he had done. Rather, at the thought of that ego of his, lifting up its head, and darting out its cobra tongue; that vanity, emerging, inviolate, fresh and new as a Pharaoh's treasure after centuries in a dark tomb, from the beatings and thumpings at the Sûreté, the questionings and shoutings, the bright lights shining and the dead hours passing. Above all, at the thought that this ego and vanity could so easily, so neatly and aptly, be related to my own. As for his crimes – in the confessional, if I ever found my way there, I should have to confess that there is no crime, however unspeakable, that I have not either contemplated, or know myself to be capable of having committed.

I read in the *Figaro* that he had been tried, found guilty and executed; not by a firing-squad, as he would undoubtedly have preferred, but guillotined – neat, sallow head with the blunt Mediterranean back to it, sliced off like a thistle's. I doubt if anyone mourned for him, unless the lady in Hull, and perhaps, in some perverse way, myself. It's a pity, maybe, that I didn't ask him for her name, for then I could have sought her out and found out what her feelings were, if any. I expect, though, that the real reason I didn't try to track her down was the certainty of discovering that she did not exist.

By this time I was settled in the Rothschild mansion in the Avenue Marigny. It was a huge, dark, sombre house, with a courtyard and a massive door opening into the street, which could be operated from the porter's lodge, where sat M. Félix, the *maître d'hôtel.* To get in or out one required M. Félix's co-operation; at his, or one of his underling's touch, the great door could be swung open, and then inexorably shut – as it seemed, excluding or imprisoning one for ever. The furniture was in keeping with the house and the gate; also heavy and sombre. Even the pictures, some of them by old masters, and, presumably, immensely valuable, hung, as it seemed to me, lifelessly on the walls; the life and light somehow drained out of them. It astonished me, when we first moved into the house, to find its contents intact and undamaged. As belonging to one of the most famous Jewish families in Europe, one would have expected it to have suffered. During the German occupation, it was taken over by a *Luftwaffe* general, who, according to M. Félix – he continued to function as a matter of course – behaved impeccably; not only refraining from tampering with the house and its contents himself, but also preventing others from doing so. When I got to know M. Félix better, I asked him how he accounted for the general's good behaviour, he being, after all, a Nazi. His reply was interesting; Hitlers come and go, he said, but Rothschilds go on for ever. He said it with a droll smile; not a man, I concluded correctly, to tell me that he had hidden RAF officers in the Rothschild cellar, along with the Mouton Rothschild. Someone, clearly, with his wits about him. We often had chats together after that.

To me, there always seemed to be a shadow hanging over the house in the Avenue Marigny, as over the Kremlin – in the one case, of money, in the other of power; though, of course, ultimately, they amount to the same thing, money being a pasteurised form of power. This shadow, I confess, is something that has haunted all my days. Seen first, perhaps, in those Doré illustrations of Dante which so fascinated me as a child; there, hanging over the nether regions where poor lost souls await release from the chains they have forged for themselves on earth. Likewise, hanging over all Kremlins everywhere – the City, Wall Street, the Vatican, the Houses of Parliament, the Pentagon, Capitol Hill, and that Krupps sanctum at whose monstrous desk I once sat shivering through a thunderstorm; hanging over all the frozen corridors along which feet tramp incessantly on their way to war, to vote, to applaud and to decry, to work and to play, to victory and to defeat. The same shadow that I envisaged, when, between Jericho and the Dead Sea, I tried to reconstruct forty days and forty nights in the wilderness, dogged by the Devil making his offers – of plenty, a Gross National Product without end; of wonders illimitable, reaching to the moon and beyond; of the kingdoms of the earth, to have and to shape. This shadow was the Devil's own, darkening the golden sand. The sun could not reach it; only another Light, not of this world, would suffice to abolish it.

For Rothschild himself, of course, the Avenue Marigny house was a home from home, but at the same time, I felt, a prison. Installed there, he was the *de facto* if not *de jure* head of the family. Other Rothschilds appeared from time to time, and offered obeisance. He both liked to feel they were looking to him, and abhorred their presence; his disposition was a curious, uneasy mixture of arrogance and diffidence. Somewhere between White's Club and the Ark of the Covenant, between the Old and the New Testament, between the Kremlin and the House of Lords, he had lost his way, and been floundering about ever since. Embedded deep down in him there was something touching and vulnerable and perceptive; at times lovable even. But so overlaid with the bogus certainties of science, and the equally bogus respect, accorded and expected, on account of his wealth and famous name, that it was only rarely apparent. Once when I was going to London he asked me to take over a case of brandy, addressed in large letters to him at his English address. In the guard's van where it was put, among the porters who carried it, wherever it was seen or handled, it aroused an attitude of adoration, real or facetious, as though it had been some holy relic – the bones of a saint or a fragment of the True Cross. Even I partook of its glory, momentarily deputising for this Socialist millionaire, this Rabbinical sceptic, this epicurean ascetic, this Wise Man who had followed the wrong star and found his way to the wrong manger – one complete with chef, central heating and a lift. I think of him in the Avenue Marigny dictating innumerable memoranda, as though in the hope that, if only he dictated enough of them, one would say something; on a basis of the philosophical notion that three monkeys tapping away at typewriters must infallibly, if they keep at it long enough, ultimately tap out the Bible. Rothschild, anyway, did not lack for monkeys. After the war I caught glimpses of him at Cambridge, in think-tanks, once in the Weizmann Institute in Tel Aviv, still dictating memoranda.

*

The *Services Spéciaux* were now installed in the Boulevard Suchet, having taken over several houses requisitioned and camouflaged by the Germans during the occupation for some sort of naval headquarters. It was an ultra-fashionable neighbourhood, where, later, the Duke and Duchess of Windsor were to reside. I had an office looking out on the Bois de Boulogne; very agreeable and convenient. Some of the original elegant furniture belonging to the dispossessed occupants remained; but when the cold, fuel-less winter months came along, in which even M. Félix had difficulty in getting supplies, a lot of this found it way into the fireplaces. I remember cheerfully consigning to the flames the carved legs of chairs and tables, which may for all I knew have been priceless antiques. At first we had 'SS' for *Services Spéciaux* on the number plates issued to us for our cars. This, with memories of the German SS troops during the occupation, soon became a subject for newspaper ridicule and abuse, so we changed to DGER – *Directorat-Général des Études et Recherches*, whatever that may have meant. Now that all the different branches, including Paiolle's, were under one roof, with Soustelle as the boss, the role of MI6, which I represented, necessarily declined. This was not a process I sought to impede, since it resulted, to my great satisfaction, in a steady diminution in the amount of paper that came my way. Most of what I had to do consisted in trying to sort out the position of purported British agents who had been arrested as collaborators by the French police. For obvious reasons, their work for us had often necessitated their being ostensibly on good terms with the German occupation authorities, for which they now found themselves under the threat of severe punishment, if not execution.

Looking back, it seems as though trying to help these people was about the only worthwhile thing I did in the whole war. It involved my visiting prisons quite a lot, especially Fresnes, and appearing in law courts which were hopelessly biased, and often dominated by Communist zealots. In Fresnes there were an extraordinary collection of alleged collaborationists, consisting of former eminent politicians, *Préfets* and other senior civil servants, officers from the three services, diplomats, writers and journalists, as well as riff-raff from the streets accused of having been informers, *agents-provocateurs* or pimps for the Germans. They were all packed tight, five or six to a cell originally intended to accommodate a single prisoner. It was a kind of Beggar's Opera scene, in which it was difficult to distinguish between some immensely distinguished admiral or general, dishevelled, but still wearing his uniform and decorations, and rogues of the Laffont type; between some famous actress from the *Comédie Française* and prostitutes who had found a lucrative clientele among German officers and other ranks. The only faces that were vaguely familiar to me were the politicians, and they mostly managed to get transferred to the infirmary, where one caught an occasional glimpse of them, seated with blankets round their shoulders like stalactites, and treated now with some degree of deference by the warders, even called M. le President again, as being on their way back to freedom and their former status.

The name of the prisoner I had come to see would be called out in stentorian tones, and down he would come, often in a state of furious indignation, which I would do my best to soothe down, explaining that I was working for his release, and needed for that purpose to ask certain questions. I made the fatal mistake of asking one of them, who I knew had been in Fresnes during the occupation, how conditions compared with the previous occasion. He laughed uproariously at my question; why, he said, under the Germans it was a *vie de château* compared with now. As for the warders, he went on, looking savagely at the one who was hovering round us – they don't change, except that now, when they went to bawl you out, they call you *tête de Boche* instead of *tête d'Anglais*. I'm glad to say he did get released, quite soon after this encounter, and managed to make his way abroad, where, as I heard, he became a very successful picture-dealer.

As it became known that I was concerned with such cases, I received appeals for help from numerous quarters, some of them very moving ones. Thus I saw a good deal, one way and another, of the *Épuration* process; described in great and truthful detail in the definitive work on the subject, M. Robert Aron's *Histoire de l'Épuration*. It was, all things considered, one of the more squalid episodes in France's history, with, as it sometimes seemed, everyone informing on everyone else. The préfectures and police stations were stuffed with accusatory letters; some even found their way to the Boulevard Suchet. A whole people's sense of guilt found expression in this unedifying passion to accuse and to punish others, which, of course, also opened the way to a great deal of working off of private grudges and envies. The truth is that under the German occupation everyone who did not go underground or abroad was in some degree a collaborator and could be plausibly accused as such. The barber who cropped the bullet heads of German soldiers, the greengrocer who sold them fruit, the waiter who served them meals, the whore who went to bed with them, the entertainer who sang to them, the clown who made them laugh, were all collaborating.

I felt desperately sorry for the individuals who were picked on for this *soi-disant* crime, especially when, as sometimes happened, I actually saw the pack going after their victim – shaving the head of some wretched girl, hunting down a German soldier who had got left behind, carrying some gibbering, trembling creature off to prison.

One case that came to my notice particularly held my attention. It concerned a French girl who had fallen in love with a German soldier compulsorily billeted on her family. First of all she had turned away whenever he spoke to her in good *Silence de la Mer* style; but in time his kindliness and good-nature had broken down their resistance, and they had all grown fond of him; she, ultimately, as a lover. After all, she said to me, his being a German didn't make him not a man, nor her being French make her not a woman. The sentiment was commonplace enough in itself, but her words continued to echo in my mind. Now, she went on, he had disappeared; an information had been laid against her as someone who consorted with German soldiers (to add to her distress, she feared that this might have been by her brother who had joined the FFI), and she lived in terror of being taken away and having her head shaved, and other horrors. 'What a Liberation for me!' she said, beginning to cry. Perhaps because she was so sweet and pretty, and, even in her sorrow, still elegant in a French way, I brooded over her case longer and more intensely than over others ostensibly more important. It seemed to me that her plight was a true image of the war, unlike those fabricated at the Ministries of Information or in the studies of statesmen; reflecting, as it did, her actual feelings, her true state of mind, rather than some fraudulent version designed to generate alternative bellicosities and bigotries to the Nazi ones.

In the end I became so preoccupied with the subject that, after the war, I wrote a play about it, called *Liberation*, partly based on this girl's story, and trying to show that through her love for her German, she really was liberated, whereas the so-called liberating armies – the Red Army fighting, looting and raping its way across Eastern Europe, the Allied Forces raining down death and destruction on Berlin and Dresden, on Hiroshima and Nagasaki – were liberating no one and nothing, but rather, bringing new servitudes in their train. By the time I had finished the play, the point I was trying to make almost ceased to have any meaning in the light of a myth that had been created, whereby Paris was liberated by French patriots to the unanimous delight of its population, apart from a few *mauvais sujets* who were faithfully dealt with. Eisenhower gave this myth a great push forward when he publicly stated that the French Resistance was the equivalent of putting into the field some twenty divisions – that is, rather more than the British contribution to the Normandy landings. I may add that I was able to help the heroine of my play a little in real life by affording her some protection, and after the war she doubtless married her German lover. In the play she fares worse; her German lover stays behind in Paris, to be shot down by the FFI with the connivance of her brother. She is left to grieve alone; but in the knowledge that she, at any rate, has been liberated.

Perhaps, especially today, the myth, as always, reigns supreme. In the case of the liberation myth, it has been possible to watch its growth; like a coral reef, gaining accretions all the time. Marcel Ophuls's film, *Le Chagrin et la Pitié*, is, perhaps, the myth's final apogee. It has been acclaimed all over the world, and received numerous awards. In it, the single intimation of any help in the way of personnel, supplies and money by the Allies is the appearance on the screen of an avowed English pederast, who describes a love affair he had in Paris with a German officer subsequently killed on the Eastern Front. The only heroes are the Communists, who are not asked to account for what they were doing during the first twenty months of the war, when the Nazi-Soviet Pact was in operation, and their party did everything possible to procure the defeat of France and a Nazi victory. If collaboration is to be regarded as a crime, then of all collaborators, the Communists bore the heaviest guilt. Criticism like mine, as I am well aware, can have absolutely no effect in counteracting the impact of M. Ophuls's film; any more than the scholarly researches of a Robert Aron. The camera has spoken, and before it tongues and pens are powerless. No instrument hitherto devised has been a thousandth part as effective in the creation and propagation of instant myths, often, as in the case of *Le Chagrin et la Pitié*, out of the most implausible material. We are far more likely to perish of a surfeit of celluloid than in consequence of any subversive conspiracy of nuclear explosion.

Another case that I got involved in, though in itself serious enough, was, because of the indomitably cheerful temperament of its central character, much less harrowing. About the third day after I arrived in Paris Trevor Wilson muttered to me, as we were walking along the Champs Élysées together, that he had just received instructions from London to keep an eye on P. G. Wodehouse, who was staying at the Bristol Hotel. Would I take this on? I agreed with indecent alacrity; not because I was an ardent Wodehouse reader, or even because of a burning desire to make up for the shabby treatment he had indubitably received at the hands of his fellow-writers at the time of his notorious broadcasts from Berlin, but, primarily, out of curiosity; to see just how he had reacted to suddenly becoming a national villain after having been for so many years a national hero, or class totem.

I made my way to the Bristol Hotel that same day in the early evening, and as I walked along I tried to remember the details of Wodehouse's alleged misdemeanour, which had occurred when I was at GHQ Home Forces. I had not, as it happened, taken much account of the broadcasts themselves at the time, but I remembered something of the row they caused – letters in *The Times* signed by A. A. Milne and others, suggestions that his honorary degree at Oxford should be rescinded, a ferocious outburst by Cassandra (Bill Connor) in the *Mirror*, expulsion from the Beefsteak Club, and – as I learnt subsequently, the only thing Wodehouse really minded – being expunged from some sort of roll of honour at his old school, Dulwich College.

At the Hotel Bristol reception desk a sleek man in a black cutaway coat gave me the number of Wodehouse's suite without displaying the slightest embarrassment or curiosity about my visit, though I suppose it must have occurred to him that, in all the circumstances, a visit by a British officer probably boded no good for him. An odd, and for obvious reasons little publicised, feature of war is how much goes on unchanged despite it. This receptionist knew better than the rest of us that when all the excitement had died down, and all the arm-bands and cartridges had been handed in, there would still be expensive hotels and their clients to whom politeness was due; Wodehouse being indubitably one such.

Nothing was working in the hotel, but the receptionist must have found some way of letting Wodehouse know that I was on my way up to his suite, because he seemed to be expecting me. 'Oh, hullo!' he said when I opened the door and stepped inside. He was standing by the window; a large, bald, amiable-looking man, wearing grey flannel trousers, a loose sports jacket and what I imagine were golfing shoes, and smoking a pipe; a sort of schoolmaster's rig. He might, I suppose, easily have been a schoolmaster if he hadn't taken to writing – Wooders. Our meeting seemed so natural that it only occurred to me afterwards that he may have thought I had come to put him under arrest. If so, he showed no signs of anxiety, but seemed perfectly at ease. When I got to know him better I asked him what sort of person he had expected to come into his room. 'Oh, I don't know,' he said, 'but not you.' This, I must say, greatly pleased me.

I should, of course, before coming to see Wodehouse, have got hold of a dossier from somewhere – there always is a dossier – and studied the text of the offending broadcasts, generally familiarising myself with the case. In fact, I had made no sort of preparation for my visit, and had no plan as to how I should approach Wodehouse. So I began with the banal observation that his books had given me great pleasure. Even this was not strictly true. In my Socialist home Bertie Wooster and Jeeves were as reprehensible figures as Sade and Casanova in a Methodist one. My feelings about him on first making his acquaintance, were, I should say, that he was a distinguished and original writer who had given a great deal of pleasure to a great many people, and that, as such, he was entitled to be kept clear of the monstrous buffooneries of war. Otherwise, I had no strong sense of partisanship one way or the other.

There was still a lot of rushing about and shouting in the street outside; even an occasional pistol shot. Wodehouse turned away from the window, and we both sat down. Then, after a short silence, I made a hesitant approach to the business in hand. I had no idea, I said, to what extent he had been able to follow what was going on in England, but there had been quite a public row about his broadcasts – a row which I personally considered to be unwarranted. All the same, in order to clear matters up, questions would have to be asked and the legal position gone into. I slipped in the reference to the legal position (about which, of course, I knew nothing) in order to stress the gravity of Wodehouse's plight – in the circumstances then prevailing, decidedly serious. Judges are as prone as anyone to swim with the tide – perhaps a bit more so – and the English, too, as the trial of William Joyce (Lord Haw-Haw) showed, were in a mood for sacrificial victims, though in their case, particular ones, rather than, as with the French, in bulk. Wodehouse might well have fared ill if he had come before a British court at that time.

From numerous talks I had with him, sometimes on walks that we took together through the streets of Paris, sometimes sitting and chatting, I was able to piece together what happened to him in the war years. When in the summer of 1940 the Germans arrived at Le Touquet, where Wodehouse and his wife Ethel had a villa in which they were living at the time, he was taken into custody as an enemy alien and transported to a prison camp at Tost in Poland. The building in which they were lodged, to his great satisfaction, turned out to have previously been a lunatic asylum. Here he lived relatively contentedly, though food was decidedly short; he found, he told me, that nourishment could be got out of match sticks if assiduously sucked. He had brought his typewriter with him, and, marvellous to relate, he continued to turn out his daily stint of words. When the war ended he had five novels, all up to his usual standard, ready for publication. I asked him whether the guards at Tost took any interest in his writing. Yes, he said, very markedly so; they would stand and watch him tapping with awe and fascination. I could quite believe it. Wodehouse has written an entertaining account of his life at Tost – what he calls his Camp Book – which he gave me to read. It must be unique in prison literature as minimising the miseries of captivity, and stressing the pleasant relations he had even with the guards, as well as with his fellow-captives, and the solaces they found to alleviate their boredom and privation.

The normal procedure is to release civilian internees when they are sixty; Wodehouse was released some months before his sixtieth birthday as a result of well-meant but ill-advised representation by American friends resident in Berlin, America not being then at war with Germany. He made for Berlin, where Ethel (who had not been interned) was awaiting him. Hearing of his presence there, the Berlin representative of the Columbia Broadcasting System, an American named Flaherty, asked him if he would like to broadcast to his American readers. For professional reasons, if for no others, the idea appealed to Wodehouse, who did not want to be forgotten in his most lucrative market. So he foolishly agreed to Flaherty's proposal, not realising that the broadcasts would have to go over the German network, and therefore were bound to be exploited in the interest of Nazi propaganda. It has often been alleged that there was some sort of bargain whereby he agreed to broadcast in return for being released from Tost. This has been denied again and again, and is in fact totally untrue, but nonetheless continues to be widely believed. Lies seem to have much greater staying power than truth.

Naturally, the broadcasts were gone through minutely by more expert eyes than mine, but no one has ever been able to find them other than blameless. They are, like everything Wodehouse writes, accomplished; in his own special vein, an amusing, wry, and well-observed account of his journey to Tost and life there – a sort of preliminary sketch for his Camp Book. Ironically enough, they were subsequently used at an American political warfare school as an example of how anti-German propaganda could be subtly put across by a skilful writer in the form of seemingly innocuous light-hearted descriptive material. The broadcasts, in point of fact, are neither anti- nor pro-German, but just Wodehousian.

He is a man singularly ill-fitted to live in a time of ideological conflict, having no feelings of hatred about anyone, and no very strong views about anything. In the behaviour of his fellow-humans, whoever they may be, he detects nothing more pernicious than a kind of sublime idiocy, and in commenting on public affairs rarely goes further than expressing the hope that this or that august personage might be induced to return to his padded-cell. I never heard him speak bitterly about anyone – not even about old friends who turned against him in distress. Such a temperament does not make for good citizenship in the second half of the twentieth century.

As we went on talking evening shadows began to fill the room we were sitting in. There was no electricity, and so no possibility of turning on a light. I have always loved sitting in a darkening room and talking with someone sympathetic; it takes the sharp edge off the exigencies of time, and, one may dare to hope, is a little like dying. The experience was sharpened in Paris on that particular evening because of the contrast between our tranquillity together and the mounting confusion and shooting outside. Wodehouse sent down for a bottle of wine which we consumed as we talked; royalties on Spanish, Swedish and other translations of his books provided him with adequate funds during the war years. Our conversation soon moved on from his Berlin misdemeanour and its repercussions. Were things still ticking along? Did clubs go on? And *The Times Literary Supplement*? Alas, yes, I had to tell him. And A. A. Milne? And *Punch*? Yes, again. Wodehouse wanted to know what books had been published and how they had sold, what plays had been put on and how long they had run, who was still alive and who dead. I satisfied him as best I could on these points, hampered, in the case of the last, by a morbid tendency to believe I had read the obituary of practically everyone; especially women novelists, eminent Quakers, popular clergymen, famous Shakespearean actors and Governors of the BBC. Bernard Shaw, I told him, was certainly alive; the news, I fancy, fell a little flat. 'And Wells?' he asked eagerly. 'He might be dead,' I said, leaving him to extract whatever joy or grief he might from my uncertainty.

The room was quite dark now, and I got up to go, promising to come again soon, if I might, to make the acquaintance of Ethel. On the way back to the Avenue Marigny I looked in at the *Cercle Interallié* where one could always find a cluster of American colonels, some with their ladies, as well as a one-armed Pole ingeniously playing snooker, and a King's Messenger or two resting between journeys. At the

Avenue Marigny I rang the bell, and after a discreet interval for inspection the great door swung open to let me in. In passing, I asked M. Félix if he had heard of P. G. Wodehouse. Yes, he had, he said; in fact he had dined at the house some years before, as the guest of M. Robert, or maybe M. Edmond. Wasn't he *un écrivain humoristique bien connu?* Correct I said, and went on to describe how I had just been to see him at the Hotel Bristol. 'They say it's a very comfortable and well-run hotel,' M. Félix sagely observed, and there the matter rested. I wish I could have presented M. Félix to Wodehouse; he would, I felt, have fitted in well with his galaxy of heroes as a sort of Gallic Jeeves.

In the following days I saw a lot of Wodehouse and Ethel, who turned out to be a spirited energetic lady trying as hard to be worldly wise as Wodehouse himself to be innocent. A bad sleeper, accustomed to wander about during the night, polishing tables and planning to pull down whatever house they happened to be occupying and re-build it nearer to her heart's desire; a mixture of Mistress Quickly and Florence Nightingale, with a touch of Lady Macbeth thrown in – I grew to love her.

When I had occasion to go over to London for a few days, Wodehouse asked me to get him some Three Nuns tobacco, and to find out from his agent, Watt, how his books had been selling. The former commission was easily fulfilled; more particularly as I had also to get some shag for George Orwell – who had turned up in Paris, to my great satisfaction, as *Observer* correspondent – of a kind that he considered to be genuinely proletarian, and so suitable for him to smoke in the cigarettes he made inexpertly for himself. The latter, however, presented unexpected difficulties; for when I called upon Mr Watt in his office in one of those little streets running between the Strand and the Embankment – a sort of no-man's land where the Savoy, Fleet Street and the Temple impinge – I found him decidedly reticent and evasive. Maybe he supposed I was collecting information to Wodehouse's discredit on behalf of MI5 or the Inland Revenue, or just considered it best, in the circumstances, to keep quite quiet about what must have been one of his most lucrative clients. There, anyway, he sat: a large sullen-looking man in an office which – to add an extra macabre touch to the scene – was lined with metal boxes bearing the names in white lettering of famous writers like Rider Haggard and Rudyard Kipling, who were all dead. In the end, with enormous difficulty, and the exercise of much persuasion, I did manage to extort from Mr Watt the information that Wodehouse's books during the war years had been having record sales, and that a large sum in accumulated royalties stood to his account, which, however, as of then, was blocked by the authorities. It pleased me, I must say, to know that all the abuse heaped on Wodehouse had only served to increase the demand for his books, providing one more illustration of how public obloquy is as much a myth as public adulation; the hisses and cheers are taped, as in recorded broadcasts.

Orwell was a great admirer of Wodehouse's writing, and I was happy to arrange for them to meet. The essay he wrote following their meeting provides, I should say, about the best treatment of the subject there is, apart from Waugh's elegant broadcast tribute on Wodehouse's eightieth birthday. The two of them got on very well, though afterwards Wodehouse said to me that Orwell seemed a gloomy sort of chap. He did give this impression at first, but, on closer acquaintance it became clear that he was really, in his own odd way, quite a happy man; as I am sure Don Quixote was, even though known as the Knight of the Woeful Countenance. We talked a lot about Wodehouse, and I mentioned, as an example of how little writers can judge their own work, that Wodehouse had told me he considered his best book to be *Mike* – an early, and, as I think, immature, school story, which first appeared in my childhood days as a serial in *The Captain*. Of it, Wodehouse said in all seriousness that it recaptured 'the ring of a ball on a cricket bat, the green of a pitch, the white of flannels and the sound of schoolboy cheers' – or words to that effect. Orwell to my surprise, said that Wodehouse was perfectly right. *Mike*, he insisted, *was* his best book.

Orwell was delighted to be in Paris in uniform, wearing it so as to give as close an impression as possible of being in a Pioneer battalion. He tried desperately hard to enlist at the very beginning of the war, but his poor physique led to his being turned down, and he had to content himself with the Home Guard. As a veteran of the Spanish Civil War, he was considered to be a gunnery expert, but someone in the same Home Guard platoon told me that in this capacity he represented a greater danger than anything they had to fear from the enemy. It was while he was in Paris that I heard of the recent death of his first wife in hospital in Glasgow, and attempted some lame conventional remarks by way of sympathy; but he brushed them aside. It was difficult to know what he felt about anything personal, though about impersonal matters no one could be more explicit. His sister Avril told me that he inherited this enormous reticence about his own emotions from his father, who had been just the same. Under his reserve, he was, I believe, absolutely shattered by his wife's death.

Early one morning, shortly after my return from London, I got a message from Jacqueline de Broglie, whom I had met with the Wodehouses, telling me that the previous night they had been arrested by the French police. Jacqueline was the daughter of Daisy Fellowes, an American Singer sewing machine heiress, and – what interested me far more – on the de Broglie side, almost certainly a descendent of Benjamin Constant via Mme de Staël. It seemed that at a dinner party given by the then *Préfet de Police*, Luiset, an English guest had remarked on how scandalous it was that two such notorious traitors as the Wodehouses should be at large in Paris; whereupon Luiset gave orders there and then that they should be arrested, and four men with sub-machine guns and wearing black leather jackets duly appeared in their bedroom at the Bristol Hotel and took them off.

I located them at a police station on the Quai d'Orléans. No one seemed to know why M. and Mme Wodenhorse (as they appeared on the warrant) were there, and I had no difficulty in arranging for Ethel's immediate release. It appeared that, using her highly individual and idiosyncratic French at its shrillest, she had reduced the whole station to a condition of panic; aided and abetted by her peke, Wonder, whom she had insisted on taking with her when she was arrested. By the time I arrived on the scene, the police, I could see, were desperately anxious to get Ethel and Wonder off the premises as soon as possible. Getting permission for Wodehouse to have his razor returned to him was more difficult, and involved filling in an enormous form whose items I only imperfectly understood. However, with some help, I managed it, and he was able to have a shave. Then I went out and bought some food, and we all cheerfully lunched together, after which I saw Ethel and Wonder into a cab, and turned my attention to ameliorating Wodehouse's lot. It appeared that the only basis on which he could be moved straightaway was if he was ill. This presented difficulties; despite his arrest and night in the cells, he looked pink and well. However, an amiable prison doctor took his pulse, shook his head, and decided that he should be transferred to a clinic. The only one with an available bed proved to be a maternity home, with mothers having babies all round him. Each day his temperature was taken, and proved to be normal; there were two guards posted at his door, with whom he played cards in the evenings. His mornings were spent, as always, at his typewriter.

Wodehouse's release from the maternity home came sooner than expected; more, I should suppose, because of the shortage of maternity beds than as a result of representations on his behalf – though these were made. After his release I took him and Ethel out to a hotel near Fontainebleau, where they lived fairly contentedly till the end of the war, when they settled in America. By this time the Wodehouse case had long since been taken out of my hands (in so far as it could be said ever to have been in them), and put into those of an inestimable barrister named Cusden, sent over to Paris by MI5 for the purpose. Cusden, in the way barristers do, went into everything with great care, treading systematically and purposefully along the paths I had so cursorily explored, and arriving, I was relieved to learn, at the same conclusion – that Wodehouse must be exonerated of everything except foolishness and one or two minor technical offences. This conclusion was weightily and lucidly set forth in a large file which Cusden produced to show for his labours. Nonetheless, blowing down his nose in a legal way, he delivered himself of the opinion that for the time being Wodehouse 'should be kept out of the Jurisdiction'; meaning, I assumed, out of England. It reminded me of Mr Jagger's advice, similarly delivered, regarding Pip's benefactor in *Great Expectations* – to secure the portable property. Out of the Jurisdiction Wodehouse was duly kept, and subsequently stayed; being always in a state of meaning to come to England, but never coming. His attitude has been like that of a man separated in painful circumstances from someone he loves, whom he both longs and dreads to see again. Perhaps it is as well; there would be little to please, and much to sadden, him in contemporary England, where, from his point of view, as he put it to me once, in a totally a-political observation, the cads have taken over.

I discussed the Wodehouse case with Duff Cooper, who was now comfortably settled with Lady Diana in the old British Embassy in the Rue St Honoré. There, they had raised the banner of pre-war smartness, and many flocked to it, some of whom for various reasons had been lying low since the Liberation. Every social situation produces its appropriate phraseology, and any vague – or, for that matter, actual – anxieties felt by millionaires, actors, writers, dress-designers, *vicomtesses* and others, coming into the gossip-writer's category of *tout Paris*, about their behaviour during the occupation, were described as *des ennuies*. The Duff Coopers' salon was a great place for shedding *ennuies*, and was much frequented accordingly. Though the guest-list caused some head-shaking and eyebrow-raising in the Boulevard Suchet, as I tried to explain to my colleagues there, the Embassy was only reacting like Maxim or Cartier, or, for that matter, the Hotel Bristol, and welcoming old clients. I was surprised, on the only occasion

I went myself, to find Picasso in this throng, looking like some strange wild ape who had strayed into a film-set where the ball on the eve of the Battle of Waterloo was being filmed. Already, he wore the look of an astute old comedian who would know how to turn even his doodles to account in augmenting the great cascade of gold which the *bourgeoisie* he so abominated and ridiculed were to rain down upon him. Picasso can scarcely have been seriously afflicted with *ennuies*, but even he may have been glad to take a purificatory dip at the British Embassy. During the occupation years, it seemed, his Paris studio had been warmed – a rare privilege – and visited by German officers; such minutiae, as I was all too well aware at the Boulevard Suchet, being collected, tabulated and seriously deliberated upon in that strange time.

Duff Cooper, as Minister of Information, had led the pack against Wodehouse, but now he showed a creditable disinclination to follow up the attack with a kill. On the contrary, he was ready to help in easing the Wodehouses' path. Wodehouse's trouble, he contended, was that all his life he had successfully evaded reality and his responsibilities as a citizen. Even paying his taxes was something about which he took a decidedly casual attitude, and when his country was fighting for its life his heart continued to be in Blandings Castle rather than on the beaches of Dunkirk or in blitzed London. This, despite the adulation, the honours and the wealth showered upon him by his fellow-countrymen. It might be so, I replied, but surely there were different sorts and levels of reality. Could we be sure, for instance, that Hitler's ravings and Churchill's rhetoric and Roosevelt's Four Freedoms would seem more real to posterity than Blandings Castle? I rather doubted it. As Evelyn Waugh put it in his broadcast tribute, in Wodehouse's world 'there has been no Fall of Man, no aboriginal calamity; the gardens of Blandings Castle are that original garden from which we are all exiled.'

Duff Cooper had a useful propensity, which now afflicted him, of seeming to fall asleep, or perhaps actually falling asleep, when a conversation went on too long, or failed to hold his attention. One became aware that his eyes had closed, his chin fallen onto his chest, his breathing become audibly regular. Then, suddenly, he would come to. When he did, I made one last point. Though so dyed-in-the-wool a noncombatant, Wodehouse had, all unconsciously, made at least one useful contribution to the war effort. The Germans, in their literal way, took his works as a guide to English manners, and used them when briefing their agents for a mission across the Channel. Thus it happened that an agent they dropped in the Fen country was wearing spats – an unaccustomed article of attire which led to his speedy apprehension. Had he not been caught, he would, presumably, have made his way to London in search of the Drones Club, and thought to escape notice by throwing bread about in restaurants in the manner of Bertie Wooster. Duff Cooper agreed that this was a notable service deserving of an OBE, but did not feel that, in the circumstances, he could recommend Wodehouse for one.

Nothing impresses the English more than to live to a ripe old age, something that sufficed to make even so ill-tempered an old lady as Queen Victoria popular. As the years have passed, Wodehouse has increasingly come to be regarded as a Grand-Old-Man-of-Letters. His stories have appeared on the television screen, his books continue to be popular, his ninetieth birthday was an occasion for public acclamation, and it may confidently be anticipated that on his hundredth he will be knighted. Whether, and if so to what extent, he remembers his time of distress, he keeps as his own secret. As with all imaginative people, there is an area of inner reserve in him which one never penetrates. The scars of his time in the stocks are doubtless hidden there. In one of his rare references to the experience, he said to me that it made him feel like a music-hall comedian, accustomed always to applause, who suddenly gets the bird. This, I think, is what it signified to him, and I daresay, what it signifies.

By this time Graham Greene had left MI6 and joined the publishing firm of Eyre & Spottiswoode, calculating – as it turned out incorrectly, as far as he personally was concerned – that the aftermath of the war would be a time of great difficulty for writers, in which it would be well to have some secure economic base. The precise occasion of his leaving MI6 was very characteristic; as part of his machinations inside Section Five, Kim Philby wanted to promote him – something that Greene considered an outrage, and indignantly refused to countenance, to the point of resigning. At the Eyre & Spottiswoode office in Bedford Street, he sat in a room with Douglas Jerrold, where I several times visited them. It would be difficult to imagine two more strangely assorted human beings; both Catholic converts, certainly, but Jerrold induced thereby to move to the extreme Right, as a supporter of General Franco, and Greene to move ever further Leftwards as a fervent advocate of Catholic–Marxist dialogue. If I had occasion to talk with one of them, I was keenly aware of the other's presence; a telephone call by either produced a sort of anguished silence in which a third person found himself listening intently to every word spoken into the receiver, however softly. Even their appearance made a striking contrast. Jerrold gave an impression of being enormous. He dressed in an old-fashioned conventional way – black coat, striped trousers, stiff collar, foot-wear noticeably hand-made for him by Lobb. His head was tiny, thinly covered with sparse hair, and altogether he looked, as Kingsmill used to say, like an inflated *hors d'œuvre*. Greene, on the other hand, was tall and slight, with the look of a perennial undergraduate engaged in working out some ingenious joke or impersonation. It is a tribute to both their characters that they managed to survive this strange proximity without a serious quarrel.

Knowing that I was going to Paris, Greene asked me to seek out François Mauriac and get him to agree to English translations of his books, to be brought out in a uniform edition by Eyre & Spottiswoode. This I gladly agreed to do, and in the very early days of the Liberation made a special point of calling at the office of Mauriac's publisher, Grasset, which I found to be in a condition of confusion. Grasset himself was suffering from acute *ennuies*, having published during the occupation numerous volumes with a decidedly collaborationist flavour, and had retired for the time being, I was given to understand, to some sort of a psychiatric institution. The firm was left in charge of his red-haired wife; a fiery lady with whom, nonetheless, I was able to establish friendly relations. Only afterwards did it occur to me that in the circumstances my appearance, unannounced and in uniform, may well have created some consternation in the Grasset office; though, actually, my mood was one of considerable diffidence. I stood for quite a while in the street outside before I could nerve myself to go in at all. Mme Grasset pronounced herself wholly in favour of the translation project, which she commended to Mauriac, and it was arranged that I should go to see him. In due course Mauriac's novels appeared under the Eyre & Spottiswoode imprint, brilliantly translated into English by Gerard Hopkins, and proved a great success.

Mauriac proved to be a frail, intense man of a kind often found among French writers and intellectuals, who seem to shake themselves to pieces with the vigour and urgency of their thoughts and words; like some ancient ricketty old car which shakes and shivers when the engine is started up, so that one constantly marvels that it can hold together at all. In his case, the impression was intensified by some impediment in his throat which caused him to speak always in a hoarse whisper, and made talking with him on the telephone an agony. Despite this, his company was enormously stimulating, and, at times hilariously

funny. Once when I called to see him he was striding up and down
dictating the obituary of a distinguished friend, who, I gathered, had
just died. He was obviously deeply moved, and, between each rotund
phrase, delivered in his breathless whisper, he would pause to get up
steam for the next – '*Encore un de la petite bande des vraiment grands* . . .
pour moi désolant . . . *pour la France une perte irréparable* . . .' As an
obituary connoisseur myself, who has enjoyed few journalistic tasks
more than fixing a sheet of paper in his typewriter, and beginning,
of some politician still very much alive: 'The death of X deprives the
Labour (Conservative) party of one of its leading figures in the House
of Commons (Lords) . . .' I rated his performance highly. It was only
because of his whispering voice, he told me, that he was elected to the
French Academy; the Academicians calculating that he must have cancer
of the throat, and so would only be briefly among them. His stories
about this august body were endlessly diverting, especially the ones
relating to General Joffre, who had sat among them, largely in im-
penetrable silence. There was only one word, he said, which should be
emblazoned in letters of fire on the Academy's walls, and he brought
it out with immense zest and verve – the word PROSTATE. Once I
asked him if it was true that André Gide was about to become a
Catholic; a look of anguished horror spread over his face as he said he
prayed heaven, if he ever did, that it would be a few seconds before
he expired.

His own Resistance record was, of course, impeccable; but what I
particularly admired was that, instead of luxuriating in this, he used
the position of authority it gave him to protest against the intolerance
and vengefulness which the Liberation had released in many of his
fellow-countrymen; especially in the irregular formations like the FFI
and FTP (*Franc-Tireurs Partisans*) who, in Paris and in many parts
of the country, were behaving as terrorists, having taken over the role,
and sometimes the actual premises and sinister gear, left behind by
the Gestapo. His articles in the *Figaro* on this theme delighted and
heartened me as they appeared. Like Alexander Solzhenitsyn's speech
on the occasion of his being awarded the Nobel Prize for literature—
an award which, incidentally, Mauriac ardently promoted shortly
before he died – they raised a lone but influential voice against the
destruction of literature and art by making them an instrument of
power rather than of truth. Applying his own principles, he defended
his arch-enemy Charles Maurras, against the vilification to which he
was subjected in the press and at his trial, and pointed out that a

Liberation which applied to the victor, but not to the vanquished was a mockery. He also did everything in his power, including a personal approach to General de Gaulle, to save the poet Robert Brasillach, who was nonetheless executed as a collaborator on 6 February 1945. When Mauriac died, I was asked by the representatives of a French newspaper if I had any particular memory of him. Yes, I had, I said, and recalled how once, when I was at Fresnes Prison, someone begged me to get in touch on his behalf with *St François des Assises* (St Francis of the Assizes), meaning Mauriac. What a marvellous nick-name to die with!

Through my contact with Mauriac and his publisher, I got to know Henry Muller and his most charming wife, at whose house I met numerous French writers many of whom were having *ennuies*, of different degrees of seriousness, as a result of what they had written, or not written, during the Occupation. One I took a special fancy to was Fabre-Luce, who boasted that he had been put in prison, successively, by Daladier, Pétain, the Germans and the Gaullists. When he went in for his Liberation stretch, the warders greeted him like an old friend; the moment he got out, he started a clandestine press with a view to exposing the absurdities of the Gaullists in power. Another French writer I particularly wanted to meet was Montherlant, whose novel, *Les Célibataires* (first translated into English, badly, as I considered, with the title *The Death of the Upper Classes*; followed, later, by an excellent translation, properly entitled *The Bachelors*, by Terence Kilmartin), I greatly admired. He, I gathered, was having really quite serious *ennuies*, and for the time being was lying very low, if not actually in hiding. Before the war, he had specialised in denouncing French degeneracy, and when France collapsed in 1940 could not forbear pointing out that it was just what he would have expected from so run-down and decadent a nation. This displeased not only the French, but the Germans as well, who felt that it belittled their victory. So he was forced to adjust his position accordingly, indicating that, after all, the French had put up a good fight. One way and another, when the Liberation came, he found himself in a difficult situation.

Nonetheless, the Mullers were able to produce him for dinner one evening. He turned out to be a taciturn taut sort of man, who had little to say, and gave an impression of being under great strain; not just because of *ennuies* – which I really don't think bothered him too much, though, other things being equal, he preferred keeping out of Fresnes to going in – but rather of some inner tension, reminding me, of all people, of Enoch Powell. He was, as I learnt, another Nietzsche admirer, though not, like Powell, to the point of emulating his soup-strainer moustache. The spiritual children of Nietzsche are mostly benighted; when I was editing Ciano's Diaries I was fascinated to find that, with his crazed sense of the fitness of things, Hitler sent Mussolini for his sixtieth birthday present a splendidly bound edition of Nietzsche's works, which the Duce opened, surely with a sinking heart, when he had become the prisoner of his despised Italian fellow-countrymen, before Skorzeny came – I was going to say, to rescue him, but, more appropriately, to take him away.

When I complimented Montherlant, too fulsomely perhaps, on *Les Célibataires*, he was not particularly pleased; the book of his that he took most pride in was *Pitié pour les Femmes*, which I considered to be an essay – and rather an unconvincing one – in that most ridiculous of all vanities, phallic exhibitionism; D. H. Lawrence being, of course, the prize exhibitor in this field. I gathered from Montherlant that he lived like a monk (France Muller confirmed this), dedicating himself wholly to his chosen work of writing; unconcerned about comfort, or food, or even heating; just sitting doggedly at his desk, and with infinite care and pains shaping words to his purpose. His taut face bore witness to this dedication; he looked like a monk – but one without laughter, bowing down in wilfulness rather than surrender, burrowing into the ego rather than escaping from it. After the war I had some correspondence with him à *propos* an article I had written on him and his work in the *TLS*, when he was little known in England, which seemed to please him. I even made some desultory efforts to promote a collected edition of his works in English, like Mauriac's – a project that met with his warm approval, if only because he was so passionately opposed to anything of the kind being undertaken in America, of which he had an obsessive hatred. Nothing, however, came of the project.

It did not surprise me that, when his *ennuies* had been dispersed – which they soon were – Montherlant's fame grew apace. The greatest craving of a scared *bourgeoisie* is for writers like Montherlant who make their secret authoritarian cravings intellectually respectable. (Their children, incidentally, achieve the same purpose by including in their proletarian fancy-dress, military tunics, German helmets and swastika arm-bands.) Thus Chesterton, Belloc and T. S. Eliot gave anti-semiticism literary credentials, as Pound did racialism – in his case, of so extreme a nature that it was calculated to make even a backwoods Afrikaner uneasy. Yeats, likewise, brought comfort and joy by writing the marching song of Franco's Irish contingent, and Lawrence by commending thinking with our blood, producing on this theme, *Apocalypse*, with its strong affinity with *Mein Kampf*. Not to mention Céline, who carried his ravings, not just to the end of the night, but to the end of the world, and still died in his bed; while Orwell's brilliant send-up of a broiler-house state was taken as applying specifically to the USSR, instead of, as was the case, to contemporary authoritarianism in all its guises. In the end, Montherlant, like Hemingway, took his own life; they were both bull-fight fanciers – that sick resort of the weak and solace of the timid.

At the Boulevard Suchet, I heard much talk, mostly cynical and facetious, about the different grades and categories of *ennuies* then being endured, and gleaned a good deal of information on the subject, of varying degrees and reliability; not least about the famous Mme Coco Chanel. As it happens, I was to be taken to see her by an old friend of hers, F, who had appeared in Paris, covered in gold braid, as a member of one of the numerous liaison missions which by now were roosting there. So I went along with F to Mme Chanel's lavish *haute-couture* and perfume emporium with a sense of being on duty as well as pleasure bent. My first impression of her was of someone tiny and frail, who, if one puffed at her too hard, might easily just disintegrate; her powdery frame collapsing into a minute heap of dust, as those frail houses had in the London Blitz. She seemed to have various pieces and shapes of shining metal about her person; like Earl Attlee in old age when he went to a ceremonial dinner, or one of the ancient men-at-arms at Windsor Castle who appear in breast-plate and armour at gatherings of Knights of the Garter. It seemed extraordinary that she should be able to support this extra weight. By way of attendant, she had with her, not, as might have been supposed, some elegant young girl, but a grey-haired lady who looked as aged as herself, to whom she gave instructions quite softly but containing a hidden note of authority which sent her scuttling off to do her mistress's bidding.

If Mme Chanel felt any uneasiness at my presence, she gave no indication of it; towards F she adopted an attitude of old familiarity, as though to say: 'Don't imagine, my dear F (she addressed him by his surname), that your being dressed up in all that gold braid impresses me at all. I know you!' Nor had she, as a matter or fact, any cause for serious anxiety, having successfully withstood the first *épuration* assault at the time of the Liberation by one of those majestically simple strokes which made Napoleon so successful a general; she just put an announcement in the window of her emporium that scent was free for GI's, who thereupon queued up to get their bottles of Chanel No. 5, and would have been outraged if the French police had touched a hair of her head. Having thus gained a breathing space, she proceeded to look for help *à gauche et à droite*, and not in vain, thereby managing to avoid making even a token appearance among the gilded company – Maurice Chevalier, Jean Cocteau, Sacha Guitry, and other worthies – on a collaborationist charge.

The three of us – gold-braided F, Mme Chanel and I – sat side by side on a particularly soft settee, in near darkness, two candles our only illumination, and were served an excellent dinner. The filet mignon was exquisitely tender, the red wine soft and mellow, the cognac silky, with other delicacies virtually unobtainable in Paris at that time, to all of which F did full justice, while Mme Chanel and I only nibbled. The elderly attendant was not permitted to sit down with us, but hovered round in case anything was required of her. Even in this dim twilight, Mme Chanel seemed immensely old and incorporeal; I had the feeling almost that she might expire that very evening, seated between F and me, and we just tiptoe away, leaving her there with the debris of our meal – the coffee cups, the billowing brandy glasses, the cigarette ends, hers stained a deep red. Actually, of course, she lived on for years and years, growing ever richer and more famous. I even had a glimpse of her villa looking down on the Mediterranean, all done up in shades of lavender-pink. Someone who worked there remarked of it: '*C'est une vie en rose là haut.*' So, I am sure it was, and for all I know still is, where-ever she may now be.

During the dinner she and F reminisced about old times. At the slightest hint of patronage in his manner, she brought him up sharply, as it were looking through his gold braid at another F she remembered, speaking and behaving in a very different style, thus effectively putting him in his place. I had heard that for a number of years she had been the regular companion of an English duke, and asked her if she often saw Churchill in those days. Oh, yes, she said, she knew dear Winston well, and used to play piquet with him, making a point, of course, of always losing, as otherwise he'd be in a bad temper (*mauvaise humeur*). She felt sure, she said, that he'd never come to Paris without seeing her. I didn't say so, but I felt equally sure that he would; in fact, had. Afterwards, I tried to draft some sort of report on my evening with Mme Chanel, but really there was nothing to say except that I was sure the *épuration* mills, however small they might grind, would never grind her – as indeed, proved to be the case. If only I had been Cusden,

I reflected, I might have found out all sorts of things – how she managed to get to and from Spain during the occupation, whether she also offered free scent to the German troops, who were her clients, associates and intimates in those years. Alas, all I had done was to listen; fascinated, and even a little awed, at the masterly way she harpooned and skinned the braided F.

When I had been in Paris some months, a directive came from London about a new MI6 department which had been set up to deal specifically with Soviet Intelligence activities, including sabotage and subversion. The directive had been drafted by Philby, who, as he recounts in his book, *My Secret War*, had managed to get control of the department in question, the person he ousted being none other than my old Lourenço Marques friend and colleague, Steptoe. It remains a nice point as to whether Soviet Intelligence had more to gain from having its own man, in the person of Philby, or Steptoe in this post – like considering whether it is more advantageous, in a football match, to bribe a man on the other side to kick balls into his own goal, or to arrange for them to choose a goal-keeper who may be relied on to let every ball through, while supposing he is valiantly keeping them out. Contrary to what was, and probably still is, believed in the Kremlin, up to this point nothing much had been done about the field covered by Philby's new department, apart from giving diplomats going to Communist countries an article to read, which had once appeared in the *Spectator*, on the Intelligence and ideological hazards likely to confront them. As the original cutting got dog-eared through passing from hand to hand, it was cyclostyled, the copies being carefully marked 'Most Secret'. The article was later expanded into a handbook, undertaken by an estimable don named Carew-Hunt. When surveys, studies, analyses and other presentations of the subject began to proliferate, especially across the Atlantic, Carew-Hunt was allowed to publish his handbook, and it duly appeared under his name.

I was supposed to refer any queries I might receive from Philby or his staff to Soustelle, and had a discussion about it with him, Passy being also present. I could see that they did not like the idea at all, and it was not difficult to guess why. The DGER – as we had at last got into the way of calling the *Services Spéciaux* – was already under heavy attack as an organ of crypto-Fascism (quite unjustly, I may say); if it came out that it was supplying anti-Soviet material to Allied Intelligence agencies, these suspicions would seem to be confirmed. At the same time, of course, I knew quite well that in the reconstructed French counter-espionage services, Soviet activities were by no means being overlooked. Philby's department sent me two token questions to put to the French: Where was the headquarters of the French Communist Party? and, Who was its effective boss? I showed the questions to Soustelle and Passy, just as they had come to me, as an example of the kind of information we should be seeking. Passy found them highly amusing; after all, he said, the answers could be got from the Paris telephone directory. I protested that this was a preposterous argument; if Intelligence agents were not to go sleuthing after information which was available in telephone directories, what future had the profession got? Soustelle and Passy assumed, of course, that we were hard at work finding out, with our usual skill, everything there was to know about Soviet espionage, and that these naïve questions were just a bluff. Whether other channels with the French were opened up, or, more probably, given that a Soviet agent was in charge of the department concerned with uncovering Soviet agents, whether the whole initiative was dropped, I have no idea, but I personally never heard any more about it.

One consequence of this abortive *demarché* for me personally was that I became acquainted with Colonel A, and, through him, was thenceforth to be a welcome visitor at a small convent in the neighbourhood of the Rue du Cherche-Midi, where my happiest hours in Paris in that last year of the war were spent. The Colonel called to see me at my office shortly after my talk with Soustelle and Passy, having somehow got to know what had passed between us. He was a large vigorous man, who stumped about energetically despite a severe leg wound received in the 1914–18 war; gruff and hearty and rumbustious. In my experience rumbustiousness is easier to bear in a foreign language than in one's own; anyway, the Colonel's did not unduly trouble me. He wanted, he said, to have a serious talk with me, but not there in the Boulevard Suchet, where – winking and looking round knowingly – *les murs ont des oreilles*. If I wanted to know more about him he would refer me to – and he mentioned numerous eminent personages whom I could not possibly have approached, as he must have known. He himself, he went on, was connected with French Intelligence, but not with these amateurs and adventurers in the Boulevard Suchet; with *les gens vraiment du métier*, to whom in due course he would be happy to present me. The rendezvous he suggested – safe, discreet, and quiet – was the little Cherche-Midi convent, and I agreed to meet him there for dinner the following evening. A few discreet enquiries about the Colonel disclosed that his Resistance record was impeccable, that he was an industrialist of sorts, in a small way, and altogether a good fellow, though with some pretty lunatic ideas, to the point of being maybe a little off his head (*un peu détraqué*), which was just about what I had thought myself from meeting him.

When I arrived at the convent I was taken straight to the Reverend Mother, who had lately been awarded the *Croix de Guerre* by General de Gaulle for her part in the Resistance, especially in hiding people on the run. Her reputation was very high at that time, so much so that when, after the Liberation, milk was exceedingly scarce, and it was decided to allocate most of what there was to nursing mothers, her nuns were entrusted with the distribution, as being, in everyone's eyes, beyond any suspicion of corruption or partiality. Their house had the particular shining cleanliness religious houses have; the Avenue Marigny shadow being noticeably absent. I noticed the same thing when Mother Teresa's Sisters of Charity took over the upper part of a condemned house in Notting Hill. It was not just that they swept and scrubbed and polished, which, of course, they did to a high degree. Somehow they made the place luminous, so that visiting there was like climbing up to Heaven. The convent in the unsalubrious Cherche-Midi district seemed likewise to have caught the light of some sun outside the universe.

It was obvious, when the Colonel arrived, that he was a favoured visitor. He cracked jokes, took liberties and paid compliments, pretending that he only entertained his guests in the convent because of the excellence of the food and wine provided, and of his stinginess, which made him appreciate not having to pay. Before sitting down to eat we attended the evening office in the chapel; the Colonel groaning and puffing as he got with difficulty onto his knees, and then when I looked sidelong at him, his old worldly, weather-beaten face wearing so serene and joyful an expression, I found myself envying him, and staring, as I so often have, at the altar, as though I hoped that enlightenment would come visibly out of it to me; maybe as a voice, or a dove descending from Heaven. This, as I well know, can never be. The process is the other way round; a purified heart has to be offered to the altar, rather than the altar dispensing purification.

The Colonel and I sat down to dinner together – an excellent dinner of fish, it being a Friday. A nun served us, and the Reverend Mother stood talking with us for part of the time, but declined to join us at table.

In her face I noted the special kind of sagacity and sense of the absurd that comes of understanding the world without being in it; of knowing within the Cloud of Unknowing – what might appropriately be called, in her case, the coquetry of Christ. I greatly appreciated her company, and was sad when she left us, the Colonel having, presumably, given her instructions that he had private matters to discuss with me. What he had to tell me was a detailed story, naming names, of ostensible Communist infiltration of the French Government, administration and security services. As he went on, I confess that my heart sank; not so much because I necessarily disbelieved him – though I largely did – as because, in my mood of contentment, I did not particularly care whether what he said was truth or fantasy. He went on and on, and finally I got up to go, promising that – for what it was worth, which wasn't much – I would send on to London the information he had given me. This I did, in a very abbreviated version, with many reservations of my own, and giving full weight to the possibility that he was a bit cracked.

From Philby I got back a contemptuous dismissal of the Colonel's allegations as so much poppycock, and a recommendation to put any further offerings from this source straight into the w.p.b. (I particularly remember the newspaper-style use of initials; as scrawled editorially on some proffered news item or syndicated feature.) Coming from such a source, the judgement might almost seem like an endorsement of the authenticity of the Colonel's disclosures. After all, from a Soviet agent's point of view, if they were purely nonsensical, the obvious tactic would be to let them seem to be taken seriously and filed away. Then, when, in due course, they were discredited, other similar reports which might have some truth in them would be automatically devalued with them. As it happens, too, one or two stories I read after the war of scandals that came to light in the French Intelligence services seemed to me to lend some support to the Colonel's allegations. Perhaps, after all, he did know something; if so, it was lost, more through my fault than Philby's. I have always been glad in any capacity – as editor, publisher's reader, journalist – to put any document in the w.p.b., since thereby I am let off having to read it. So, for this inglorious reason, if for no other, Philby's instruction about communications from the Colonel was scrupulously observed by me. Into the w.p.b. they went, unread.

All the same, I did go on seeing him, and visiting the Cherche-Midi convent, where for a while he lay quite seriously ill and in considerable pain. I would sit beside his bed, usually with one of the sisters present in case he needed anything – medicine, or a bed-pan, or to have his temperature taken. Sick and weak as he was, he managed to go on complaining, with such voice as he could muster, about France's steady decline since the Dreyfus case, if not since the Revolution, Blum's *Front Populaire* Government being a significant milestone on this road to ruin. He imagined a vast, elaborate international network of financiers, Communists, Free Masons, Leftist intellectuals and Americans, whereby a spell had been cast over Christendom, making fair foul and foul fair – as those three notable precursors of Women's Lib, the Horrid Sisters in Macbeth, put it. England alone, the Colonel considered, could break the spell, and Churchill alone lead Christendom back to its true path and destiny. I must be the intermediary, and *l'Intelligence Service* the instrument, for bringing about this splendid transformation. Without delay, I should go to London; to 'C', to Buckingham Palace, to Downing Street, to Westminster, bearing the message. It was useless trying to explain that I should make a ludicrous emissary – as though Noah, instead of sending out a dove from the Ark to see if the floods had subsided, had sent a frog to croak and enjoy the high water.

When the Colonel was better, I brought Duff Cooper to dine with him at the convent, first picking him up at the British Embassy where Lady Diana had a little group of worshippers gathered round her, she statuesque among them, like her namesake of the Ephesians – dons, photographers, dress-designers, film-makers, wits and wisecrackers, with a place, albeit lowly, for the merely rich. Duff Cooper extricated himself from this company, not too unwillingly, I thought, and we reported together in an Embassy car.

The dinner at the convent was not a success; the Reverend Mother was not as impressed as I hoped she might have been with a visit from the British Ambassador, and indirectly with me for bringing him, and the Colonel, having started by being excessively flattering and affable, got involved in a tirade about Yalta, which touched off in Duff Cooper one of his sudden spasms of rage – the counterpart of his equally sudden bouts of falling asleep – when his usually mild and genial features became distorted with fury, the veins standing out, the eyes misted over, if not slightly bloodshot, the teeth grinding, the voice rising to shrill heights. All this, of course, in French, which he knew well, but which, as he spoke it, was ill-suited to such stridency.

We left early, and I looked in at the Embassy for a farewell drink. Duff Cooper spoke of his political future, about which he had obviously been thinking a lot. His assumption was that Churchill must win a general election when it came, and would offer him, at best, only a mediocre job. Why not, then, stay on in Paris, where he was well content? It seemed like a sound argument at the time, and in Paris he stayed. If, of course, he had known that the cards would fall the other way, he would have given up his Paris job, returned to the House of Commons, and been an important figure on the Opposition Front Bench, with a good chance of a major post when the next Conservative Government came to be formed. In politics, as in playing patience, a single mistake is usually ruinous – though in this particular case ruinous is a relative term, involving, as it did for Duff Cooper, trivial but lucrative duties on behalf of the *Wagons-Lits* and Sir Alexander Korda, rather than, say, becoming Home Secretary.

An encounter at the convent that passed off more satisfactorily was with a certain M. Jacques, about whom the Colonel and the Reverend Mother frequently spoke, as someone who stayed there from time to time, and whom they would particularly like me to meet. This was duly arranged, and I went to the convent one evening to dine with him. He was obviously in some sort of disguise; his long hair and moustache did not fit his face, and his clothes – old and shabby – seemed wrong. He turned out to be Paul Baudouin, first de Gaulle's colleague in the Ministry of Defence under Paul Reynaud, and then Pétain's Foreign Minister. I enormously admired the Reverend Mother for hiding him, as she had hidden people in the Resistance during the German occupation. To take risks for a particular cause by providing sanctuary for its fugitives can be heroic, but to take risks on behalf of all fugitives, whoever they may be, and whatever the cause, is the prerogative of saints rather than of heroes. I was also greatly flattered that the Reverend Mother should have considered it perfectly safe to present me to M. Jacques, thereby disclosing his identity to me, when he was very much on the run.

He struck me as being a cool, able, managerial sort of man, who by accident had strayed into the world of politics and power; like a well-trained circus lion straying into the jungle. Even now he seemed somehow bewildered; as though he still could not understand how he, who sat so contentedly in board-rooms and in ministries, should have come to find himself, shabbily dressed and with unbecomingly abundant whiskers and hair, lurking in a convent near the Rue du Cherche-Midi, with a prison conveniently at hand into which he might so easily, at any moment, be popped. About Pétain, the author of his misfortunes, he spoke with a kind of wonder; as it might be an accomplished steeple-chaser brooding over a pedigree horse which, instead of winning the Grand National, had thrown him at the first fence. The Marshal, he said, still dropping his voice respectfully in mentioning his name, was unfortunately only lucid for certain periods during the day, which grew shorter and shorter as time passed. I imagined Baudouin lurking in his ante-room with carefully prepared documents in his hand, hoping to catch the Head of State during one of his moments of lucidity. Subsequently, he was arrested and imprisoned briefly in Fresnes.

After the war, when he published a volume of reminiscences of his political life, he asked me to write a Foreword to the English edition, which I did. For some reason, Professor Namier was very taken with the book, and asked me for a specimen of Baudouin's handwriting, which I provided. This he submitted to some necromancer, who specialised in deducing people's characters from their handwriting. To my considerable surprise Namier attached great importance to his findings, which he incorporated in a long front article he wrote in the *TLS* on the book. It was this article that he read aloud to me in a slow flat voice, with the deliberation of an artillery barrage; which, however, I endured with such cheerfulness as I could summon up, out of affection for the dear, solemn, preposterous man. I saw Baudouin once more, in paris, at an office he then occupied in the Boulevard Victor Hugo. We had a somewhat distant chat from which it did not emerge what precisely his office was concerned with, though I assumed it was something to do with money. He told me that he had received several feelers from de Gaulle about joining him, but always declined. About this, I was, and remain, dubious. I think his vague embarrassment when I was with him was due to the fact that my presence reminded him of a time which he wished to forget. Shortly afterwards I read he had died. He was a man I should, perhaps, have found more interesting than I did.

It was around this time I received an intimation that Kim Philby was coming over to Paris in connection with his new duties as head of the department concerned with Soviet espionage, and that he wanted to see me. He stayed in the Avenue Marigny house, and we arranged to dine together. This proved to be a very strange, though by no means unhappy, evening; certainly, it is one that I can never forget. We went to a restaurant to eat, and Kim, being very fond of food, ordered a lot of exotic dishes; whereas I, never having taken the slightest interest in gastronomy ordered my usual melon, omelette and fruit and cheese. I drank a fair amount, however, as also did Kim, and whether as a result of this, or for some other reason, for once we felt at ease with one another. Kim's stutter was less marked than usual, which of course made things easier; I asked about his family, especially his wife Eileen, and he responded in the style of an affectionate father and husband. Then I asked about people in the office, and we laughed over some of the famous comics; like Colonel Vivien; who had actually given me an account – which I imitated – of how one of his agents, executed by the Turks, had managed to send a message: 'Tell the Colonel I kept the faith.' I regret to say that I also threw a lot of ridicule on poor Steptoe, whom Kim had just scuppered and sunk without trace. The ostensible reason for our getting together – Kim's new job, and what might be expected of me and my contacts with the French in connection with it – remained virtually unmentioned. This, in my experience, often happens when a meeting has been arranged for a particular purpose; like seeking someone out with a view to borrowing money, or effecting a seduction, and then finding oneself talking loquaciously about everything under the sun to avoid coming to the point.

When we left our restaurant in the Champs Élysées (HMG footed the bill), the evening seemed very mild and agreeable, the lights very bright, the people strolling about and sitting in the cafés, very delightful. It was one of those occasions when you seem to hear, underlying the noise of life, music mysteriously playing in the far distance – a kind of heavenly *muzak* coming from loudspeakers posted along the Milky Way, and you wonder how it has come about that there are so many beautiful women in the world. Instead of returning to the Avenue Marigny, we strolled by the river, and Kim pointed up to a block of flats, saying that he had lived there with his first wife. This was the first time he had ever mentioned a previous wife to me; and it was only afterwards, when his past came to be minutely explored, that I learnt that she had been a German Jewess and Communist Party member, whom he had met while covering the Spanish Civil War on the Franco side for *The Times*, and who was generally assumed to have played an important part in his development into a party activist and Soviet agent.

Quite suddenly Kim said: 'Let's go to the Rue de Grenelle.' I didn't know then (though I should have) that this was where the Soviet Embassy was situated, and supposed he might have in his mind some favourite café or night-spot. Anyway, I was in a mood to go anywhere, so we set off. Kim now began at last to talk about his new responsibilities, and I realised, at the time without any particular amazement, that we were making for the Soviet Embassy. How are we going to get in there? Kim kept saying, and went on to expatiate upon the special difficulties of penetrating a Soviet embassy as compared with others – no chance of planting a servant when all the staff, down to the lowliest kitchen-maids and porters and chauffeurs are imported from the USSR, and sometimes, in reality, hold quite senior positions in the Intelligence *apparat*. Tremendous obstacles, too, in the way of bugging the place; they never let foreign electricians or builders, anyone like that, into the embassy. Listening devices, observation posts, inside agents, all ruled out; the staff themselves, high and low, rigidly controlled, only certain picked members allowed to circulate freely, and even they are often kept under surveillance. Look at it! – by this time we were in the Rue de Grenelle – every blind drawn, every door locked, every window with its iron grating, the very fire-escape contained in steel-netting; even so, behind the doors and windows, round-the-clock guards, burglar alarms, every imaginable and unimaginable security precaution.

He carried on like this in an almost demented way; not exactly shaking his fists, but gesticulating and shouting at the hermetically sealed embassy, standing so insulated and isolated in a Paris street, as though it had been just dropped there out of the sky, to be removed, intact, when its purpose had been served. While all this was going on, we were in full sight of the embassy, and of the two *flics* posted at its main entrance. Despite my fuddled state, I had my wits sufficiently about me to register in my mind that this was most irregular, if not reprehensible, behaviour on the part of a senior MI6 officer, to whom we were not allowed to refer by name, but only by symbol, even in a coded message. When I awoke the following morning I saw it as, not only irregular or reprehensible, but inconceivable. Had it really happened? I was forced to conclude that it had; I had neither dreamed nor imagined it – the two of us in the Rue de Grenelle, loitering there in so noticeable a way, and Kim behaving so strangely and uncharacteristically.

Even now I have no convincing explanation to offer. That Kim was just drunk and didn't know what he was doing? – quite ruled out; if he had been subject to that sort of thing he would have given himself away long before, and anyway, back at the Avenue Marigny, he was perfectly calm and collected. That he had some special purpose? – but what? To exhibit me to his pals at the Embassy? My ego, inflated as it easily becomes, wouldn't stretch to that supposition; I was, as they say in the trade, 'known' to the Soviet security services as a result of my time in Moscow, and of things I had written, but there was no reason on earth why so strange a procedure should be followed just to take a look at me. That Kim wanted to test me out, with a view perhaps to using me and my connections with the DGER in some way?—I scarcely think so; after all, it was not as though we didn't know one another, and anyway, he was my boss, and could give me instructions. Was there even, perhaps, some vague notion in his mind that I might be involved in his double-cross? This, on consideration, seemed absurd, if only for the reason that Kim was sufficiently familiar with my record as an Intelligence officer to know that I should be worse than useless in such a role. Even Burgess, for whom Kim nourished a romantic admiration – disastrously for him, as it turned out – in the end proved a liability. So did Whitaker Chambers. The best traitors are the most ostensibly diligent and attentive to their betters – like Donald Maclean and Alger Hiss, and, for that matter, Kim himself. Set an Establishment to catch an Establishment.

No, the only convincing explanation I can find for an otherwise inexplicable incident is that in some peculiar way it arose out of the seeing double which is inescapable in the role Kim had taken on. To an infinitely less degree than he, I experienced the same sort of thing in Lourenço Marques as a result of the various stratagems and masquerades I involved myself in there; all that *jouant la comédie*, as Serge put it. Thus, I well remember vaguely considering whether, if I went home via Lisbon, I might not look in at the German Embassy there – they would certainly have heard of me from Wertz's reports – with a view to making my number with them. To what end? None, actually, though I could easily have worked out something that would have satisfied Section Five – or so I thought. It was not that I wanted to be a traitor, or, for that matter, a patriot or hero; just that establishing contact with the German Embassy in Lisbon would give a new twist to my script, introduce some fresh characters, and open up the possibility of quite new episodes. When I spoke to Johann about this notion, he looked, for once, really agitated. 'You mustn't think of such a thing,' he said: 'you simply don't understand. Our people mean business, they'd skin you alive, they'd have you talking as you've never talked before.' He spoke obviously from experience, and I promised to heed his words of warning. Anyway, I didn't go home via Lisbon.

What happens, as it seems to me, in playing the double-agent game, is that the magnetic field of one's mind gets dispersed, with the particles flying here, there and everywhere. Instead of straining after an integral self, one becomes first two, then maybe several selves, functioning independently. Which of them happens to be uppermost at a particular moment depends on circumstances; on the chance of a mood, whimsical or otherwise, pushing one in this, that or the other direction. It is rather like living, instead of writing, a novel; being each character in turn, experiencing their adventures, their hopes and disappointments and moments of exaltation, as, for instance, Dickens did when his novels – sometimes two or three at a time – were being serialised while he was writing them. Indeed, the nearest I came to getting back into the double-agent state of mind after the war was when I used to walk round Regent's Park most afternoons with Tony Powell at the time he was writing the first volume of his *Music of Time*, and we would discuss, as we went along, the forthcoming adventures of his characters. Had the time come for A to seduce B? And if C got to know, how would he react? And D – what, if anything would she feel if C, as he was bound to, told her about it? By the time our walk was over, I had to jerk myself back into my own identity, so absorbed had I become in these fictional beings.

If one sees Kim's double-cross in these fictional rather than ideological terms, an episode like the one in the Rue de Grenelle becomes more comprehensible – as an interlude, perhaps even comic relief, in a plot moving majestically on to its *dénouement*, with Kim not just the author and only begetter, but the villain and the hero as well, whichever might be which. He, the hawk-eyed Secret Serviceman, infinitely resourceful and audacious, and also the star Soviet agent, one day to have his head on a Russian postage-stamp, like the famous Sorge. Dedicated, ruthless, inscrutable, with all sorts of minor roles as well – Bohemian boozer and amorist with Burgess, Arabist and persona-grata in mysterious Mecca like his father, and so on, including the brief essay in pure farce in the Rue de Grenelle.

As it happened, quite a number of dossiers of double-cross practitioners, both French and British, passed through my hands while I was in the Boulevard Suchet with the DGER, the problem in each case being to decide whether the double agent in question leant more heavily on our or the enemy's side. In most instances, it was an impossible problem to resolve for the very simple reason that the agent himself, by virtue of his circumstances, never had occasion to decide definitely where his allegiances lay. Like a man with a wife and a mistress, he maintained a position of fluidity, giving his heart to both – or to neither. One particular dossier, relating to a certain P von Q, an Austrian attached to the *Abwehr* in Paris, has stayed in my mind as a perfect example of the *genre*. The dossier could have been published as a novel almost as it stood, so vividly did the central character, von Q himself, emerge, as well as the nature of his various relationships with subsidiary characters, such as his superior officers in the *Abwehr*, representatives of the Resistance and of Allied Intelligence services, fashionable and aristocratic French ladies for whom he had a great fancy. At *Abwehr* headquarters they were clearly dazzled by his exalted social connections; his command of travel facilities was a boon to Resistance fighters and Allied prisoners-of-war on the run, and the fashionable and aristocratic ladies found him, as far as one could judge, an agreeable and effective lover. His own central purpose, as it seemed to me, was just to remain in Paris with his charming circle of friends rather than be sent to the Eastern Front, where he would almost certainly be killed. To this end, he skilfully leant, now in this direction, now in that, concerned only to remain on his feet; the most subtle fidometer (if there were such a thing) would have been unable to indicate any marked preference for one loyalty over another. Had the Nazis won the war instead of the Allies, I felt quite sure that an *Abwehr* officer would have been thumbing over more or less the same dossier as I was, probably also in the Boulevard Suchet, and finding it equally impossible to exonerate or to accuse von Q. In the end, he would doubtless have been permitted to return to his native Vienna, as happened as a result of our side's inconclusive scrutiny, there, as I should suppose, to live out his days cheerfully enough. If anyone ever asked him what happened to him in the war, he could say with the Abbé Sieyès: '*J'ai vécu!*'

Would Kim perhaps have preferred the cards to have fallen this way for him? His 'K' and his Order of Lenin simultaneously awarded; an honoured visitor at Lords and at Lubianka, in the Royal Enclosure and in the Kremlin. It is possible. If so, he was more unfortunate than von Q. Or possibly just less adroit. To judge from his dossier, I cannot imagine von Q considering it expedient to associate with Burgess, as Kim did. In any case, it is easy to see why both of them, in their different ways, are in the category of folk heroes today, this being the age of Hamlet rather than of Henry V, of Judas rather than of his Master. Our contemporary Casabianca is the first, not the last, to leave the burning ship; if, indeed, it is not he who set fire to it.

The Liberation by now belonged to yesterday. All the lights had gone on, water flowed from the taps, and the *flics* had recovered their assurance, blowing their whistles, directing traffic and grabbing miscreants with their accustomed verve and venom. Bicycles had given way to cars, heat had come back to icy rooms and offices, the Bourse reopened, and the newspapers sorted themselves out – *Temps* into *Monde*, *Peuple* into *Combat*, and so on; only the ultra-bourgeois *Figaro* and ultra-Communist *Humanité* remaining unchanged. Bank accounts were unblocked, villas unshuttered along the Côte d'Azur, restaurants refurbished, and the gaols delivered up their notabilities – M. le President presidential again, songsters clearing their throats, comedians dusting down their jokes, and whores reappearing in their familiar haunts, the shaved ones wearing wigs. The old Chamber of Deputies was reborn as the National Assembly, with veterans like Mm. Herriot, Léon Blum and Vincent Auriol back at the rostrum, their voices a shade hoarser than heretofore and occasionally quavering, but still able to hold forth vociferously and interminably. Mme Coco Chanel discreetly removed from her window the notice announcing that scent was *gratuit pour les GI's*, while M. Félix, hearing that a move was afoot in the Air Ministry to take over the house in the Avenue Marigny, waited upon the then Minister, a Communist. Whether as a result of his representations, or of other pressures, Rothschild remained securely in possession.

The war was still going on, of course, but as far as Paris was concerned, ever receding. At the time of the Ardennes offensive there was a momentary recurrence of panic, and once again cars loaded with mattresses and other household goods were to be seen headed south. I even heard it suggested in the Boulevard Suchet that de Gaulle should be given command of the Allied forces 'to finish the job'. This crisis, however, proved short-lived; the Ardennes offensive soon spent itself, and at last the day came when General Eisenhower's elephantine headquarters laboriously removed itself from Versailles, and was soon lost to view, moving in the direction of Germany. By then it was clear that the war was as good as over, and though young Frenchmen continued to be mobilised and sent to the front ('*ne te fais pas casser la figure*,' I heard a mother say to her son as she saw him off), Parisians were chiefly concerned to resume their peacetime existence, and forget both the occupation and the Liberation – two almost equally distasteful memories.

There remained the drama's centrepiece – blitzed Berlin. Who that set eyes on this extraordinary spectacle can ever forget it? The vast expanse of rubble, with the Brandenburg Gate rising up, stark, amidst it; a wasteland of utter desolation, like the Mountains of the Moon, which at first sight gave an impression of being denuded of all life – no living creatures great or small, no birds, no insects even, no branch or leaf or anything growing, nothing that could possibly associate the scene with our human condition or existence. Just the grotesque hulks of what had once been buildings – maybe the Adlon Hotel, Unter den Linden, the Reichstag, who could tell? – and hanging over it all, long after hostilities had ceased, a stench of rotting corpses, sickly-sour; the cadaver side of our mortality, and stinking at that. Closer inspection revealed that, contrary to the first impression, there were actually human beings burrowing into this rubble like badgers, constructing for themselves little rickety shelters out of it; as you sometimes find in some grim, forgotten cave that bats have made a home there, blindly flying to and fro and emitting tiny squawks. The rubble-dwellers were the liberated citizens of Berlin, who in some mysterious way managed to acquire food of a sort to sustain life, engaging in a weird kind of commerce, with Lucky Strike and Players cigarettes for small change, Spam for the larger pieces, and their bodies, if presentable enough, for currency notes of varying denominations.

Was all this, I asked myself, the realisation of our war aims – on the one hand, getting the *Banco di Roma* going again; on the other, the creation of a non-place where once Berlin had been? Did it represent the triumph of good over evil? In Paris, the shavers of heads chastising the sinful, and the shaved chastised for their sins? The Red Army coming in from the East bringing freedom on its wings; the Allied forces coming in from the West with enlightenment on theirs? Was Paris, now that it had a *Monde* instead of a *Temps* to read, an Assembly instead of a Chamber to debate in, a de Gaulle instead of a Daladier or Laval to preside over the Government, full of renewed zeal for liberty, equality and fraternity? Had Berlin, in being reduced to rubble, become a citadel of democracy? Or were there, as before, just victors and vanquished, with some uncertainty as to which was which, and justice once more a fugitive? I inclined to the latter view, myself, and doubted very much whether restoring the *Banco di Roma* was going to underwrite Roosevelt's Four Freedoms, any more than being liberated by the Red Army was going to seem, in the eyes of the beneficiaries at any rate, readily distinguishable from a new and harsher servitude. A Restoration that restored the *Banco di Roma*, but not Rome, would not, in my opinion, amount to much; any more than would a Liberation that liberated governments (Herr Ulbricht's, for instance), but not the governed.

*

There was really nothing more for me to do in the Boulevard Suchet, or anywhere else that I could see. The house in the Avenue Marigny, in any case, would soon be reverting to its rightful owners; it was time for me to go, as even M. Félix, in the nicest possible way, indicated. At this point I did something which strikes me now as altogether extraordinary, but at the time seemed the most natural thing in the world. Acting on an impulse, I simply went home, took off my uniform, got a job in Fleet Street, and resumed my peacetime life, without reference to anyone in MI6 or the DGER, or trying in any way to regularise my position as a serving officer by getting myself posted anywhere or put on anyone's strength, however nominally, or even looking in on Section Five to see Cowgill or Philby. I just wound up my military service myself, becoming, I suppose, technically a deserter, until some months later, I received my demobilisation papers, went along to Chelsea Barracks and collected my discharge and civilian suit and message of appreciation from the King, as though, like everyone else, I had come there from some military posting in which I had been impatiently awaiting this joyous deliverance.

Thus, my war service, such as it was, ended as irresponsibly as it began. Looking back on it, I cannot join the chorus of regrets at five years lost; they were just lost years in a lost life, indistinguishable, essentially, from the five preceding and the five succeeding ones. I might, it is true, have improved my French, which remained as execrable when I was demobilised at Chelsea Barracks as when I enlisted at Mytchett Hutments. Or kept a regular journal instead of scribbling down a few very occasional notes. Or cultivated less fitfully the literary figures I met at the Mullers'; perhaps even, as it were, buying up some Sarrautes and Robbe-Grillets at the bottom of the market with a view of disposing of them later at a substantial profit. (The only venture of the kind was to send a copy of Camus's *l'Étranger* to Eyre & Spottiswoode, but by that time Graham Greene had ceased to be active in the firm, and it fell on stony ground.) Altogether, I might have spent less time and energy in foolish pursuits and self-indulgences, and more in wresting some mental or professional benefit from the barren fatuities of war. Otherwise, the difference between writing leading articles in the *Guardian* or propaganda ones in the Ministry of Information, between walking about the streets of wherever I happened to be and marching up and down the barrack-square at Mytchett, between news-gathering in Moscow or Intelligence-gathering in Lourenço Marques, seemed no more than a nuance.

As for the war itself, just as it had no beginning, so it had no end. V-E Day, when it came – a two-day event, as though extending its duration might somehow enhance its significance – was a repeat performance. Remembering so vividly the first production in 1918, the 1945 version had, for me, a nightmarish quality about it. The abandonment more unrestrained, but also more desperate; faces more lavishly made-up, bodies heavier and ampler; a middle-aged bacchanalia – as, indeed, it very largely was, the young still being called-up and kept in the forces. On the former occasion, I had been a schoolboy; now I was middle-aged and white-haired, well past my half-way mark. In my forty-two years, there had been two wars, with an uneasy interlude in between. Or rather, one war that was still continuing. I saw little to rejoice over.

It happened that, at the *Daily Telegraph* where I was now working, I got hold of some tickets to take my family to a production of *As You Like It* at the Old Vic. We had moved up to London from Whatlington, sold our house there, and found very cramped accommodation in a flat in Buckingham Street looking onto Temple Gardens and the Embankment. I gave Kitty the tickets for herself and the children, but was only able to get to the theatre myself after the performance had begun. Not wanting to create a disturbance by making my way to my seat, I stood at the back waiting for the end of the first act. I could see Kitty and the children quite clearly. In that perspective, the four of them seemed to be grouped round her rather than seated side by side in a row; their faces riveted by what was happening on the stage, not just attentive, but utterly absorbed. There they were, caught up, compacted, by the enchantment of Shakespeare's comedy; and there was I, looking at them, and recalling that it was thirty years since I had likewise sat in that auditorium as a child, and been enthralled by *As You Like It*. On this occasion, the theatre was still very battered from the Blitz; part of the auditorium roped off as dangerous, and the stage similarly restricted, the roofing reinforced by a tarpaulin, but in places the sky and the stars nonetheless clearly visible. A very gallant and splendid effort, I thought, to have a performance at all; like a ship limping into port after battling its way through a terrific storm. The actors were very young – they might even have been RADA students – but they spoke the lines charmingly, bringing the Forest of Arden to pass in Waterloo Road, and Rosalind to life amidst the debris of a war fought and a victory celebrated. After all, then, something *had* been salvaged from the world's wreck, as there still might be something to salvage from my life's wreck. At the back of the Old Vic auditorium, I had my own private V-E day, and then, when the lights went up, joined the others.

The office of the *Daily Telegraph* in Fleet Street, where I now worked, seemed oddly detached and secluded from the turbulent, confused world – the raw material which we were required to process and package for distribution to our readers. Each edition of the paper, as it came out, I used to think, might be compared with an eminently respectable man, wearing a bowler-hat and carrying an umbrella, who went racing after a furiously driven bus; just managing to jump aboard, and then settling into his seat, a shade breathless, but otherwise unruffled. Travelling each morning, as I did, from Battle to Charing Cross, I could observe our readers for myself; especially the large contingent that got in at Tunbridge Wells. How they opened the paper with great placidity, sipping its columns like a cup of hot cocoa rather than quaffing them like a glass of champagne, or gulping them down like a bloody Mary. News on the *Guardian* was script-material for yet another instalment in an interminable western, in which, for the umpteenth time, the Good Guy and the Bad Guy confront one another. On the *Evening Standard* it was fed back to our little old reader, cooked and garnished, as we hoped, to his taste; on the *Daily Telegraph* it blew where it listed, except that we had double-glazing and air-conditioning to ensure that no one was incommoded.

This atmosphere of serenity and detachment was reflected in the character, and even the appearance, of our editor, Arthur Watson; brother, incidentally of the Alfred Watson who had been shot at when he was editor of the *Calcutta Statesman*. He was a large, benign man, with a shining, pink face, abstemious in his ways and measured in his speech; a superb newspaper technician, with, beyond a vague liberalism, no particular views on anything. He had never travelled, sought no tête-à-têtes with the great, wrote legibly, read little, and sat patiently in his editorial chair without a break from the early afternoon till he had seen the first edition through the press. I met with nothing but kindness and consideration at his hands, and remained always devoted to him. Each day some three or four of us would gather round him for an editorial conference to consider possible subjects for comment. The space at our disposal was very limited owing to paper rationing, which was still in force – a restriction I could endure with equanimity. Our discussions were not particularly lively, and sometimes I found myself dozing off as they proceeded. The weighty political leaders were undertaken by

Colin Coote, a migrant from *The Times*, and later Watson's successor; the ones about economic matters by J. C. Johnstone, a survivor from the *Morning Post*, which by this time had been taken over by the *Daily Telegraph*, and I usually dealt with out-of-the-way topics – like an old man in Georgia who claimed to be 130, or the elimination of the Tsetse fly in Africa, which would make available vast new supplies of frozen meat. My copy invariably came at the bottom of the leader columns – sometimes column – and so was convenient for cutting as and when required.

I shared a room with Johnstone, who, despite a boyish, easy-going appearance, held to his old-fashioned conservative opinions with ferocious tenacity and expounded them with steely implacability. Composing a leader or feature article, he would pace up and down our room with a rapt expression on his face, oblivious to all interruptions; then sit at his typewriter and tap out his piece without a pause, only breaking off when he needed to make use of his slide-rule. He applied the same concentration of purpose to edging a lawn or verge in his own or anyone else's garden; an occupation to which he was greatly addicted. Though, in sharing a room in a newspaper office, there are infinite possibilities of strife, I cannot recall a single cross, or even irritable, word ever passing between us. To my great distress he died of cancer in 1954, when I was editor of *Punch*. I visited him in hospital shortly before his death, and even then he sternly corrected me when I was imprudent enough to refer carelessly, in my hit-or-miss way, to an approximate date.

Watson's editorial authority was strictly limited, the effective control of the paper being in the hands of the Berry family, who owned it, and under whose direction its circulation had climbed from a hundred thousand to over a million. This meant, in those days, Lord Camrose, with, for supernumaries, his two sons, always referred to in the office, in true Victorian-patrician style, as Mr Seymour and Mr Michael. Sometime after our editorial conference, Watson would be summoned to the fifth floor to give an account of his editorial intentions, and receive his instructions. Later, the news-editor would be similarly briefed. In this way, the two satrapies were kept separate and independent of one another. Occasionally, I ran into Watson in the lift on his way up to the fifth floor, looking for all the world like a trusted family solicitor called in for consultation by some wealthy client. The notes he brought back with him for guidance often included an actual phrase to be worked verbatim into a leader.

Later, in America, when I was *Daily Telegraph* correspondent in Washington, and on my return when I was made deputy-editor of the paper, I got to know Camrose quite well, and to like him. Compared with the two other newspaper magnates I worked for – C. P. Scott and Beaverbrook – he was straightforward and honest; altogether a simpler person. His aspirations had been well satisfied by becoming rich and a lord, whereas the other two continued, till the days of their deaths, to be tormented by unrealised hopes and unaccountable fears. Camrose, it is true, might have liked to go a notch or two up in the peerage, or accumulate another million or two, but as long as his brother and former associate, Lord Kemsley, didn't, it bothered him little. This contentment with his achievement and status made him seem more like a lord than most lords. He told me once how, travelling in an American plane, a fellow-passenger, hearing he was a lord, asked him where his castle was. I could see the questioner's point; Camrose looked like a man who lived in a castle. The nearest he got to actually living in one was to acquire Curzon's former residence; a huge, rambling house near Basingstoke called Hackwood. In my experience, aspirants quite often make more convincing versions of what they aspire to be than the originals they copy – for instance, Isaiah Berlin as a don, Evelyn Waugh as a country gentleman, Orwell as a proletarian and Camrose as a lord. For one thing, they take more trouble over their costumes and getting word perfect.

During the election campaign of July 1945, my services were in little demand on the paper, which, of course, campaigned hotly for a Conservative victory and Churchill's return to power. Practically everyone expected this to happen, including the numerous Labour supporters on the staff. When it didn't, there was great consternation. Even Watson seemed troubled; not in himself – I don't think he cared much either way – but at the thought of having to venture up to a stricken fifth floor. My own feelings were very mixed. It was the moment my father and his friends had dreamed of and lived for – a Labour Government in power with a huge majority, and here was I in the office of a Conservative newspaper, and taking no joy in the occasion beyond a certain satisfaction at the confusion of all the pundits and the overthrow of a government in office. I cannot recall a single election in which I have not hoped for the defeat of the incumbent side. This might seem a very negative and irresponsible attitude, and the only justification I can offer for it is that, since being able to turn a government out is almost the only advantage parliamentary democracy offers, one might as well enjoy it as often as possible. As for the sense of being in the enemy camp – it didn't weigh much with me, since I had no expectation that Attlee and his colleagues would be able, or even seriously try, to achieve the things that had seemed so wonderful a prospect when I was lurking in the red cosy-corner in our Croydon sitting-room to avoid being sent to bed, and listening enthralled to the Saturday evening talk of my father and his friends. Moreover, a good many of the likely candidates for posts in Attlee's Government – John Strachey, for instance – had been foremost in believing the lies of the Soviet bosses and covering up their evil deeds. Of them I could expect nothing good.

A figure whose part in the campaign and in the victory fascinated me was Harold Laski, whom I had vaguely known in Manchester, where his father, Nathan Laski, was a highly respected orthodox Jew and resident on Cheetham hill. Later, when I began to work for the BBC, I quite often encountered him, and we became in a sort of way friends. What I found very endearing in him was something which many of his admirers either did not notice, or, if they did, tried to overlook – a Walter Mitty-ish strain, whereby he would invent incidents and personal relationships, and quote from purely imaginary conversations and even letters, all designed to make him seem important; as hob-nobbing with the great, consulted by them, and the recipient of their confidences. He was liable, for instance, when he had gone out of the room to take a telephone call, to say on his return: That was Stanley Baldwin, or Bob Cecil, or Lloyd George – almost anyone of eminence. There were no ideological implications. He would as readily recount, in direct speech, a conversation with Lord Halifax as with Stalin; and his long correspondence with the American Supreme Court Judge, Oliver Wendell Holmes, is laced with obviously mendacious stories. Holmes himself, who seems to have been a pompous, self-consciously erudite, rather asinine figure, no doubt, on his side of the correspondence, engaged in his own kind of fantasy; the unwritten, unspoken bargain between them being to believe each other's, which they did, most earnestly, over the years. Such bargains are common enough in all sorts of human relationships, including matrimony.

The difference was that, whereas the judge's fantasy was plausible, and as habitual with him as wearing his Supreme Court gown, Laski's was poetic, variegated, Chaplin-esque. Indeed, with his hat always a shade too large so that it was well down on his ears, his little moustache and large spectacles, he looked a bit like a campus Charlie, and continued, despite all his fame and success, to convey some of the other's woebegone air. In his company, one would wait for it – how he had just come from the Foreign Office, where Anthony Eden had called him in to ask his advice. Or about how that very morning he had received a long letter from F.D.R., even, maybe, quoting a bit from it; about how the President hoped to be in London before long, when they'd have a chance of getting together, but adding that he wasn't going to 'eat any of your damned brussels sprouts'. Even before I was editor of *Punch* I had a fancy for old chestnuts, and I found it touching that Laski should have fallen back on the sprouts to give his Roosevelt letter verisimilitude.

In all follies there is always an appropriate pay-off lurking about somewhere, and in Laski's case it was that, as he grew to be more and more of a celebrity, life had a disconcerting way of catching up with – even overtaking–his fantasies. As an American lawyer named Thurman Arnold put it to me once in Washington, he was becoming so important that he was getting to know some of the people he'd known all his life. I caught a glimpse of him once in the British Embassy in Washington standing at the foot of the large stairway and looking up at a portrait of a past ambassador – I think Bryce. It made me realise how he would have loved to be the Ambassador himself. The only thing he ever asked Attlee for was a life peerage, which, however, was refused him. Thinking of the people who have been given life peerages, I confess I can't see why. It was typical of Churchill, who was capable of such brilliant leadership, and, at the same time, could be so politically inept, to mistake an aspiring poor man's Disraeli like Laski for a dangerous revolutionary. When he accused him, in an election broadcast, of wanting to set up a Gestapo, it must have lost him a lot of votes.

It was from Arthur Watson that I first heard the news of the dropping of atomic bombs on Hiroshima and Nagasaki. He was walking along a corridor in the direction of the news-room, at what was, for him, an accelerated pace, with a news-agency flash in his hands. Without a word he showed it to me, and I read it – the bare announcement of what had happened. It meant nothing to me except that a new powerful weapon had been developed which was calculated to bring the war in the Far East to a speedy end. This, I think, was most people's reaction; I personally came across no one in any walk of life who had moral qualms at the time. Attlee subsequently disclosed the fact that he had never, in all the War Cabinet's deliberations, heard talk of fall-out. Truman was in an even worse case, Roosevelt having told him nothing about the war-time atomic weapons programme. I remember seeing a memorable newsreel of Truman, shortly after he became President, reading a statement about dropping the bomb in the monotonous tone of voice of a village policeman giving evidence at a court of petty sessions. A primary school doomsday.

Later, the hysteria was worked up, and in some degree affected almost everyone. I myself had perfectly sensible friends who sold up their homes and left their jobs to settle in some outlandish place, there to await the inevitable nuclear apocalypse. Others, given to dissolute behaviour, found an excuse in the dreadful potentialities of nuclear weapons, which, they were liable to say in their cups, 'caused something inside them to snap'. As they had behaved in very much the same way before the alleged snapping, I was unimpressed. For some reason I never experienced this particular *bouleversement*. It seemed to me that just having an enormously more powerful weapon altered nothing; it was the will to destroy rather than the means which mattered, and if human destructiveness had reached the point that our very earth itself could be turned to dust, this danger would not be averted by agitating for nuclear disarmament, any more than poor Arthur Henderson's Disarmament Conference at Geneva had averted the danger of Nazi aggression. I remember reading a statement from the Vatican at the time of the invention of the cross-bow to the effect that Christian men never would, or should, use so diabolically destructive a weapon; but, of course, it was used, even to settle disputes between Christians. The cross-bow is only different from nuclear weapons in degree, not in kind. Nonetheless, it became increasingly clear that for some time to come the mushroom cloud was to be the most favoured backdrop to the contemporary scene, and I was correspondingly thankful that my first introduction to it should have been under the cool, professional aegis of Arthur Watson, rather than of some *Guardian* or other *exalté*.

The Watson, as distinct from the Bertrand Russell, attitude was sustained by a visit I paid to Hiroshima in 1946. I went there from Tokyo, along with other journalists, in a special train in which the Emperor Hirohito and his suite were travelling; this being the first time he had visited the city since the atomic bombing. The Emperor wore a trilby hat, which, whenever he appeared in public, he continuously raised, his American advisers having told him that he was no longer a Sun God but a democratic monarch, and that democratic monarchs wore ordinary hats which they raised. They neglected to point out, at the same time, that hats should thus be raised only for a particular reason, as in response to cheers; and he just raised and lowered his all the time – like working a pump-handle. His suite consisted of some twenty or thirty seemingly identical men in black cutaway coats and white gloves, who on all possible occasions clapped their hands and shouted '*Banzai!*' in unison. When we got to Hiroshima we all climbed to the top of a tower, which was almost the only edifice still standing. There, the Emperor was shown a blue-print of the town as it was going to be rebuilt. While he was examining it, the men in cutaway coats kept up a non-stop chorus of *Banzais*, but failed thereby to give this weird occasion a touch of drama. My persistent efforts to have a sight of some of the strange phenomena widely publicised in alleged eye-witness accounts of what happened when the bombs were dropped – for instance, the outline of an incinerated hand on a stone wall, and of an incinerated body on one of the bridges – were all fruitless. The only survivor of the raid I have actually talked with is the present General of the Jesuit Order, who happened to be in Hiroshima at the time; and he, too, failed to notice many of the high-lights in the vast literature on the subject.

As a basis for studying the shaping and propagation of a modern myth, some of this material is incomparable. Particularly interesting is the tragi-comedy of Claude Eatherly, billed as a much decorated American Air Force major who led the raids on Hiroshima and Nagasaki; then repented of what he had done, couldn't face a hero's welcome in his native Texas town, turned to a life of petty theft in the hope of getting punished and so drawing attention to his contribution over what he now saw as a monstrous crime, and ended up in a military psychiatric institution. The story was publicised and embellished all over the world; poems celebrating it were recited on the BBC, best-selling books written about it, and a film based on the theme was made and shown. Then it turned out that Eatherly didn't lead the raid, hadn't had any combat experience, wasn't decorated, and hadn't – at least, not until psychiatrists told him he had – experienced any remorse about the raids on Hiroshima and Nagasaki. It was all pure fantasy. The interesting thing was that no one invented the story. It just emerged, ready-made; begotten by the Media out of the prevailing nuclear hysteria.

Kitty's father and mother were living near us in Whatlington, having settled there in 1939, when once more, as in 1914, the exigencies of war brought to an end their nomadic life between Swiss mountain resorts, sea cruises and picturesquely placed *pensions* offering advantageous out-of-season terms, and forced them to return to their native land and the extortions of the Inland Revenue. As it turned out, their wanderings were never to be resumed; Whatlington was their positively last port-of-call. For Mr Dobbs this meant being subjected to his wife's cooking, housekeeping and company without a break. There was no longer the possibility, which his job with Lunn's Tours had always provided, of being able to disengage from time to time, and, as it were, retire to a rest-camp where he could re-equip and recover his morale. I must say, he stood up manfully to a situation which might well have broken a lesser man; concentrating his efforts on maintaining a small, limited area of order of his own in their disorderly household, from which he would emerge as spry, well-groomed and turned out, as ever.

For her part, Mrs Dobbs, in so far as it was possible in their new circumstances, resumed her habitual ways. She could no longer paint her favourite subjects, like the Chateau de Chillon and the Dent du Midi, in situ, but she could, and did, make copies of past water-colour sketches of them. She also did some local painting, seated on her camp-stool and dipping her brushes in the cup of water from which she occasionally absent-mindedly took a sip to drink. Her efforts in the kitchen produced the familiar concoctions, with safety pins and other foreign bodies liable to turn up in her cakes and puddings. There was little neccessity now for her essays in dilution – water in the soup and the marmalade – as guests were increasingly a rarity. Her familiars were dying off, and old age and the strain of war made the survivors less able to face the rigors of her household. One thing that she did I found very appealing – the portraits she painted in oils of our eldest son Leonard and youngest son Charles. The one of Leonard is particularly striking, and quite different from the general run of her work. There was something even then – he was about twelve at the time – in his character akin to hers, but purified, transfigured, to which she responded. He was the only one of us never to be exasperated by her; whose amusement at her antics was never unkind, and who was able by his mere presence to pacify her. When I saw this happening, I used to think of David similarly pacifying with his music a troubled Saul. Her portrait of Charles is not so good, as a portrait, but precious to us because he was killed in a ski-ing accident when he was just about to be twenty-one.

In the village Mrs Dobbs became a familiar and much-liked figure. Her eccentricities – like stretching out for a nap wherever and whenever she felt like it; under a hedge or by the road-side, and once on a tomb-stone in Battle churchyard – caused fewer stares among country-people than they would have in a town. Likewise, her weird apparel – like an old gipsy-woman's – which, when she was travelling on the bus to Battle or Hastings, often led some kindly fellow-passenger to offer to pay her fare – an offer she readily accepted. Actually, her wardrobe had been augmented substantially when her sister, Beatrice Webb, died in 1943, bequeathing her all her clothes. These consisted mostly of elegant dresses, coats and suits, cut to her taste, and mostly in grey – Mrs Webb's favourite colour. Mrs Dobbs soon made them her own by wearing them constantly, often back-to-front or upside-down, spilling food and paint over them, and generally assimilating them, thereby pulling off one of her unconscious parodies; in this case, of the kind of high-minded elegance her famous sister practised. Her capacity for producing such parodies amounted to genius.

With Beatrice's death, Mrs Dobbs was the last remaining Potter sister; the last exponent of their explosive combination of passionate living and dedication to good causes. Only, in her, the mixture was so weirdly blended that the result was more bizarre than, as with the others, either tragic or farcical. During Beatrice's last months the two sisters drew together. That is to say, Mrs Dobbs would descend upon Passfield Corner at fairly regular intervals, to be received affectionately by Mrs Webb, and stoically by Sidney, who was still partly incapacitated as a result of a stroke he suffered in 1938. She had various techniques for disconcerting them; one being to borrow Mrs Webb's spectacles (Mrs Dobbs could, seemingly, see through anyone's, and when hard-pressed would buy a pair for herself at Woolworth's); and another, to sit in Sidney's chair, specially low-built so that his short legs did not dangle. To take some of the sting out of her presence, she was lodged in a nearby inn rather than in the house.

It was always a nice question, with Mrs Dobbs, whether it was more painful when she agreed with one or when she disagreed. I myself, as it happened, was nearly always in the latter case; try as I would, I very rarely achieved even a show of agreement, and this only by advancing on a very wide philosophico-mystical front – as that I was confident all life would ultimately become one. Developing this point with her once in Kingsmill's presence, he let out a strangled: 'Yes, but not for a very long time!', appalled at the prospect, in any measurable future, of becoming one with Mrs Dobbs through all eternity. The Webbs had to bear the full force of Mrs Dobb's eager accord. This was particularly burdensome to Mrs Webb when applied to their views on politics, as she considered her sister to be, politically speaking, a kind of imbecile. At the same time, she had an uneasy feeling that Mrs Dobbs might have chosen the better part in her wilfulness and easy surrender to sensual

living, which, after all, had left her with a tribe of children and grand-
children, as against the row of what Mrs Webb always referred to as her
and Sidney's unreadable books. She even remarked to me once, out of
the blue, that perhaps Rosy had been right – an enigmatic observation
which might as well have related to the much-frowned-upon period
between her marriages, when, in the outraged estimation of the Potter
family, she was considered to have lived loosely, as to the years of
troubled but fruitful domesticity which followed.

Even Mrs Dobbs, I think, realised that Beatrice's last months were
deeply melancholic, and that she longed to die. In the last entries in her
immense journal, written during the sleepless hours of the night, she
poured out her misery, seriously considering taking her life – VWL, she
called it, or Voluntary Withdrawal from Life – only refraining out of
consideration for Sidney. A veiled suggestion that they might make it a
joint enterprise met with no response. Nor, in her secret communings
with herself, did she derive any comfort from either the new civilisation
in the USSR that she and Sidney had proclaimed (though she recorded
with satisfaction the continued attentions of the Soviet Ambassador,
M. Maisky), or from the launching of the Beveridge Plan, which was
generally considered to be the implementation of their ideas. Whatever
she might say in public, doubts assailed her, when she was alone with
herself, as to whether the fulsome adulation of Stalin, obligatory among
his subjects, and enforced by ever more through-going and brutal
terrorism, really amounted to a flowering of socialist brotherliness and
humanistic virtue. As for the Beveridge Plan – her severely practical
side, inherited from her father, made her realise at once that handing
out unconditional largesse to the citizenry of a universal suffrage
democracy would have grave moral and social implications. Also, I
think, very humanly, she felt some heart-burning at the limelight
which shone upon Beveridge himself, who, in his London School of
Economics days, had so often pained and irritated the Webb Partnership as they toiled away on behalf of notions which, as embodied in his
Plan, now bore his name, not theirs. In the very last entry in her journal
she describes her sense of melting away into nothingness ('The garden
will disappear and all our furniture, the earth and the sun and the
moon. God wills the destruction of all living things, man and even a
child . . . we shall not be frozen or hurt, but merely not exist'); and
shortly afterwards, I am sure to her infinite relief, she participated in
this process.

What exactly Sidney felt at being deprived of his companion and partner over so many years, could not, with his stumbling speech and partially paralysed faculties, find any clear expression. At one point, when Mrs Dobbs was staying with him, he gave her quite a turn by suddenly remarking: 'That's Beatrice, you know!', at the same time, pointing excitedly at what seemed to be a large vase placed over the fireplace, which turned out, on closer inspection, to be the urn containing his late wife's ashes. One odd consequence of finding himself on his own was that he started signing his letters 'Passfield' in the style of his peerage; during Beatrice's lifetime he had stuck to 'Sidney Webb'. Another was that he took to eating a hearty breakfast of bacon-and-egg, which, during the years of matrimony, had been prohibited. Who knows what, if anything went on behind that still placid exterior – goatee beard, pince-nez on a black ribbon, abundant hair carefully brushed, tiny feet in well-made boots, neat suit; all just as when, in 1929, as the first, and only, Lord Passfield, he settled into the late Joseph Chamberlain's seat at the Colonial Office. A laconic exchange with Kitty when she visited him, reflects something of his state of mind:

'What are you reading, Uncle Sidney?'

'I am reading the novels of Walter Scott.'

'Do you like them?'

'No!'

Some four years after Beatrice's death, a second urn containing his ashes was placed beside hers in a little shrine set up at a spot in their garden that she had designated for the purpose. There they would have remained, becoming, perhaps, the focus of a minor cult, with ageing Fabians, visiting American liberals and an odd attaché from the Soviet and satellite embassies putting in an appearance from time to time to honour their memory, and maybe lay a wreath. This was not to be, due largely to the efforts of Bernard Shaw, who wrote a letter to *The Times* urging that they should be re-interred with due ceremony in Westminster Abbey.

As was so often the case with Shaw, his precise motives for promoting this strange happening, are not easy to discern. Was it, perhaps, a kind of Shavian joke, aimed, equally, at the Abbey's Dean and Chapter, and Attlee's Labour Government; at the old and new Establishment? In his letter to *The Times* he argued that, although the Webbs, admittedly, had expressed a wish to be buried in their garden, where, in fact, their ashes then lay, the nation owed it to itself to have them disinterred and brought to the Abbey. Furthermore, that whatever objections the Dean and Chapter might raise, the reason for their transfer was not to honour Sidney and Beatrice Webb (they being beyond being pleased or displeased by anything of the kind), but to confer an additional distinction on the Abbey itself. Anyway, his persuasion, specious or seriously intended, proved acceptable, and arrangements were made for a re-burial in the North Aisle of the Nave, at the foot of the memorial to Charles James Fox, at whose roystering ways Mrs Webb would surely have sniffed as noisily as she did at mundane contemporaries like Margot Asquith, the first Lord Birkenhead, and even the sometime fellow-Fabian to whom she invariably referred as 'poor little Wells'. Another near-by memorial might be considered more appropriate – that of Joseph Chamberlain, the only man with whom she could be said ever to have been, in ordinary terms, in love.

I should very much have liked to be present at the deliberations of the Dean and Chapter on the matter. Did one of them, I wonder – if only some doddering old Canon soon to retire – raise the question of Webb's atheism, and intense dislike of what he sibilantly called 'spiritual exercises'? Or even of his and Beatrice's ardent joint adulation of the world's first professedly atheistic State, in which the practice and propagation of the Christian religion had been put down so ruthlessly and rigorously? If so, no word of it got out; and no serious objections were publicly raised to Shaw's proposal, in the columns of *The Times*, or anywhere else. Few can have known, or anyway remembered, how, in her younger days, Mrs Webb used quite often to turn into the Abbey, from her restless pacing along the Embankment, to wrestle there in peace and quietness, quite often on her knees, with the questions that so insistently intruded themselves upon her other preoccupations – the Why? questions, as distinct from the How? ones.

No such considerations arose on this occasion, when her ashes, along with Sidney's, were brought to the Abbey. Despite the ecclesiastical setting, the proceedings were almost exclusively secular, with a little sacerdotal dressing provided by hymns (Scott Holland's 'Judge eternal, throned in splendour', and G. K. Chesterton's 'O God of earth and altar', with its, in the circumstances, particularly appropriate line 'The walls of gold entomb us'), and carefully chosen readings – from Ecclesiasticus: 'Let us now praise famous men . . .'; and from the First Epistle of Peter: 'But the end of all things is at hand . . .', which might be considered as providing a scriptural basis for revolutionary sentiments. On one side of the aisle there were distinguished visitors, led by the Prime Minister, Mr Attlee, and a contingent from his Government, including the Chancellor of the Exchequer, Dr Dalton, who, of course, unlike others present, knew from his early Windsor days how to come in strong with the responses. Fabians and London School of Economics alumni were present in strength. On the other side of the aisle there was a large turnout of members of the family. Sir Stafford Cripps, as a nephew and President of the Board of Trade, could legitimately have taken his place on either side, but chose to sit with the Government. It was altogether a goodly company, with no evident intimations of pro-letarian affiliations. Not a single cloth cap; no red ties even, – that convenient slide from 'Forty Years On' to 'The People's Flag'. Bour-geois through and through, a casual observer would have concluded. The organ notes swelled loudly, the Dean was especially unctuous as he intoned: 'Like as a father pitieth his own children; even so is the Lord merciful unto them that fear him.' It was the Abbey at its glorious best – re-bury the great Webbs with an empire's lamentation.

There was one notable absentee – the compère, G.B.S. Never mind! a worthy stand-in was at hand. With her familiar shuffling step, attired in Mrs Webb's best grey costume, now decidedly the worse for wear, strands of disorderly hair breaking out of a tall straw hat decorated with bunches of artificial fruit, and perched on the very top of her head, Mrs Dobbs, as the only surviving sister, made her way to the front of the family reservation, announcing in a loud grating voice: 'Well here I am!' A seat was hurriedly found for her. The address, as was fitting, was delivered by the Prime Minister. His tiny figure in its black cutaway coat perched in the pulpit was like some strange, shrilly twittering little bird. Everything the Webbs worked for, he said, looking down complacently on his Chancellor of the Exchequer, his President of the Board of Trade, and the rows of lesser colleagues, had now come to pass. Someone less attuned to the occasion might have considered the then parlous state of the world – the millions of still displaced persons, the new frontiers savagely drawn without reference to history, ge-ography or even ethnic considerations, the widespread famine and disorder, the menacing rival power line-ups – and wondered just what the speaker had in mind. It is doubtful if any among those present so reflected. They knew perfectly well what he meant – that what the Webbs had worked for was the coming to power of himself and his colleagues. And there they were – His Majesty's Government. Was that not an achievement worthy of a place in the Abbey? He went on to say that millions were now living fuller and freer lives thanks to the Webb Partnership; not, however, adding that its crowning achievement had been to commend to their fellow-countrymen and the whole world as a new civilisation a system of servitude more far-reaching and comprehensive than any hitherto known.

His little words seemed to be swallowed up in the swelling organ notes that followed, and, in due course, the more eminent members of the congregation made their way to the grave that had been prepared to receive the two urns. It was here that Mrs Dobbs made her only contribution to the proceedings; looking at the urns, she asked in a troubled voice: 'Which is Sidney and which is Beatrice?' Then, recollecting herself, she added that her sister's urn must be the little dirty one, which had stood so long beside Beatrice's herbal cigarettes on the mantelpiece in the Passfield sitting room. Her final comment, muttered but perfectly audible, was: 'They should have left them where they were.'

Such scenes as this pin-point history; like the tiny aperture in a camera taking in a wide scene. Doubtless they occur to help us to understand – a sort of tabloid parable. And as with parables, they disintegrate in your hand the moment you try to explain them. *Vide* St Augustine's rather enchantingly laboured exposition of the parable of the Good Samaritan – 'The inn is the Church. . . . The two pence are either the two precepts of love, or the promise of this life and that which is to come. . . . The Innkeeper is the Apostle Paul. The supererogatory payment is either his counsel of celibacy, or the fact that he worked with his own hands. . . .' Let me, then, content myself with saying that the set – the Abbey – seemed as perfectly chosen as the characters – including the two off-stage, Sidney and Beatrice – were perfectly cast. Where was there a better compère, even *in absentia*, than Shaw, the old Irish jester? What better musical accompaniment than the great organ? Who more appropriate than the Dean to give his blessing to the materialist conception of history as expressed in two urnsful of ashes, to be deposited with all the other illustrious bones and ashes in his Abbey. Or than Mr Attlee to pronounce the eulogy of two such estimable upholders of Stalinist dictatorship? Above all, than Mrs Dobbs, after her superb entry, to ring the curtain down with her riveting last line. For me, the story that began on those walks with my father through Park Hill Recreation Ground to East Croydon Station, was now, once and for all, over. Another Way had to be found and explored.

Index